EDUCATIONAL THEORY

EDUCATION IN A COMPETITIVE AND GLOBALIZING WORLD

Additional books in this series can be found on Nova's website
under the Series tab.

Additional E-books in this series can be found on Nova's website
under the E-books tab.

EDUCATION IN A COMPETITIVE AND GLOBALIZING WORLD

EDUCATIONAL THEORY

JALEH HASSASKHAH
EDITOR

Nova Science Publishers, Inc.

New York

Library of Congress Cataloging-in-Publication Data

Educational theory / editor, Jaleh Hassaskhah .
    p. cm.
Includes index.
ISBN 978-1-61324-580-4 (hardcover)
1. Education--Philosophy. 2. Education and state. I. Hassaskhah, Jaleh.
LB14.7.E3967 2011
370.1--dc22

               2011013679

Published by Nova Science Publishers, Inc. † New York

CONTENTS

PREFACE

Educational theory can refer to either speculative educational thought in general or to a theory of education as something that guides, explains, or describes educational practice. In this book, the authors present current research in the study of educational theory including the role of peer social capital as a predictor of adolescent academic outcomes; constructivism as educational theory; educational technology experiments and pre-service mathematics teachers perceptions about the nature of problem-solving.

Chapter 1 - Little attention has been paid to the role of peer social capital in the school context, especially as a predictor of adolescent academic outcomes. The present study uses multilevel models and a nationally representative sample to address this issue. Results reveal that in addition to those factors typically associated with academic outcomes (e.g., school composition), peer networks also had a significant impact on educational achievement and attainment. As in many prior studies, school composition was a significant predictor of achievement for students of all racial/ethnic groups. Although academic attainment was worse in schools where low-income students were concentrated, for some racial/ethnic groups educational attainment increased with higher concentrations of minority students. Furthermore, peer social capital, measured as the average achievement of a peer network, was a significant predictor of both educational achievement and attainment for all racial/ethnic groups. In addition, and counter to some earlier studies, results revealed that segregated peer networks among African-Americans may lead to better academic achievement and attainment than school settings with more integrated friendship networks.

Chapter 2 - Constructivism is a major referent in education, although it has been understood in various ways, including as a learning theory; a philosophical stance on human knowledge; and an approach to social enquiry. In terms of informing teaching, constructivism has variously been seen by different commentators as a basis for progressive, mainstream or failed approaches to pedagogy. This is unfortunate, as the different ways the term has been interpreted have confused debate about the potential of constructivism to contribute to planning effective teaching. This chapter sets out the basis of one version of constructivism: that which is informed by findings from both cognitive science, and from educational studies exploring learners' thinking about curriculum topics and about classroom processes. A key concept here is the way in which new learning is contingent on features of the learner, the learning context and the teaching. This version of constructivism (which has been widely embraced) offers a theoretical basis for designing effective pedagogy that is accessible to classroom teachers.

The chapter will explain that although constructivism understood this way certainly offers the basis for learner-centred teaching, it is far from 'minimally-guided' instruction, as caricatured by some critics. Rather, a feature of this approach is that it does not adopt doctrinaire allegiance to particular levels of teacher input (as can be the case with teaching through discovery learning, or direct instruction) but rather the level of teacher guidance (a) is determined for particular learning activities by considering the learners and the material to be learnt; (b) shifts across sequences of teaching and learning episodes, and includes potential for highly structured guidance, as well as more exploratory activities. When understood in these terms, constructivism provides a sound theoretical basis for informing teaching at all levels, and in all disciplines.

Chapter 3 - The aim of this chapter is to present educational technology experiments with school students, organized as laboratories. Among these laboratories, we introduce arrangement and findings of the Virtual Theatre and the Edutainment Robotics Laboratories, also presenting that based on the construction of Chua's circuits. Regarding the first one, the objective has been the manipulation of virtual contents, as well as the measure of both acceptation of technology and learning. In particular, we have tested a Virtual Theatre software as an educational tool in grammar classes of different schools in Cosenza (Italy). The system has been presented and a list of tasks has been provided, including the manipulation of: - the content "script of the story" in a group writing laboratory; - sounds for the recording of dialogues; - virtual agent to model/animate on the basis of the script to perform; - the performance in the virtual theatre.

As regards the Edutainment Robotics Laboratory, the objective has been the investigation of the cognitive strategies showed by students in building and programming a Lego MindStorms Robot, adopting a systematic methodology in data collection. The aim has been the leading of subjects in the acquisition of new knowledge as well as the development of advanced cognitive skills in problem solving, in thinking strategies and in the acquisition of new concepts. The Robotics Laboratory has consisted in two parts: the first phase has foreseen some key theoretical lessons about Robotics and the programming language; in the second phase, the task "to build and program a robot able to cross an arena in order to take part in a race" has been assigned to each group. At the end of the educational activities, subjects have tested the robot behaviour and presented a project report (a documentation on each phase of the work). Reports have showed the work strategies, the modalities of problem solution, as well as the cognitive strategies adopted by students in programming the robot.

Regarding the laboratory devoted to the construction of Chua's circuits, its aim has been the dissemination of new science concepts among young students during the project "Chaos at School: building a Chua's circuit, simulating its behaviour and using it to create sound and music". The purpose of the project was to familiarize high school students with chaos and complexity related concepts, motivating them to build the physical circuit, simulate its behaviour and then to create patterns and music by software applications. Results have showed that the direct contact with the circuit has encouraged students to think, to formulate hypotheses and to test their hypothesis through experiments. Hence, results of all experiences have shown that an active learning can remarkably enhance students' learning efficiency; moreover, a rich interaction can provide fruitful feelings of participation in the educational process. In this view, the tension between new forms of learning and old forms of schooling could not be solved with the victory of one on the other, but through a bridge between the two.

Chapter 4 - Introduction: This study aims to follow a typical night of high school night in a public school, trying to demonstrate its characteristics from the perspective of students and especially from the classroom. Intends to analyze to the relevant literature.

Method: We used the observation as the main instrument of research. The issues findings were used in guided interviews with students, intending to develop a qualitative analysis.

Results and Conclusions: Students, counselors and teachers resent the educational policies that sought to reduce repetition and suit the age, such as accelerated classes. The students revealed a desire by teachers who meet with their proposals, which are severe and prepare their lessons, although occasionally give signals that take advantage of the loopholes of the lack of limit to have fun. It is necessary that the high school to review their roles and allow the issues revealed by his young students, such as the necessity for compliance with basic objectives can be analyzed and answered promptly.

Chapter 5 - Problem solving is an important component of mathematics education, mainly because it provides an environment for students to reflect on their conceptions about the nature of mathematics, and develop a relational mathematical understanding. Due to its powerful characteristics, problem solving has been given value in mathematics education as a skill to be taught, as a goal for mental development, and as a method for teaching. Especially, for the last three decades, there have been attempts all around the world to make problem solving the focus of school mathematics rather than being an isolated part of mathematics curriculum. This study aimed to investigate pre-service elementary mathematics teachers' beliefs about mathematics problems and the nature of problem solving. The sample of the study consisted of 244 senior undergraduate students studying in Elementary Mathematics Teacher Education programs at 5 different universities in Turkey. The data were collected during the spring semester of 2005-2006 academic years. Participants completed a survey composed of three parts as demographic information sheet, questionnaire items, and non-routine mathematics problems. The results of the study indicated that, in general, pre-service teachers held positive beliefs about mathematical problem solving. However, a number of pre-service teachers held several traditional beliefs about problem solving, such as following predetermined sequence of steps while solving mathematics problems and the importance of computational skills in mathematics education. In addition, it was found that a number of pre-service teachers did not value problems that do not cover any topic in the curriculum, problems that do not involve any number and problems that take a long time to solve.

Chapter 6 - The Patchwork Text is a recent assessment innovation that seeks to enhance students' synthesis of learning over a period of time through engagement with progressive tasks culminating in a final synthesized assignment. However, this is not dissimilar to a form of plagiarism known as 'Patchwriting', wherein students unfamiliar with academic convention resort to paraphrasing pieces of published text and representing the consequent miscellany of text as their own. It is argued that students may likewise resort to Patchwriting in Patchwork Text assessment. In this article, the Structure of Observed Learning Outcomes ('SOLO') taxonomy is used to explain how certain forms of Patchwork text design may lead to Patchwriting, and suggests how Patchwork text assessment may be designed to minimize such risks. An example of minimizing Patchwriting is provided in the form of a Patchwork Text assessment for English Literature.

Chapter 7 - Some reflections which proceeds from teaching and research on the areas of Mathematics and Computation, which have taken the author to conclude that both fields lose perspective and potential when they are kept disconnected, and only they have felt when they work coordinated, looking each of them for the natural support in other one.

Chapter 8 - Arguments over the nature and purpose of theory have abounded within and beyond educational fields. One counterproductive scenario is to leave education atheoretical and conceptually unguided. The opposite counterproductive scenario is to have education dominated by a grand hegemonic but inadequate, narrow theory. The phenomena of interest in education are highly varied and complex; consequently, educational fields require guidance from multiple theoretical perspectives, which can shed light on specific phenomena. Only an interdisciplinary search covering multiple levels of analysis can bring into play an adequate array of theories that can illuminate the intricate, complex, multiple dimensions of learners, educators, classrooms, school systems, and the sociopolitical, ideological, and economic contexts that influence them. Employing the concept of cognitive diversity, this chapter describes the conceptual territory from which useful theory can be drawn. This territory includes levels of disciplinary scope from macro-societal to immediate contextual, to the level of the individual, to the organic-biological, to the cellular biological, to the molecular-genetic, and possibly even to the subatomic. Examples of theoretical perspectives from these various levels are provided, along with some ways in which they can guide the work of educational researchers and practitioners.

In: Educational Theory
Editor: Jaleh Hassaskhah, pp. 1-38

ISBN 978-1-61324-580-4
© 2011 Nova Science Publishers, Inc.

Chapter 1

ADOLESCENT EDUCATIONAL OUTCOMES: DO PEER NETWORKS MATTER?

Igor Ryabov and Franklin Goza
Bowling Green State University,
Bowling Green, Ohio, USA

ABSTRACT

Little attention has been paid to the role of peer social capital in the school context, especially as a predictor of adolescent academic outcomes. The present study uses multilevel models and a nationally representative sample to address this issue. Results reveal that in addition to those factors typically associated with academic outcomes (e.g., school composition), peer networks also had a significant impact on educational achievement and attainment. As in many prior studies, school composition was a significant predictor of achievement for students of all racial/ethnic groups. Although academic attainment was worse in schools where low-income students were concentrated, for some racial/ethnic groups educational attainment increased with higher concentrations of minority students. Furthermore, peer social capital, measured as the average achievement of a peer network, was a significant predictor of both educational achievement and attainment for all racial/ethnic groups. In addition, and counter to some earlier studies, results revealed that segregated peer networks among African-Americans may lead to better academic achievement and attainment than school settings with more integrated friendship networks.

The United States continues to become more ethnically and racially diverse (U.S. Census Bureau 2000) and this is especially so among the school-age population (Bean and Stevens 2003; Hirschman 2001; Orfield, Eaton, and Jones 1997). Between 1991 and 2001 the white share of public school enrollment fell from 67.4% to 60.3%, while the percentages of African-American, Latino, Asian, and Native American youth all increased (U.S. Department of Education 2002). Paradoxically, there was a simultaneous increase in school racial segregation for the first time since the 1955 *Brown v. Topeka* decision. Harvard's desegregation project found that the percentage of black students attending high-percent minority schools fell from 76.6% in 1968-69 to 62.9% in 1980-81, but by 1996-97 had increased to 68.8% (Orfield and Yun 1999). Furthermore, by 2003 the enrollment of black students in predominantly white schools was lower than in any year since 1968 (Frankenberg, Lee, and Orfield 2003). In fact, today many inner city schools are more racially segregated than they were in 1955 (Orfield, Eaton, and Jones 1997). However, today the most segregated minority group is Latinos, not blacks, and their segregation levels have steadily increased over the past thirty years (Orfield and Yun 1999).

Despite the fact that many schools are racially and/or ethnically segregated, their student bodies remain extremely diverse (Clotfelter 2001). According to Bankston and Caldas (1998: 534), although "segregated schools are not and have never been the products of self-segregation by minority group members" the vast majority of teens is homophilic and prefers in-group associations (Joyner and Kao 2000; Kubitschek and Hallinan 1998; Moody 2001). Even when schools have diverse populations, students may not be integrated to the extent that members of distinct ethnic groups regularly interact with one another (Cohen 1975; Epstein 1985; Maran 2000; Tatum 1999). Thus even relatively diverse student populations do not ensure high levels of interracial contact among students.

Numerous studies have examined the relationship between school social composition and educational outcomes. However, prior research has not paid enough attention to the possible effects of school-based *friendships* and *networks* on educational outcomes. Thus the question of whether school-based racial and/or ethnic social capital can explain adolescent educational outcomes remains unanswered. This research will analyze the importance of various school-level factors on student academic achievement while controlling for other family- and individual-level measures. The school-level predictors to be examined include peer network segregation, school socioeconomic status, and school racial/ethnic composition. These enable us to address the following questions: (1) Do youth with more racially and/or ethnically segregated peer networks have worse academic achievement than those with less segregated peer networks?; (2) Do youth in schools with higher percentages of minority enrollment have lower academic achievement than those in schools with smaller percentages of minority enrollment?; (3) Do youth in high socioeconomic status (SES) schools have better academic achievement than those in low SES schools?; and (4) How do the results for the first three questions vary across racial/ethnic groups?

This study is both conceptually and empirically significant. First, it updates and expands the implications of earlier research by incorporating more recent theoretical developments, empirical findings, and statistical techniques (Bryk and Raudenbush 1992; Raudebusch and Willms 1995). By so doing, we capture the essence of the school context by viewing adolescent networks and school composition as intertwined rather than isolated from one another. Second, we examine school-level effects differentially by race and ethnicity. As this is done we explore the tenets of oppositional culture theory, which posits that the orientation of friendship ties towards co-ethnic and co-racial peers hurts minority achievement (Ogbu 1981). Third, the present study draws on nationally representative data which are analyzed using multilevel modeling techniques. Fourth, school-level characteristics are examined while controlling for measures of family background and family social capital. Fifth, the present study examines academic performance both cross-sectionally and longitudinally. Sixth and most importantly, we examine both race and class, two key "family background" components, as individual- and school-level predictors of academic achievement.

This chapter proceeds by first reviewing relevant literature on school segregation and peer networks. Next is a discussion of the data and methods used as we also describe the individual- and school-level independent measures to be analyzed and the hypotheses examined. This is followed by our results and conclusions.

RELEVANT RESEARCH ON SCHOOL SEGREGATION

Although most scholars agree that education is an important mechanism for social mobility, some also believe that schools reproduce social inequality (Bankston and Caldas 2002; Carnevale 1999; Kahlenberg 1996; Roscigno 1998). The influences of race and social class extend well beyond the family realm, as they shape school attendance patterns and contribute to the creation of highly segregated school contexts, all of which affect academic achievement. Many of the mechanisms regarding how segregation affects achievement remain unknown. One intuitive explanation often advanced is that because school racial composition determines one's ability to make friends with students from other racial and ethnic groups, an integrated school would provide the best possibility for frequent interracial contact and interracial information transfer (Bankston and Caldas 1996; Coleman et al. 1966; Longshore and Prager 1985; Mahard and Crain 1983; Schofield 1993). Thus the importance of interracial peer contact in schools has been of particular interest to social scientists. It has also served as one rationale for pursuing school desegregation.

In the 20th century the political issues surrounding racial/ethnic integration, generally, and school desegregation in particular, aroused intense debate as numerous social scientists attempted to document how school (de)segregation affects the academic achievement of both minority and majority students. Thus far the evidence on the effects of desegregation has been mixed. Some studies observed short-term positive effects of desegregation on the math and verbal scores of black students (e.g., Hoxby 2000; Schofield 1993), while others found little or no evidence linking racial segregation to academic achievement (Armor 1995; Ascher 1992; Crain and Mahard 1978; Jencks 1972; Leake and Leake 1992; Rivkin 2000). Efforts to synthesize research findings on the effects of desegregation have led some to conclude that the evidence is so mixed or contradictory that reliable conclusions are impossible (e.g., Bankston and Caldas 2002). One explanation for the apparent ambiguity of much of this research is that the effects of desegregation vary enormously from community to community and from school to school.

Others suggest that the best indicator of school quality is not level of integration, but rather socioeconomic composition (e.g., Kahlenberg 1996, 2001). Much evidence shows that high-poverty schools reduce the educational performance of children, even when controlling for children's own class and race (e.g., Bankston and Caldas 1996; Entwisle and Alexander 1992). As such, the collective evidence accumulated by desegregation research made Orfield (1978:78) conclude: "Educational research suggests the basic damage inflicted by segregated education comes not from racial isolation but from the concentration of children from poor families." The most influential study to date, the *Coleman Report*, found that the "beneficial effect of a student body with a high proportion of white students comes not from racial composition *per se* but from the better educational background and higher educational aspirations that are, on the average, found among whites" (Coleman et al. 1966:307). Using data from over 600,000 students and teachers across the country, the report found that educational outcomes were primarily influenced by individual factors, such as a student's adaptation to school and the student's family background. Although the *Report* noted that individual factors supersede school-level factors, it also confirmed that low-income students experience greater achievement gains when they attend middle-class schools than when they attend high-poverty schools. The *Report* further found that the socioeconomic composition of a school's student body is more highly related to achievement, independent of students' own social background, than any other school factor. Accordingly, both poor blacks and whites should benefit from attending a middle-class black school, whereas poor blacks would not enhance their academic achievement by attending schools largely populated by poor whites.

A number of criticisms that may be raised regarding both the Equality of Educational Opportunity (EEO) data used in the *Report* as well as the methodological approach undertaken (see Jencks 1972 and Madaus et al. 1979). For instance, most of the school-level analyses were reduced to analyses of correlation-covariance matrices where the order of inserting variables often determined the magnitude of correlation coefficients. Another important criticism of the *Coleman Report* is that, although it had access to student scores on standardized tests and grades, it used verbal ability as the primary dependent measure (Madaus et al. 1979). Perhaps it was the media's oversimplification of the *Report*'s findings that lead to the controversy about it and the belief among some that schools do not make a difference. Indeed, the methodological limitations discussed above may have lead to an underestimation of the school effect.

Numerous studies conducted after the *Coleman Report* concurred that the social class of a student's classmates matters more than their race. In 1972, using the same EEO data, Jencks repeated the Coleman analyses and found that poor sixth-graders, regardless of race, attending a high-poverty school were academically years behind their poor peers who attended a middle-class school. Jencks (1972), like Coleman, did not find significant racial differences in this regard. Jencks' study, however, is subject to the same criticism as the *Coleman Report*, as he also used a number of standardized tests as measures of achievement. Later studies would revisit these research questions with more complex statistical techniques.[1] Among these studies, those that employed multilevel modeling are of special attention as they tend to produce more accurate estimates of the school effect (Raudenbush and Bryk 2002; Raudenbush and Willms 1995). Bryk and Raudenbush (1992) pioneered the use of Hierarchical Linear Models (HLM) for the purpose of producing more accurate statistical inferences from complex multilevel data. Using HLM and a sample of 7,185 students from 160 schools, they estimated that between-school variance accounted for 18 percent of the total variance in student math tests. Moreover, almost 70% of total between-school variance was explained by a single factor, the mean school SES. We caution against emphasizing the significance of this finding as Bryk and Raudenbush (1992) did not control for the schools' racial/ethnic composition, a factor which is typically found to be one of the most significant school-level predictors of educational achievement (Bankston and Caldas 2002). However,

---

[1] For instance, Chubb and Moe (1990), using longitudinal data, found the average SES of a school's student body to be strongly associated with gains in academic achievement among high school students. More recently, Sui-Chu and Williams (1996) examined factors influencing the math and reading scores of eighth-graders and concluded that the effect of a school's SES was as strong as that of the family SES. Lastly, Puma et al. (1997:73) analyzed a nationally representative sample of schools and concluded that "the poverty level of the school is negatively related to standardized achievement scores."

Bryk and Raudenbush (1992) did control for school type (i.e., private/public), a factor sometimes found to be significant, which may partially explain their high estimate of the variance explained by average school SES. The fact that Bryk and Raudenbush (1992) did not include extensive individual-level controls may also account for their high estimate of between-school variation in math test scores (i.e., approximately 20% as compared to only 10% in the studies by Coleman and Jencks). Building on Raudenbush and Bryk's (1992) study, we will use the same software (i.e., HLM), but a different analytical strategy that satisfies the call for a more elaborate methodological approach to monitor the school effect.

RELEVANT RESEARCH ON PEER NETWORKS

School segregation affects students in ways that go far beyond the effects of class isolation. To begin, the peer networks students develop and the friendships they form are important consequences of the school they attend. Recent research (Haynie 2002) suggests there is much to learn about these networks as they are far more complicated that previously believed. Furthermore, relatively little is known about how peer networks affect educational outcomes. The unique data used in this chapter will enable us to examine two aspects of adolescent networks believed to be important determinants of academic behavior. The first is peer network social capital, an individual-level measure, while the second, peer network segregation, is determined at the school-level. Each is briefly discussed below.

Peer group theory predicts that the prospects for adolescent school success will vary depending on the peer group with whom adolescents most often come into contact (Coleman et al. 1966; Hallinan and Sørensen 1985). The peer group is the context in which adolescents are exposed to others, including role models. It involves contemporaneous behavioral influences and is always reciprocal (Coleman 1988; Coleman et al. 1966; Schneider and Coleman 1993).

Chubb and Moe (1990:109) consider peer friendships at school to be a critical link between families and schools because "through their peers, students are influenced by the families of other students in a school." The acquaintances and communications between students foster social capital because they make possible network connections among sets of individuals (Hallinan and Sørensen 1985; Harris et al. 2002; Kubitschek and Hallinan 1998; Morgan and Sørensen 1999). However, this social capital may be used to promote either positive or negative outcomes (McCarthy and Hagan 1995). Thus although peer groups may provide members with the opportunity to form positive skills and relationships, including those that may make them academically successful, they may also transmit less desirable behaviors such as those that make adolescents more likely to fail academically (Berndt and Keefe 1995; Wentzel and Caldwell 1997) or to engage in delinquent behavior (Haynie 2002).

Various theoretical ideas have been advanced to describe the positive and negative aspects of peers on academic achievement. For instance, Ogbu (1978, 1981) has used oppositional culture theory to describe a cultural pattern within African-American and Latino communities whereby peers disparage academic achievement because it is perceived as "selling out" or "acting white" (Fordham and Ogbu 1986; Ogbu 1991). Ogbu (1978) argues that minority students tend to develop a collective oppositional culture, a frame of reference that actively rejects mainstream behaviors and undermines academic achievement. In other words, children in this situation are often ostracized for conforming to the educational system. As a result, Steinberg et al. (1992) argue that minority students receive less support for achievement from their peers of the same ethnic background and consequently do not fare as well in school as non-Hispanic white students.

Just as links have been established between negative peer influence and academic outcomes (Berndt and Keefe 1995; Berndt et al. 1990), similar linkages may be established between positive academic outcomes and peer influence (e.g., Epstein 1983). For example, Carter (2003) reported that while black and Latino students rejected certain styles of speech, dress, and music as "acting white," they nonetheless valued behaviors conducive to academic success, such as studying hard, getting good grades, and making the honor roll. The present study will determine which, if any, of these possibilities best describes how peer networks affect academic outcomes.

A related way of examining the potential positive impact of networks on adolescent academic achievement is to examine the effect of ethnic social capital on academic outcomes. Borjas (1992, 1995) locates ethnic social capital within the ethnic group and its networks. This notion of ethnic social capital has primarily been used in studies of immigrants and assimilation (e.g., Portes 1998; Portes and Rumbaut 2001). Borjas hypothesizes that immigrant and minority children may experience increased chances of economic success when they develop in social environments with greater amounts of ethnic social capital. Ethnic groups and networks provide intergenerational transmissions of social and human capital, norms regarding educational attainment, as well as educational and employment opportunities. Those ethnic groups that resist acculturation and maintain high levels of ethnic solidarity may provide better opportunities for younger generations through the creation and diffusion of ethnic social capital.

Because minority youth are often disadvantaged regarding other forms of social and financial capital, ethnic social capital may be a beneficial form for the educational outcomes of these adolescents, especially given their occasional reliance on peer based social capital to compensate for the lack of family social capital (Lin 1990; Zhou and Bankston 1998). However, thus far the lack of appropriate data (Haynie 2002), as well as the typical view that co-racial and co-ethnic peer influences among adolescents were considered liabilities, have meant that this possibility has not yet been systematically examined. This chapter, however, will carefully analyze the effect of ethnic social capital within the school context to determine how it affects the educational achievement and attainment of minority youth. In a related vein, various measures of family social capital (described below) will also be considered in multivariate analyses.

The second aspect of peer networks this study will examine is peer network segregation. According to Hallinan (1982), the racial/ethnic composition of a student body determines the probability of interracial friendship formation by influencing the composition of friendship pools from which students draw. Most researchers consider interracial friendships beneficial for the academic performance of minority students (Chubb and Moe 1990; Coleman et al. 1966; Hawley and Smylie 1988; Roscigno 1998). The *Coleman Report* explained the benefits of school integration as the transmission of values. More specifically, socially acceptable patterns of behavior were diffused from the more privileged racial group to the less privileged one *through* interracial contact (Coleman et al. 1966; Gerard 1988). Other scholars stressed the importance of information transfer, which is facilitated in integrated environments (e.g., Chubb and Moe 1990). Still others (e.g., Hawley and Smylie 1988) argue that interracial friendships provide minorities with access to resources, means of self-presentation, and patterns of communication acceptable to the majority.

In essence, virtually all prior research extols the virtues of integration and interracial friendships and suggests that they lead to improved academic performance. However, the lack of adequate data made it impossible for prior studies to systematically examine this oft made assertion. Below we examine the effects of peer network segregation to determine how it is related to both adolescent educational achievement and attainment.

HYPOTHESES

Several of the hypotheses examined in this chapter have already been tested before using different data sets and techniques. However, what is unique about the present study is that these research questions are now examined together with still others that have never before been addressed. The primary hypotheses examined in this study may be stated as follows:

1. Like prior studies of segregation (e.g., Bankston and Caldas 2002; Coleman et al. 1966; Jencks 1972), we incorporate school racial and ethnic composition as a key independent variable and hypothesize that it will affect adolescent achievement and attainment. More precisely, we expect that attendance at a school with high minority enrollment will be negatively associated with academic achievement and attainment.

2. Based on earlier research (e.g., Entwisle and Alexander 1992; Kahlenberg 1996, 2001; Orfield 1978), we hypothesize a direct relationship between average school SES and the academic achievement of its students. More specifically, attendance at a high SES school is expected to be associated with high academic achievement and vice versa.

3. We hypothesize that differences in academic performance are influenced by friendship preferences, especially with respect to race and ethnicity. Based on Borjas' (1992, 1995) notion of ethnic social capital, and contrary to oppositional culture theory (Ogbu 1978, 1981; Fordham and Ogbu 1986), we expect to see significant interactions between race/ethnicity and one's orientation towards ethnic social capital, as proxied by the peer network segregation index. In other words, minority youth preferences for inter-group rather than intra-group ties may positively affect their academic achievement and attainment. The additive and multiplicative effects of this possibility are analyzed below for all racial/ethnic groups considered.

4. Following Coleman (1988), who suggested social capital manifests itself not only in the structure of social groups and networks but also in the quality of relationships and the amount of support they provide, we hypothesize that the amount of social capital present in networks is directly related to academic success. Since we proxy this amount as network achievement, we expect to find a positive association between network achievement and an individual student's achievement and attainment.

5. Research suggests that family based social capital is one of the most important factors influencing adolescent educational success (Dornbusch et al. 1987; Israel, Beaulieu and Hartless 2001; Stevenson and Baker 1987). Various scholars (e.g., Coleman 1990; Teachman et al. 1996) have distinguished between the structural

(e.g., family structure and size) and relationship components (e.g., the quality of parent-child relationship) of family social capital. An increasing number of studies suggest that the presence or absence of a parent, as well as family size may affect adolescent educational outcomes (Bridge et al. 1979; Hetherington 1998; McLanahan and Sandefur 1994; Nelson et al. 2001; Schneider and Coleman 1993; Tienda and Angel 1982; Thomson et al. 1994). Similarly, adolescent academic performance has been linked to instrumental parental practices that stimulate and monitor children's educational progress (Conger et al. 1997; Galambos et al. 2003; Israel et al. 2001; McNeal 2001; Muller 1995; Steinberg et al. 1992; Zhou and Bankston 1998). Therefore, we hypothesize that adolescents from non-traditional (i.e., single parent and non-parent) and large families will do less well academically than adolescents from two-parent nuclear families. Second, we expect that all types of family social capital (i.e., parental expectations, involvement and supervision) will have a positive effect on students' academic achievement.

Data and Methods

The data used to investigate the aforementioned hypotheses is the National Longitudinal Study of Adolescent Health (hereafter, Add Health). This nationally representative, school-based data set was collected in three waves, in 1994-95, 1996 and 2001-2002, respectively. A sample of 80 high schools and 52 middle (feeder) schools from the U.S. was selected with unequal probability of selection.[2] During Wave I all students present in the 132 selected schools the day the self-administered questionnaire was conducted were surveyed (N=90,118). These data were supplemented with information supplied by an official at each of the surveyed schools. A subset of students was randomly selected from the 132 schools (N=20,745) for in-home interviews, as was a parent or parent-figure. With the exception of educational attainment, which comes from Wave III, we rely on the Wave I data as they provide the most complete information on all variables of interest. Those cases with missing values on educational attainment in Wave III were excluded. Applying this selection criterion reduced our final sample size to 19,117 students from 129 schools. Auxiliary univariate analyses revealed that this reduction did not affect the distribution of sample.

These detailed data enable us to rigorously measure peer networks in ways that were not possible with earlier datasets (Haynie 2001, 2002). The Add Health data are distinguished by their hierarchical structure. This structure enables us to interpret the multifaceted nature of student achievement as a function of individual- (e.g., sex and age) and school-level factors (e.g., school racial and ethnic composition). For our analyses the Hierarchical Linear Models (HLM) statistical package will be used since it incorporates such factors more efficiently than ordinary least squares regression. HLM also takes into account the error structures present at

---

[2] Initially, 80 high schools were selected from a sampling framework of 26,666. Of these, 52 were eligible and agreed to participate. The other 28 schools were replaced by randomly selected similar high schools that matched on eight criteria (school size, school type, level of urbanization, percent white, grade span, percent black, census region, census division). A total of 52 feeder or middle-schools that matched the attributes of the selected high-schools were used. As a result, the composition of middle and high schools in the Add Health sample are very similar (Chantala and Tabor 1999). Our analyses indicate that key school-level variables (e.g., school composition and peer network segregation) in middle schools are not significantly different from those of the high schools.

each level (see Bryk and Raudenbush, 1992 or Raudenbush and Bryk, 2002) for more information on HLM).

Dependent Variables

This study will estimate both short- and mid-term school effects on the educational progress of middle- and high-school students. Accordingly, this project's dependent variables are educational achievement, measured as GPA, and attainment, measured as high school graduation. These two variables are theoretically distinct. Although attainment as conceptualized by Blau and Duncan (1967) and Sewell and Hauser (1975) is a function of family background, and, to some degree, intellectual abilities, achievement is also related to one's ability to adapt to their educational context (Bridge et al. 1979; Lareau 1989). More importantly, the aforementioned classical studies (Blau and Duncan 1967; Sewell and Hauser 1975) document that educational achievement has a long-term effect on attainment, which, in turn, has a profound effect on one's children and so forth. Therefore, while achievement may determine attainment, the opposite is not true. Because of these conceptual differences between achievement and attainment, distinct analyses will focus on each dependent variable. Achievement was computed based on the grades adolescents reported they earned the prior year in four subjects (English, math, science and social studies). These four responses, ranging from 1 (D or F) to 4 (A), were averaged across subjects and converted to a standard 4-point GPA. Although slightly inflated, self-reported grades are highly correlated with grades reported on official transcripts (Dornbusch et al. 1990). Table 1 shows that the average GPA in Wave I was about 2.8. The measure educational attainment is culled from the Wave III results, which helps to address concerns about causal ordering. At that time respondents, then young adults between the ages of 18 and 26, were asked about the highest grade of regular school they had completed. Their answers range from "6th grade" (the lowest score) to "5 or more years of graduate school" (the highest score). Note that this measure is cohort-specific and censored from above and below. In other words, attainment and age are inextricably linked. Hence, although the variable's distribution is approximately normal, it is because of factors unrelated to attainment. Controlling for age alone does not eliminate the problem of cohort-specificity. Because of this and the fact that the median and mode for Wave III attainment approximates graduation from high school, we transformed the original Add Health measure into a dichotomous outcome variable with at least high school graduation equal to 1. Thus, in contrast to achievement, which monitors GPA, educational attainment provides information about an educational transition this cohort may have experienced.

INDEPENDENT VARIABLES

Individual-Level Measures

Peer Social Capital. In this study, we employ two measures of peer social capital. One, discussed below in the section School-Level Variables, captures the structural component of peer social capital. The other is an individual-level measure computed as the mean GPA of a student's peer network (henceforth peer network GPA). This measure relates to the actual amount of peer social capital and, hypothetically, peer support available to an individual student. Pre-constructed by the Add Health, this variable does not account for unequal network sizes. In other words, in those cases where networks are relatively small, peer network GPA is likely to approximate an individual student's GPA, thereby creating a source of collinearity with the individual student's achievement. To eliminate this bias we transformed the Add Health peer network GPA measure according to the following formula:

$$New\ Network\ GPA = \frac{UNGPA \times NS - Individal\ Student's\ GPA}{NS - 1},$$

where UNGPA = untransformed network GPA and NS = network size.

Other individual-level variables are examined in an attempt to control for personal and family factors that might impact academic achievement. These include race/ethnicity, gender, age and frequency of involvement in extracurricular activities. Race and ethnicity are determined based on student responses. From these responses we created a series of dichotomous race/ethnicity variables for the categories African-American, Asian, Latino, and non-Hispanic white.[3] The latter serves as the reference category in these analyses. Gender is a dummy variable with male serving as the reference category. Age is measured in complete years at the time of interview. We monitor the variable involvement in extracurricular activities because high-achieving students typically spend more time engaged in learning activities both in and outside of school than do lower-achieving students (Blum and Reinhart 1997). In the Add Health extracurricular learning activities may include reading, writing, arts and crafts and other activities. Information on these activities comes from the question: "During the past week how many times did you do hobbies, such as collecting baseball cards, playing a musical instrument, reading, or doing arts and crafts?" Response categories range from 0 "not at all" to 3 "5 or more times."

Table 1 reveals that the sample's sex ratio is balanced with approximately equal proportions of male and female students. The average age of Wave I respondents in the summer of 1995 was 15 years. Approximately 65% were non-Hispanic white, 16% African-American, 14% Hispanic, and 5% Asian. The modal score for extracurricular activities was 1 meaning that this group participated in 1-2 extracurricular activities during the past week.

Prior research shows that adolescent educational outcomes were associated with immigrant generational status (e.g., Kao and Tienda 1995, Orfield and Yun 1999). This is not surprising given that theories of immigrant adaptation have long predicted differential outcomes across immigrant generations (see Hirschman 2001 for more information about theories of immigrant assimilation). "Straight-line" assimilation posits continuous improvement with each successive generation while segmented assimilation theory (Portes and Zhou 1993) emphasizes contexts of reception. Because all assimilation theories underscore the significance of generational status, we created three dummy variables to monitor respondents' generational status.

---

[3] Asian and Latino adolescents were not divided into distinct ethnic origin groups (i.e., Chinese, Cubans, etc.) because these groups are too small to make statistically significant inferences about their educational achievement.

Table 1. Descriptive Statistics of Study Variables (N=19,117) [a]

	Weighted Mean	St. Deviation	Minimum	Maximum
Peer Social Capital				
Peer Network Segregation Index [b]	0.25	0.10	0.48	0.75
Peer Network Achievement	2.81	0.69	1.00	4.19
School Composition				
Average SES	0.85	0.02	0.96	0.65
Percentage of Minority Students [b]	0.26	0.18	0.00	0.69
Percentage of High-School Students	0.62	0.48	0.00	1.00
Dependent Variables				
Educational Achievement	2.82	0.76	0.77	4.17
Educational Attainment	0.86	0.35	0.00	1.00
Race/Ethnicity				
African-American	0.16	0.36	0.00	1.00
Asian	0.05	0.23	0.00	1.00
Latino	0.14	0.35	0.00	1.00
Non-Hispanic whites	0.65	0.45	0.00	1.00
Family Structure				
Two-Parent Household	0.59	0.50	0.00	1.00
Single-Parent Household	0.24	0.43	0.00	1.00
Non-Parent Household	0.17	0.38	0.00	1.00
Large Household	0.20	0.40	0.00	1.00
SES				
Parents' Education	6.84	2.11	0.00	10.85
Family Income [b]	5.27	1.48	0.26	14.21
Family Social Capital				
Parents' Educational Expectations	4.33	0.89	1.00	6.58
Parents' Involvement	0.43	0.29	0.02	1.82
Parents' Supervision	3.83	0.70	1.00	5.67
Individual-Level Controls				
Age	14.98	1.66	11.00	21.00
Male	0.49	0.01	0.00	1.00
Immigrant Generation 1	0.05	0.21	0.00	1.00
Immigrant Generation 2	0.10	0.30	0.00	1.00
Immigrant Generation 3	0.85	0.36	0.00	1.00
Extracurricular Activities	1.39	1.56	0.00	22.00

[a] All variables are from Wave I except for educational attainment, which is from Wave III.

[b] Percentage of minority students, peer network segregation index, and family income were transformed by the Box-Cox method in order to satisfy the multilevel normality condition of HLM (see more on HLM in Raudenbush and Bryk 2002).

Foreign-born adolescents are coded as immigrant generation one. U.S.-born children with at least one foreign-born parent are distinguished as generation two and generation three is comprised of those born in the U.S. with two U.S.-born parents.

Socioeconomic Status (SES). Household income and parents' education are included in an attempt to control for family SES, a factor often linked to adolescent academic achievement (e.g., Bridge et al. 1979; Conger et al. 1997; Lareau 1989; McLoyd 1998). The income measure was obtained from the parental response to the question: "About how much total income, before taxes did your family receive in 1994? Include your own income, the income of everyone else in your household, and income from welfare benefits, dividends, and all other sources." Responses are coded in units of 1000 and range from 0 to 999. Those cases with negative income were recoded as zeros because reports of negative household income, as opposed to individual income, may indicate debt and, thus, differ in nature from the income measure.[4]

The parental education measures came from items asking: "How far did she [mother] go in school?" or "How far did he [father] go in school?" This is a measure of the highest level of education completed. Response categories range from "eighth grade or less" (coded 1) to "graduate training beyond a four-year college or university" (coded 9). Parents' education is recoded as the highest educational attainment of both parents. In order to account for family structure all family social capital measures, except parents' education, were constructed as the average response for both parents, if available, and as simple measures if responses for only one parent were available. Multiple imputation was used to fill in missing values for both parental income and education.

Family Social Capital. Like others (Coleman 1988; Teachman et al. 1996), we conceptualize family social capital as having quantitative (e.g., family structure) and qualitative (e.g., parental interactions) components. Earlier research suggests that both of these components are associated with adolescent educational achievement (e.g., Hetherington 1998; Israel et al. 2001; Morgan and Sørensen 1999; Patterson et al. 1992; Tienda and Angel 1982).

Family Structure and Size. Family structure is believed to affect well-being by influencing family functioning (McLanahan and Sandefur 1994; Thomson et al. 1994). For this reason a series of dummy variables were constructed based on the household roster. We use these to contrast youth who live with biological or adoptive parents (reference) with those residing in either a single parent or non-parent situation. Similarly, research on household composition suggests a link between household size and adolescent well-being, as adolescents in smaller households exhibit better educational achievement (e.g., Bridge et al. 1979, Nelson et al. 2001). Therefore a dummy variable that controls for household size is also incorporated. The reference group consists of households that contain no more than four members.

Parent-Child Relationships. Both affective and instrumental ties between adolescents and their families and the parenting behaviors associated with them are viewed as a potential resources or forms of family social capital (Laosa 1982; Schneider and Coleman 1993; Smith et al. 1992; Stanton-Salazar 1997). Components of parent-child relationships, such as parents'

---

[4] To reduce the skewness of the original income variable in the Add Health Parents data set family income was transformed using the Box-Cox family of transformations where $Income = \dfrac{(Income+1)^{0.2} - 1}{0.2}$. For more on Box-Cox transformations, see Box and Cox (1964).

expectations for their children's further education, or parental supervision and involvement have been documented to influence the educational outcomes of adolescents (e.g., Conger et al. 1994; Israel et al. 2001; Laosa 1982; Lee 1993; McLoyd 1998; McNeal 2001; Patterson et al. 1992). The index monitoring parents' educational expectations was created from two items asked separately about mother's and father's expectations. Respondents were asked how disappointed each parent would be if they failed to graduate from college and high school. Responses range from low (1) to high disappointment (5). The reliability coefficient for these items is 0.82. Responses were averaged to create an index. Parental educational expectations capture cultural variation in the family's emphasis on educational achievement, a family context characteristic that is often linked to immigrant academic success (Vernez et al. 1996). Parents' involvement is constructed from nine items that inquire into the activities that parents and adolescents did together over the past four week period. For each parent adolescents were asked if they had done any of the following together: gone shopping, played a sport, attended a religious service or related event, talked about life, talked about a date or party attended, attended a movie, sports event, concert, play, or museum, talked about a personal problem, discussed grades or school work, worked on a school project, and talked about other school activities. Response choices are "yes" and "no." The activities undertaken by the adolescent and at least one parent were then summed to form the index. The parents' involvement scale has a Cronbach's alpha of 0.72. Parental supervision is a variable that ranges from 0 to 3. It is constructed by summing affirmative responses to three items that indicate whether a parent is present in the home most or all of the time when the adolescent (1) goes to school in the morning, (2) comes home from school in the afternoon, and (3) goes to bed at night. The parental supervision scale has a Cronbach's alpha of 0.68.

School-Level Variables

The school-level variables examined monitor two fundamental aspects of each school's student body: its racial/ethnic make-up and its socioeconomic composition. Although measures of school racial and ethnic composition (percentage Hispanic, percentage Asian, etc.) are not provided by the Add Health data, they can be directly calculated from the race/ethnicity responses of the student body. School-level race/ethnicity codes for these calculations are defined using the same codes earlier described for individuals. Note, however, that although we consider Asians as a distinct racial category in our analyses, they do not comprise part of our minority designation. Instead, our school-level measure monitoring the proportion of minority students in each school includes only Latinos and blacks. We do this because Asians are the nation's most highly educated racial group and they attend the most integrated schools (Orfield and Yun 1999). Analyses presented in Table 4 further document the higher average academic achievement of Asian students vis-à-vis non-Hispanic whites.

To understand the importance of school-level SES this study employs the composite measure average SES, which was created by combining two school-level characteristics. More specifically, at the school-level the standardized scores for parental income and education were summed to create average SES.

This is appropriate as these two variables are strongly intercorrelated at the school-level (Cronbach's alpha = 0.90). Because both of these school-level SES measures are strongly skewed, they are transformed using the Box-Cox family of transformations. However, at the individual-level we consider it important for the present study to analyze these two indicators separately. This is done because some immigrant and minority groups experience status inconsistency, meaning that their educational attainment does not correspond with the occupations they occupy or the income they earn. This may explain why the reliability of the aggregate individual-level SES measure is lower (Cronbach's alpha = 0.71) than that of the school-level.

According to Blau (1994), students cannot form friendships with students of other racial and ethnic groups if schools are homogenous. Interracial contact is a prerequisite for the formation of interracial friendships. For this reason, we included a measure of network segregation within schools.

Many students named as friends are also members of the sample. This allows friends and their characteristics to be matched based on their survey responses. Both the Add Health in-school and in-home questionnaires asked students to list their five best male and female friends (including girlfriends and boyfriends). For each participating school the Add Health obtained a roster of its students and assigned them identification numbers. These rosters enabled students to find their friends in their school and a sister school. These identification numbers permit the direct determination of the race/ethnicity of adolescents' friends. On the basis of friendship preferences, the Add Health constructed the modified Freeman's race segregation index (1978). This school-level index is calculated as follows:

$$Segregation\ Index\ =\ \frac{Expected\ Ties\ -\ Observed\ Ties}{Expected\ Ties}$$

where *ties* refers to the total number of ties sent from a network member sharing the same race/ethnicity to all network members of other races or ethnic origins, summed across all race/ethnicity categories. The segregation index has a theoretical minimum of -1 (pure out-group preference) and a theoretical maximum of 1 (pure in-group preference, or total segregation). A value of 0 indicates no group-preference, i.e. friendship ties are set randomly with respect to race/ethnicity.

Table 2 presents the means for the dependent variables educational achievement and attainment when cross-tabulated with independent variables monitoring school-level SES, percentage of minority students, and the peer network segregation index. These continuous independent measures were divided into categories that correspond to high, medium, and low SES levels based on the 25th and 75th percentiles of their respective distributions.

Table 2 demonstrates that at both times schools with the lowest SES and the highest percentage of minority students had the lowest GPAs. However, those attending schools with the highest level of peer network segregation had the highest GPAs. These results suggest a positive association between school SES and educational outcomes. Likewise, they also imply a positive association between peer network segregation and educational outcomes. However, the association between percent minority and educational outcomes is likely to be negative.

Table 2. Average Educational Achievement and Attainment in Schools with High, Medium and Low School SES, Percentages of Minority Youth and Peer Network Segregation Index (N high school=80; N middle schools=49)

School-Level Variable	Wave I Educational Achievement	Wave III Educational Attainment
School SES		
High	2.98	14.03
Medium	2.79	13.10
Low	2.66	12.38
Percentage Minority in School		
High	2.66	12.49
Medium	2.80	13.08
Low	2.87	13.39
Peer Network Segregation Index		
High	2.92	13.51
Medium	2.86	13.12
Low	2.65	12.04

Auxiliary analyses indicate that the school-level variables percentage minority and peer network segregation index are slightly skewed. Skewed variables can produce heteroscedasticity and inflated standard errors of regression estimates. These problems reduce the statistical power of significance tests and result in larger confidence intervals, which make the rejection of the null hypotheses more difficult (Stevens 1996). To remedy this potential problem we transformed the percentage of minority students and the racial segregation index using the Box-Cox family of log-linear transformations (Box and Cox 1964).[5] Additionally, as a requirement of HLM, all school-level variables were school-mean centered.

Analytic Strategy

The regression analyses presented below are performed using HLM. If we denote i as the ith student (level-1) and j as the jth school (level-2), the individual-level (level-1) model can be presented as follows:

$$Educational\ Outcome = \beta_{0j} + \beta_{1j}X_{1ij} + \beta_{2j}X_{2ij} + ... + \beta_{nj}X_{nij} + \rho_{ij},$$

where $\beta_{(0\text{-}n)j}$ are regression coefficients of individual-level factors $X_{(0\text{-}n)ij}$ and ρ_{ij} is normal error with mean 0 and variance σ^2.

The generalized formula of the school-level (level-2) intercept is:

---

[5] We used the following formulas: $Percentage\ Minority = \dfrac{(Percentage\ Minority + 1)^{-0.2} - 1}{-0.2}$, and $Segregation\ Index = \dfrac{(Segregation\ Index + 1)^{-2} - 1}{-2}$. These transformations were obtained by running "Box-Cox" macro from the SAS library.

$$\beta_{0j} = \gamma_0 + \gamma_1 Y_{1j} + \gamma_2 Y_{2j} + \ldots + \gamma_n Y_{nj} + \omega_{0j}$$

where $\gamma_{(0-1)}$ are regression coefficients of school-level factors $Y_{(0-n)j}$ and ω_j is the school-level error.

Assuming no meso-level covariates, as we do in Tables 3 and 4, the regression coefficients $\beta_{(0-n)j}$ of individual-level factors are modeled as:

$$\beta_{1j} = \gamma_1 + \omega_{1j}, \; \beta_{2j} = \gamma_2 + \omega_{2j} \text{ and, in more general form: } \beta_{nj} = \gamma_n + \omega_{nj}.$$

When approaching the question of constructing 2-level HLM models, we used two modeling techniques available in HLM. The first is a linear model. It suits the interval/ratio character of the first dependent variable – academic achievement. Because the other dependent variable – academic attainment – has a dichotomous outcome, a Bernoulli model for binary data with logit link function was used to estimate the chance of graduation from high-school. One and possibly the most significant drawback of using a Bernoulli model is the inability to use sample weights. Therefore, Wave I grand sample weights were used to estimate achievement in Table 3, but not attainment in Table 4.

Below we present three sets of analyses. In the first two we model educational achievement and attainment (see Tables 3 and 4, respectively) while examining the effects of individual-level controls, family structure and social capital, peer social capital, and school contextual characteristics. The third set of analyses (see Table 5) determines the effect of meso-level interaction terms on achievement and attainment. These terms monitor interactions between race/ethnicity (individual-level measures), mean school-level SES and peer network segregation (school-level measures).

Parallel analyses are estimated for the achievement and attainment models. Table 3 presents results for all achievement models while Table 4 displays all attainment findings. Model 1 documents the effects of race/ethnicity and individual-level controls (age, gender, generational status, and frequency of involvement in extracurricular activities). Models 2, 3 and 4 add, respectively, family size and structure measures, parents' SES effects, and family social capital variables. Together these three models test hypothesis V, where we expect that all types of family social capital will have a positive effect on student academic achievement. Model 5 adds the individual-level measure peer social capital as a way of testing hypothesis IV. Recall, we hypothesized a positive association between peer social capital and an individual student's academic outcomes.

To examine this hypothesis we treat peer network achievement as a proxy for peer social capital and monitor its relationship with student achievement and attainment. The final three models incorporate school-level factors, one at a time. Models 6, 7 and 8, respectively, add percentage of minority students, school SES and the peer network segregation index. These models test the hypotheses I, II and III, while controlling for the effect of individual-level factors.

RESULTS

The first model of educational achievement consists primarily of individual-level demographic predictors (see Table 3). Model 1 demonstrates that many of these measures were significant in the predicted directions. Blacks and Latinos are predicted to have significantly lower grades (p<0.001) than non-Hispanic whites, while Asian marks are not significantly different from those of the white contrast group. These race/ethnicity patterns remain in all Table 3 models. The variable monitoring first generation immigrant status reveals that this group significantly outperforms the native-born (p<0.001). This generational effect remains in all other achievement models, as well as all educational attainment models (see Table 4). The observed immigrant advantage may be due to ethnic resilience (Ogbu 1981) or the ethnic social capital present in immigrant networks (Bankston et al. 1997; Borjas 1992). Similarly, achievement among the second generation is typically higher than the native-born, but below the foreign-born first generation.

Among the individual-level controls, frequency of involvement in extracurricular activities is positively associated with GPA (p<0.001), a result that remains constant throughout Table 4. Age is insignificant in this and other Table 3 models, however, its importance is pronounced in Table 4 models predicting high school graduation. Finally, gender is insignificant in this baseline model but becomes very significant in higher-order models predicting GPA.

Model 2 adds measures monitoring family structure and sizes. Results generally conform to expectations as the educational achievement of children in both single-parent and guardian families (i.e., homes headed by relatives other than parents) is significantly lower (p<0.001) than for children reared in two-parent households. These findings are consistent with prior research that indicates family structure has a powerful impact on achievement (Cox et al. 2001; Muller 1995; Nelson et al. 2001). Family size, however, does not exert a significant effect on achievement in this model, nor in any other predicting either GPA or educational attainment (see Table 4).

Model 3 adds two individual-level measures of SES, family income and parents' education. As hypothesized, both were positive and usually highly significant (p<0.001) in this and all other models predicting achievement and attainment (see Table 4). These results clearly document the powerful effect family SES has on both GPA and high school graduation. The introduction of family SES results in a major decline of magnitude for black and Latino effects as they fell from -0.19 to -0.13 and -0.20 to -0.11, respectively.

Not only does family SES mediate the effects of race/ethnicity on grades, but it also documents a significant reduction in the GPA "race gap" for blacks and Latinos whose parents have income and education levels similar to non-Hispanic whites.

The same effect is observable for the family structure measures as single-parent and non-parent households fell from -0.14 to -0.06 and from -0.12 to -0.07, respectively. Hence, the achievement disadvantage experienced by blacks, Latinos and students from single-parent and non-parent households is partially attributable to family SES. Model 3 also reveals that the immigrant achievement advantage is stronger when family SES is controlled. Specifically, the first immigrant generation effect increases nearly 40 percent, while the corresponding boost for the second generation was 50 percent. Clearly, generational effects are larger once family SES is considered.

Table 3. HLM Regression Models of School- and Individual-Level Predictors on Wave I Educational Achievement (N students=19,117; N high school=80; N middle schools=49)

	Models															
	1		2		3		4		5		6		7		8	
Individual-Level Factors																
Race/Ethnicity																
African-American [a]	-0.24	***	-0.19	***	-0.13	***	-0.14	***	-0.11	***	-0.05	**	-0.08	**	-0.07	*
Asian [a]	0.07		0.08		0.04		0.02		0.04		0.01		0.03		0.02	
Latino [a]	-0.22	***	-0.20	***	-0.11	***	-0.12	***	-0.06	*	-0.03		-0.11	***	-0.09	***
Individual-Level Controls																
Age	-0.04		-0.04		-0.04		-0.04		-0.11		-0.09		-0.05		-0.09	
Female [d]	0.10		0.09		0.10		0.10		0.16	*	0.19	***	0.23	***	0.21	***
Immigrant Generation 1 [e]	0.21	***	0.23	***	0.32	***	0.31	***	0.28	***	0.19	***	0.20	***	0.19	***
Immigrant Generation 2 [e]	0.02		0.03		0.06	*	0.06	*	0.07	*	0.05	***	0.03		0.06	***
Extracurricular Activities	0.14	***	0.14	***	0.12	***	0.11	***	0.08	***	0.11	***	0.08	***	0.09	***
Family Structure and Size																
Single-Parent Household [b]			-0.14	***	-0.06	***	-0.09	***	-0.06	***	-0.08	***	-0.07	***	-0.09	***
Non-Parent Household [b]			-0.12	*	-0.07	***	-0.08	***	-0.09	***	-0.11	***	-0.14	***	-0.09	***
Large Household [c]			-0.09		-0.04		-0.04		-0.00		-0.01		-0.04		-0.02	
Socioeconomic Status																
Parents' Education					0.07	***	0.07	***	0.07	***	0.09	***	0.06	***	0.09	***
Family Income					0.07	***	0.08	***	0.09	***	0.10	***	0.05	***	0.08	***
Family Social Capital																
Parents' Educational Expectations							0.08	***	0.08	***	0.09	***	0.08	***	0.09	***

	Models							
	1	2	3	4	5	6	7	8
Parents' Involvement				0.10	0.03	0.05 *	0.01	0.06 *
Parents' Supervision				0.06 ***	0.05 ***	0.05 ***	0.03 *	0.04 ***
Peer Social Capital								
Average GPA of Peer Network					0.67 ***	0.52 ***	0.43 ***	0.62 ***
School-Level Factors								
Percentage of Minority Students						-0.29 ***	-0.16 ***	-0.10
Average SES							1.77 ***	1.58 ***
Peer Network Segregation Index								0.22 *
Constant	3.08 ***	3.36 ***	2.71 ***	2.01 ***	1.02 ***	0.96 ***	0.91 ***	0.86 ***
Model Comparison Test(df)[1]		468 ***	810 ***	366 ***	614 ***			
models compared		1 and 2	2 and 3	3 and 4	4 and 5			

*p<0.05; **p<0.01; ***p<0.001. Reference Categories: a – non-Hispanic white; b – two-parent household; c – household of up to four residents; d – male; e – two native born parents.

[1] The test is analogous to the nested F-test for OLS regression models. It is based on the difference between the deviance statistics (defined as -2 ln likelihood function value at convergence) of the models contrasted. It has a chi-square distribution with degrees of freedom equal to the difference in the number of parameters estimated in the models. The model comparison test is not applicable for models that differ only in the number of level-2 factors or cross-level interactions.

Table 4. HLM Regression Models of School- and Individual-Level Predictors on Wave III Educational Attainment (N students=19,117; N high school=80; N middle schools=49)

								Models								
	1		2		3		4		5		6		7		8	
Individual-Level Factors																
Race/Ethnicity																
African-American [a]	-0.19		0.12		0.32	***	0.47	***	0.47	***	0.14		0.13		0.14	
Asian [a]	0.71	***	0.75	***	0.47	***	0.43	***	0.42	***	0.19	*	0.13		0.15	*
Latino [a]	-0.59	*	-0.53	*	-0.19		-0.10		-0.11		-0.07		-0.08		-0.11	
Individual-Level Controls																
Age	0.11	*	0.15	**	0.11		0.12		0.15	*	0.29	***	0.21	***	0.23	***
Female [d]	-0.11	*	-0.11		0.17		0.15		0.14		0.11		0.09		0.03	
Immigrant Generation 1 [e]	0.19	***	0.27	***	0.75	***	0.74	***	0.72	***	0.68	***	0.71	***	0.42	***
Immigrant Generation 2 [e]	0.06	*	0.11	***	0.24	***	0.26	***	0.27	***	0.21	***	0.19	*	0.11	
Extracurricular Activities	0.41	***	0.40	***	0.31	***	0.25	***	0.23	***	0.26	***	0.19	***	0.12	***
Family Structure and Size																
Single-Parent Household [b]			-0.52		-0.21		-0.19		-0.19		-0.12		-0.15		-0.14	
Non-Parent Household [b]			-0.56		-0.33	*	-0.33	*	-0.32	*	-0.36	***	-0.34	***	-0.33	***
Large Household [c]			-0.33		-0.14		-0.12		-0.11		-0.14		-0.13		-0.15	

	Models															
	1		2		3		4		5		6		7		8	
Socioeconomic Status																
Parents' Education					0.24	***	0.19	***	0.19	***	0.21	***	0.23	***	0.22	**
Family Income					0.33	***	0.30	***	0.31	***	0.28	***	0.29	***	0.30	***
Family Social Capital																
Parents' Educational Expectations							0.18	***	0.16	***	0.14	***	0.15	***	0.15	***
Parents' Involvement							0.06		0.03		-0.05		-0.06		-0.02	
Parents' Supervision							0.08		0.08		0.06		0.02		0.03	
Peer Social Capital																
Average GPA of Peer Network									1.07	***	0.94	***	0.52	***	0.78	***
School-Level Factors																
Percentage of Minority Students											3.96	***	2.08	***	2.15	*
Average SES													1.77	***	11.86	***
Peer Network Segregation Index															-0.12	
Constant	-0.05	*	-0.63	*	-3.15	***	-4.40	***	-6.28	***	-8.30	***	-8.91	***	-16.81	***
Model Comparison Test(df)[2]			68		567	***	113	*	747	***						
models compared			1 and 2		2 and 3		3 and 4		4 and 5							

*p<0.05; **p<0.01; ***p<0.001. Reference Categories: a – non-Hispanic white; b – two-parent household; c – household of up to four residents; d – male; e – two native born parents.

---

[2] The test is analogous to the nested F-test for OLS regression models. It is based on the difference between the deviance statistics (defined as -2 ln likelihood function value at convergence) of the models contrasted. It has a chi-square distribution with degrees of freedom equal to the difference in the number of parameters estimated in the models. The model comparison test is not applicable for models that differ only in the number of level-2 factors or cross-level interactions.

Model 4 incorporates the three individual-level family social capital variables. Two of these measures, parents' supervision and educational expectations, are highly significant (p<0.001) and, as expected, positively related to achievement. These family social capital measures remain significant in all other Table 3 models. The inclusion of family social capital measures results in a 50 percent increase of the magnitude of the single-parenthood effect on grades. This is suggestive of a suppression effect whereby the negative association between single parenthood and grades is stronger when controlling for family social capital.

Peer social capital, measured as the average GPA of one's peer network, is added in model 5. This variable is very significant (p<0.001) and positively related to school performance. Furthermore, this measure remains significant for all models of educational achievement, as well as those estimating educational attainment (see Table 4). These results were earlier hypothesized and clearly demonstrate the importance of this measure. A comparison of models 4 and 5 reveals that the African-American and Latino disadvantage vis-à-vis non-Hispanic whites diminishes once peer network achievement is controlled. In the case of Latinos this disadvantage is reduced by 50 percent and declines in significance from p <0.001 to p <0.05. As such, the disparity in grades between blacks and Latinos and non-Hispanic white students is partially attributable to peer social capital. When controlling for peer social capital gender also is significant. More specifically, in model 5 females have better grades than males, whereas in models 1 to 4 the effect of gender is suppressed. Model comparison tests indicate that the inclusion of each successive block of individual-level measures significantly improves upon the preceding model.

Models 6 to 8 incorporate school-level factors one at a time. Model 6 adds the variable percentage of minority students, a proxy measure for school racial composition. Its effect is negative and significant (p<0.001) suggesting that higher concentrations of minority students result in lower grades. More specifically, this effect may be interpreted such that white non-Hispanic students who attend a school with a minority concentration 1 standard deviation higher than the mean are predicted to have a GPA 0.29 points lower than students who attend schools with the mean percentage of minority students. The addition of this school-level measure also causes coefficients for blacks and Latinos to become less significant, as the African-American coefficient declines from p<0.001 in model 4 to p<0.01 in model 6, while the Latino coefficient is now statistically insignificant. However, the effects of female, second generation status, and parent's involvement all increase in significance. This mediation effect suggests that the measure percentage of minority students partially accounts for the effects of those variables.

Model 7 incorporates the second school-level measure, mean SES. This factor is positive and significant (p<0.001), demonstrating that school-level SES exerts a powerful influence on the achievement of individual students. When school-level SES is added to the model percent minority retains its prior significance, however, its effect declined nearly 50 percent from -0.29 to -0.16. Not only does this reveal that socioeconomic composition is a more powerful predictor of achievement than a school's minority composition (p<0.001), but also that the mediation effect of racial/ethnic composition is partially explained by socioeconomic composition. Clearly, attending a school with a higher concentration of students from wealthy families increases one's predicted GPA.[8] In addition, with the exception of Asians, the inclusion of school-level SES raised the significance and magnitude of the race/ethnicity

---

[8] The exact percentage of change is difficult to estimate because the constant in HLM models is not interpretable.

effects and significantly increased the "race gap" between non-Hispanic white and African-Americans and Latinos. The achievement disadvantage of these groups vis-à-vis non-Hispanic whites appears to be muted without the school-level SES control. Also note that once school SES is controlled, the effects for parents' involvement and second generation status are insignificant. Thus the second generation advantage over native adolescents is partially explained by the socioeconomic composition of their schools. The positive association between parents' involvement and achievement is also somewhat explained by the school-level SES effect. Lastly, the introduction of school-level SES also explains some of the influence that individual-level SES has on adolescent achievement as the magnitude of both family income and parents' education decreased by approximately 50 percent. This mediation effect and the fact that individual and school SES are correlated in the individual-level sample (Pearson correlation coefficient = 0.61) indicate a link between school and family. This link suggests that supportive parental networks are formed along social class lines.

Model 8 of Table 3 includes the final school-level variable, the peer network segregation index. Its effect is positive and significant ($p<0.05$). However, its inclusion reduces the effect of percent minority at a school to insignificance. Hence, the peer network segregation index might be a mediator variable that explains the effect of racial/ethnic composition on academic achievement. In other words, close friends may have more effect on GPA than school composition. Similarly, the addition of the network segregation index results in an increase of the significance and magnitude of the effects for second generation status, peer network GPA and family social capital (parental involvement and supervision). In model 7 these effects are suppressed as network segregation is not accounted for. This implies that when controlling for school-level network segregation, the second generation has a certain achievement advantage over native-born adolescents, and that parental supervision and involvement have strong and positive effects on grades.

Generally speaking, all individual-level variables included in the Table 3 models conformed to expectations and to prior research. The school-level factors, however, are more problematic. The percentage of minority students is significant until controlling for peer network segregation. However, the other two school-level measures, mean SES and peer network segregation, were always significant. Also, as more school-level controls were added, the African-American effect became less significant, while the Latino one became more significant. Hence, without controls for school-level effects the gap between blacks and whites appears larger than it is, while the gap between Latinos and whites appears smaller.

According to a popular argument first put forward in the *Coleman Report* (Coleman et al. 1966) and since supported by other research (see Kahlenberg, 2001 for a review), it is school socioeconomic, not racial, composition that matters most for adolescent academic outcomes. The analyses presented in Table 3 clearly support this argument, as school-level SES is a more significant predictor of GPA than school racial composition. However, Table 3 also reveals the powerful, positive effects of two peer network variables not examined by Coleman et al. (1966). The first, peer network achievement, is always a highly significant ($p<0.001$) predictor of achievement in Table 3 models, even after controlling for numerous individual- and school-level factors. The second, the peer network segregation index, is also a significant predictor of achievement in our full model. This result suggests that net of numerous other individual- and school-level characteristics students with homogenous racial/ethnic friendship groups perform better in school than students with mixed friendship networks. This somewhat surprising result is examined in additional detail below.

In Table 4 we repeat the above exercise using educational attainment, more specifically at least high school graduation, as our dependent variable. Consequently, several distinct results emerge. Model 1 documents the effects of the core subset of individual-level predictors. This variable grouping suggests the disappearance of the "race gap" (Jencks and Phillips 1998) between blacks and non-Hispanic whites, and indicates Asian are more likely ($p<0.001$) to graduate from high school than the non-Hispanic white reference group. Still, the "race gap" between Latinos and non-Hispanic whites remains, although less pronounced than in Table 3. These results, however, will change with the addition of other variables in later models. Model 1 also reveals that all individual-level controls are significant. Age, males, first and second generation immigrant status, and involvement in extracurricular activities are all positively associated with attainment as all increase the chances of graduating from high school. Once school-level measures are introduced in later models, age becomes even more significant ($p<0.001$). The pronounced effects of first generation status and involvement in extracurricular activities remain throughout Table 4, while those of second generation status would fall to insignificance in the full model.

The addition of family structure measures in model 2 did not result in an improvement over model 1, as none of the newly added variables are significant. The inclusion of the family structure variables does, however, increase the magnitude and significance of age, from $p<0.05$ to $p<0.01$, as well as making gender insignificant. The only family structure variable to become significant in the subsequent models is non-parent household. Once school-level measures are introduced those present in these households become much less likely ($p<0.001$) to graduate from high school than those in two parent households.

Model 3 incorporates two SES measures, family income and parents' education. As in Table 3, both of these measures are significant in the hypothesized positive direction, further evidence of the effect and importance of SES on educational outcomes. These results remain constant in all Table 4 models. The inclusion of family SES variables significantly alters race/ethnicity effects. The magnitude of the African-American effect increases 2.6 times, while its significance increases to $p<0.001$. Further, the Asian effect declines nearly 50 percent, and the Latino effect becomes insignificant. Thus, in contrast with the Table 3 findings, the Latino disadvantage vis-à-vis non-Hispanic whites disappears, while Asians and African-Americans become more likely ($p<0.001$) than whites to graduate from high school. The inclusion of family SES also significantly increases the magnitude of the first and second generation advantage over the native-born regarding high-school graduation. Likewise, family SES partially explains the positive effect of involvement in extracurricular activities, as evidenced by a 25% decrease in the magnitude of this effect. Model 3 is a significant improvement over model 2.

Model 4 incorporates three family social capital measures. One of these, parental educational expectations, is always a strong predictor of achievement and attainment ($p<0.001$), while the other two, parental involvement and supervision, are always insignificant predictors of attainment. This model is a significant improvement over model 3 and it results in a 50 percent increase in the magnitude of the black effect.

The last individual-level effect, peer network GPA, is incorporated in model 5. The peer network effect on high school graduation is significant ($p<0.001$) and positive in this and all remaining Table 4 models. This finding provides support for hypothesis IV, the higher the achievement of a peer network, the more likely an individual will graduate. The inclusion of peer network GPA also results in the positive effect of age becoming significant ($p<0.05$). Model 5 is a significant improvement over model 4.

Model 6 adds the first school-level measure, percentage of minority students. In this model and the next percent minority is a very significant ($p<0.001$) and positive predictor of high school graduation. With two exceptions, all individual-level measures in the model maintained their prior significance. Those declining in significance are black and Asian, suggesting that mean school SES exerts a mediating effect on previously significant race/ethnicity effects. As such, the earlier observed disparity in attainment between African-Americans and non-Hispanic whites is now insignificant, while the Asian effect is less significant. Thus although it appears that Asians have better chances of graduating from high school than their non-Hispanic white peers, the Asian advantage in attainment diminishes when accounting for school socioeconomic composition. Likewise, once percent minority is controlled African-Americans and whites are predicted to have roughly equal chances of high school graduation. Only after controlling for school-level racial/ethnic composition do the chances of high-school graduation for the various racial/ethnic groups correspond with national-level graduation rates (U.S. Department of Education, 1999). The apparent paradox is explained by the fact that the most important school-level effect, SES, is not accounted for until model 6. The other significant change between models 5 and 6 is in the effect of age. The magnitude of this effect nearly doubles as its significance increases from $p<0.05$ to $p<0.001$, a result that remains in next two models. Hence, controlling for racial/ethnic school composition reveals a positive and powerful association between age and attainment, a finding that agrees with expectations. The effect of non-parent households also is more significant, suggesting that this effect is suppressed unless school racial/ethnic composition is controlled. Thus, as we expected, adolescents from non-parent households are less likely to graduate from high school than adolescents from two-parent households.

Model 7 incorporates the variable mean school-level SES. This measure is another strong ($p<0.001$), positive predictor of high school completion. This model documents the effects of school composition (both racial/ethnic and SES) and demonstrates that both mean school SES and percent minority positively and significantly ($p<0.001$) impact high school graduation. With the inclusion of school SES, the magnitude of the coefficient for peer network achievement declines from 0.94 to 0.52. This suggests that school SES explains much of the positive influence of peer network achievement on individual achievement. A similar effect is visible as the Asian student advantage vis-à-vis non-Hispanic whites becomes insignificant once school SES is controlled. Hence, it can be argued that Asian adolescents are more likely to graduate from high school than native-born non-Hispanic whites because Asian youth are more likely to attend schools where the majority of students come from high- and middle-class backgrounds. A similar decline in significance for second generation status suggests this group's attainment advantage is partially attributable to the fact that native-born and second generation adolescents attend schools with distinct socioeconomic compositions.

Model 8 includes the final school-level measure, the peer network segregation index. This full model shows that two school-level measures, socioeconomic and racial/ethnic composition, significantly impact academic attainment while peer network segregation does not. Recall, this last result is the opposite of that presented in Table 3 where the peer segregation index was a significant and positive predictor of achievement. The inclusion of the peer segregation index caused the peer network achievement effect to increase from 0.52

to 0.78. This suppression effect implies that the positive influence of peer networks increases once friendship networks are controlled. Similarly, Asian also is significant in this model. Controlling for peer network segregation also diminishes the advantage of immigrant adolescents over natives, as in the first generation case, or causes it to disappear, as in the case of the second generation [9].Among important effect of model 8 is the ten-fold increase in magnitude of school SES. This implies a suppression effect, similar to that of peer network achievement.

Results from analyses of variance (not shown) document that school SES accounts for the largest share of between-school variance in attainment. This finding corresponds with Table 4 results where the effect of mean school SES on attainment is much stronger than that of percent minority. In the case of achievement, socioeconomic composition also matters more than racial/ethnic composition, as the effects of the latter are insignificant in the full model. Thus socioeconomic composition is a more significant school-level factor than racial/ethnic composition for both achievement and attainment. Other studies of school context (Coleman et al. 1966; Crain and Mahard 1978; Jencks 1972) report similar findings. Moreover, auxiliary regression analyses using different race/ethnic reference groups reveal that peer network achievement is still significant, implying that this factor impacts educational outcomes regardless of students' race/ethnicity. Percent minority was also a significant positive predictor of attainment in every model it was included. Unexpectedly, the effect of racial/ethnic composition was positive, not negative as predicted by the *Coleman Report* (Coleman et al. 1966) and the abundant research literature that followed in its footsteps (e.g., Caldas and Bankston 1998; Crain and Mahard 1978; Gerard 1988; Hawley and Smylie 1988; Longshore and Prager 1985). In other words, one long-term effect of attendance at a school with a high percentage of minority students is an increased likelihood of high school graduation, an educational outcome directly related to better occupational opportunities, increased earnings and so forth.[10] This important finding underscores the importance of continuing to monitor the long-term effects of desegregation (see more about long- and short-term effects of desegregation in Kahlenberg 2001).

Many individual-level measures that are significant predictors of achievement were insignificant predictors of attainment (e.g., Latino, gender, single parenthood, parent's involvement and supervision). Similarly, one school-level factor, peer network segregation, was a significant predictor of achievement, but not attainment. On the other hand, two individual-level factors, age and Asian, and one school-level measure, percent minority, were significant predictors of attainment but not achievement. The most likely explanation for this is that some factors have more of a short-term or immediate effect on educational outcomes, while others have more of a long-term effect. Another possible explanation for the divergent effects of these factors on achievement and attainment rests in the nature of GPA as a measure of educational achievement. Grades are strongly influenced by school policies, tracking, and teachers' expectations and attitudes. Since information on these factors is not available in the Add Health data it was not possible to control for these possibilities.

---

[9] We cannot ascertain whether non-white immigrant adolescents have an advantage over their co-ethnic peers and to what extent this advantage, if it exists, it can explained by the socioeconomic composition of schools because the further division of Hispanic, Asians and African-Americans into immigrant generations leaves extremely small-size groups and any differences among them is not statistically reliable.

[10] The interactions of race/ethnicity variables and percentage of minority students are discussed below (see Table 5).

Table 5. HLM Regression Coefficients of School-Level Factors, Race/ethnicity and Their Interactions. [a] (N students=19,117; N high school=80; N middle schools=49)

| | | Educational Achievement Wave I | | | | Educational Attainment Wave III | | | |
| | | Models | | | | | | | |
		1		2		1		2	
Panel A. Interaction Effects of Race/Ethnicity and Average School SES									
School-Level Factors									
Percentage of Minority Students		-0.10		-0.00		2.15	*	1.87	*
Average SES		1.58	***	1.05		11.86	***	7.11	***
Peer Network Segregation Index		0.22	*	0.19	*	-0.12		1.16	*
Race/ethnicity									
African-American		-0.07	*	-0.08	***	0.14		-0.08	
Asian		0.02		-0.01		0.15	*	0.18	**
Latino		-0.09	***	-0.12	***	-0.11		-0.16	
Interactions of:									
African-American	Average School SES			0.69				2.39	***
Asian	Average School SES			1.11				0.45	
Latino	Average School SES			-1.12				1.68	***
Panel B. Interaction Effects of Race/ethnicity and Percentage of Minority Students									
School-Level Factors									
Percentage of Minority Students		-0.10		0.07		2.15	*	3.98	***
Average SES		1.58	***	2.08	***	11.86	***	4.04	*
Peer Network Segregation Index		0.22	*	0.10		-0.12		-0.29	
Race/ethnicity									
African-American		-0.07	*	-0.21	***	0.14		-0.05	
Asian		0.02		0.05		0.15	*	0.28	***
Latino		-0.09	***	-0.17	*	-0.11		-0.21	*
Interactions of:									
African-American	Percent Minority			0.03				0.09	
Asian	Percent Minority			-0.00				-0.74	*
Latino	Percent Minority			0.11				0.63	*
Panel C. Interaction Effects of Race/ethnicity and Peer Segregation Index									
School-Level Factors									
Percentage of Minority Students		-0.10		-0.18		2.15	*	2.76	*
Average SES		1.58	***	0.68		11.86	***	4.16	**
Peer Network Segregation Index		0.22	*	0.11		-0.12		0.03	
Race/ethnicity									
African-American		-0.07	*	-0.03		0.14		0.16	
Asian		0.02		-0.06		0.15	*	0.16	
Latino		-0.09	***	-0.23	***	-0.11		-0.27	***
Interactions of:									
African-American	Peer Segregation Index			0.47	***			1.55	***
Asian	Peer Segregation Index			-0.10				0.07	
Latino	Peer Segregation Index			0.07				0.21	

*p<0.05; **p<0.01; ***p<0.001.

[a] Model 2 controls for all individual-level factors, including educational achievement in the Wave III models. Regression coefficients of the control variables are not shown for the sake of parsimony.

Table 5 presents the results of three sets of HLM analyses undertaken to determine the effects of various interactions on academic achievement and attainment. The interactions considered are: average school SES x individual-level race/ethnicity variables (see part A), percentage of minority students x individual-level race/ethnicity variables (see part B), and the peer network segregation index x individual-level race/ethnicity variables (see part C). Model 1 for both achievement and attainment is identical to model 8 of Tables 3 and 4. Model 2 adds the interaction terms. Because of space limitations and theoretical interest, only the initial variables in each model are presented.

In panel A, the interactions of average school SES and race/ethnicity are always insignificant for Wave I achievement. However, in the attainment model the interactions between school SES and African-American and Latino were very significant ($p<.001$). In other words, as school SES increases each of these groups becomes more likely to graduate than non-Hispanic whites. These results underline the long-term positive effects these minority students can receive from attending higher quality schools (if school quality can be defined in terms of a school's average SES). These results are compatible with those of others who also found that educational attainment was positively associated with the socioeconomic status of schoolmates (e.g., Bankston and Caldas 1998; Coleman et al. 1966; Kahlenberg 2001). The significant interaction effects contained in panel A are displayed in Figure 1. Witness that African-American and Latino students experience the biggest boost from attending high SES schools, while for Asians and non-Hispanic whites the effect is much lower, such that even when the latter group attends a school with an SES two standard deviations about the mean their odds ratio is only 0.5.

Panel B presents the interactions between race/ethnicity and percentage of minority students at a school. Although these results are always insignificant predictors of achievement, they do attain statistical significance for several attainment measures. First, Latino x percentage of minority students shows that as minority concentrations increase, Latinos become more likely to graduate than non-Hispanic whites ($p<.05$). This suggests that student educational outcomes are not necessarily worse in high-percent minority schools, something suggested by others (Caldas and Bankston 1998; Crain and Mahard 1978; Longshore and Prager 1985; Hawley and Smylie 1988).

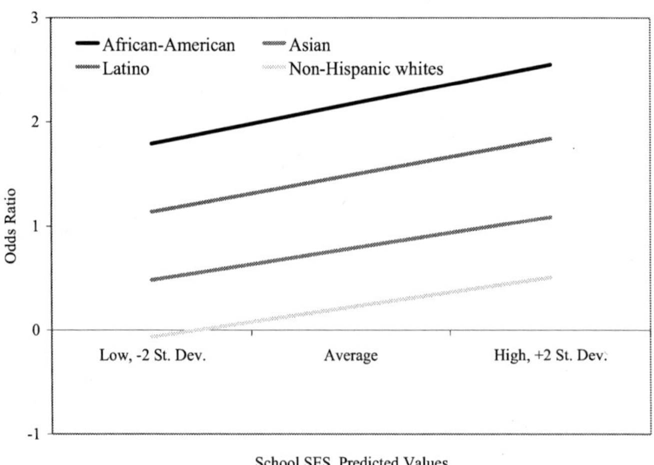

Figure 1. Predicted Values of Educational Achievement by Race/Ethnicity and School SES.

These findings also suggest that the effects of school composition (i.e., race/ethnicity) differ depending on the specific group in question. For instance, the Asian interaction term in panel B reveals they become less likely than non-Hispanic whites to graduate from high schools with large concentrations of minority students, just the opposite of what occurs among Latinos. The significant interaction effects contained in panel B are displayed in Figure 2. The African-American and non-Hispanic white lines are virtually indistinguishable from one another. However, Latino students experience the largest increase from attending high SES schools, one that is significantly higher than for non-Hispanic whites. Although Asians are less likely than non-Hispanic whites to graduate high school when attending a school with a large concentration of minority students, note that for all four groups the odds of graduating high school are positively associated with the percentage of minority students at the school attended.

Panel C of Table 5 presents the interaction effects of race/ethnicity and the peer segregation index. This interaction term only affects African-Americans and it is highly significant (p<.001) and positive for both achievement and attainment. It is also the only interaction term to be significant when predicting achievement. Auxiliary analyses reveal that regardless of the control group, these results always occur for African-Americans Together these findings suggest that for blacks both the long- and short-term impacts of peer network segregation are beneficial. These findings diverge from some commonly held assumptions about the impact of peer characteristics on black achievement. For instance, oppositional culture theory maintains that an orientation towards co-racial peers harms the educational progress of black adolescents (Fordham and Ogbu 1986; Ogbu 1974).

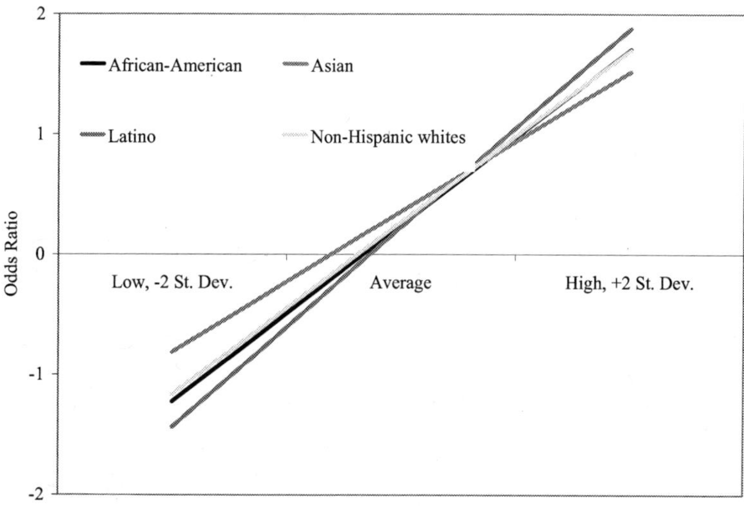

Figure 2. Predicted Values of Educational Achievement by Race/Ethnicity and Percent Minority.

While the contradiction between oppositional culture theory and these results is not easily explained, we suggest that the effects of co-racial peers on black achievement should not be deemed a priori to be negative. Rather, as documented above, co-racial peers may provide greater support for achievement than other types of peer networks. Another possibility is that prior patterns and outcomes have evolved such that they no longer apply.

Figure 3 presents the interaction effects contained in panel C. As in panel C, the Latino and Asian results are not significantly different from those of non-Hispanic whites. Furthermore, degree of network segregation appears to have little effect for any of these three groups. The African-American effect, however, is much different than that of non-Hispanic whites and the other groups. Specifically, as network segregation increases the odds of graduating high school continue to increase, such that those African-Americans with highly segregated peer networks (i.e., two standard deviations above the mean), are 50 percent more likely to graduate than those with the mean level of segregation and 200 percent more likely than those whose networks are two standard deviations below the mean.

The findings presented in Table 5 dispute several commonly accepted notions about the influence of the school context and peer influence on educational outcomes (e.g., Ogbu 1974; 1991). First, although panel A documents that all groups benefit from attending richer schools, some groups benefit more than others. More specifically, the positive effect attendance at a wealthier school had on high school graduation was greater for African-American and Latino students than it was for the non-Hispanic white contrast group. Second, educational attainment is not necessarily lower in schools with greater concentrations of minority students. Rather, our results suggest that Latinos experience a modest benefit from attending a high-percent minority school, although the effect for Asians is slightly negative. These findings emphasize the need to examine the long-term effects of desegregation, considerations often overlooked (e.g., Armor 1995; Ascher 1992; Leake and Leake 1992; Rivkin 2000).

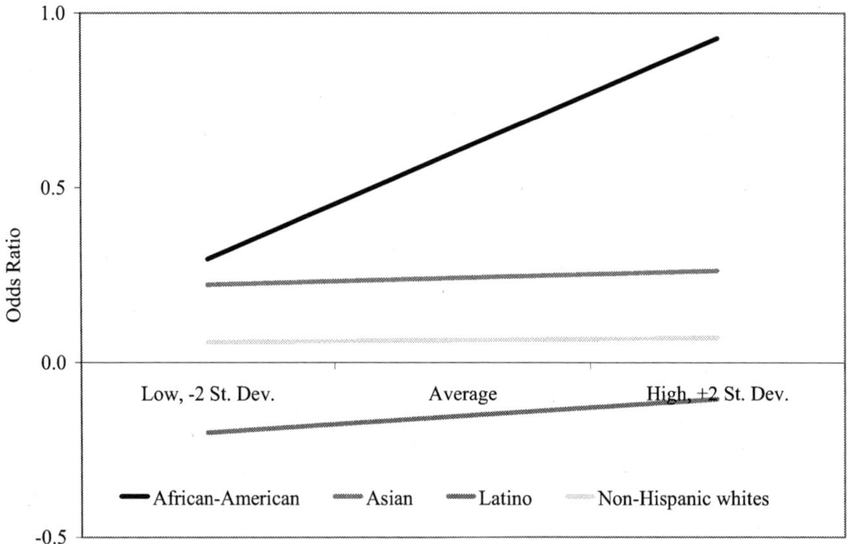

Figure 3. Predicted Values of Educational Achievement by Race/Ethnicity and Peer Network Segregation Index.

These results highlight the need to further examine the differential effects of school racial/ethnic composition on educational attainment. Third, contrary to the tenets of oppositional culture theory (Ogbu 1974, 1991), co-racial friendships do not necessarily harm the academic outcomes of black adolescents. In fact, blacks with a higher degree of peer network segregation are predicted to experience significantly higher achievement and attainment than African-Americans with more integrated peer networks.

Although these results have important implications, they also have several limitations. First, the Add Health school-level measures were only collected during Wave I. Clearly, this poses no problems for our examination of achievement. However, because no updates are available, we must proceed as if school compositions have remained unchanged throughout the period under consideration. Although the assumption of uniformity is potentially problematic for our examination of attainment, at a minimum, the results presented herein call attention to the possibility of the important findings discussed above. On the other hand, because some (Willms and Raudenbusch 1989) have demonstrated that school effects are stable over time, while still others indicate that the composition of school districts changes slowly (Kahlenberg, 2001; Schofield, 1993), it is possible that our results are the same as those that would emerge with more desirable data. Second, the Add Health transcript data were not used in this study because they were unavailable to us at the time this study was prepared. These data provide detailed information on students' grades, courses taken and school policies. Potentially, the use of the transcript data could shed light on other aspects of the school effect, such as grading policies and placement.

In order to better understand how individual- and school-level variables affect academic achievement, future research should consider incorporating additional measures not present in this study. Examples of such variables could include: administrators' attitudes, teachers' attitudes, tracking and school policies. Together these measures might help explain other potential sources of difference among schools.

CONCLUSIONS

This study of peer networks began with a review of prior studies examining the effects of school-level SES and racial segregation. Next, we provided a substantive and methodological update of this important research using recently collected national level data. Results from this update generally reinforced earlier findings and documented that adolescents in low-SES schools continue to be more likely to experience lower educational outcomes than their co-racial counterparts in high-SES schools.

We extended prior research by examining additional school-level measures. Although the other measures considered, peer network structure and school racial/ethnic composition, are also significant predictors of educational achievement and attainment, the socioeconomic status of fellow students was the most powerful of the three.

In addition to examining peer networks, we also analyzed the effect of peer social capital, measured as the average GPA of one's peer network. While both peer predictors are significant, peer social capital was the most powerful as it was always a highly significant ($p<.001$) and positive predictor of achievement and attainment. Findings for the peer network structure variable (i.e., the peer network segregation index), however, were mixed. To begin, blacks whose peer networks primarily consisted of other African-Americans were predicted to have better academic achievement and were also more likely to graduate from high school than were black students whose friendship networks were less segregated. In other words, both black achievement and attainment were positively related to peer network segregation.

Hence, peer segregation index appears to enhance the educational success of black students. Additional tests revealed that these positive outcomes for segregated peer networks were not observed among any other racial/ethnic group. Perhaps this apparent inconsistency with prior research is explained by noting that earlier studies did not distinguish peer network effects from compositional effects. Consequently, the structural autonomy of the former is ignored, a point Blau recognized with his *macrosociological theory of social structure* (Blau 1977, 1994; Blau and Schwartz 1984). Stated another way, the racial composition of a school's student body provides the opportunity for interracial contact, while the structure of peer networks reflects student behavior toward utilizing this opportunity. These results suggest that it is not necessary to see co-ethnic and co-racial friendships as obstacles to the educational assimilation of minority youth. Rather, it is essential to objectively evaluate the potential of such friendships to enhance and advance one's education and to serve as a locus of school-level ethnic social capital.

Another unexpected result emerged as we documented how the level of a school's minority enrollment is positively related to high school graduation, especially in the case of Latino students. The implications of these findings are certain to be met with skepticism; nonetheless, their policy relevance is undeniable, and our multilevel analyses of national data suggest that this is what happened in US schools, at least during the 1994-2002 period.

These results further suggest that school racial desegregation benefits not only minority students, a conclusion earlier reached by many other scholars, but also other groups, including whites. Rather than desisting from their racial desegregation plans, these findings suggest that policymakers should instead continue to strive for school-level integration, as such policies have the potential to enhance the educational attainment of all students. However, such a recommendation clearly seems somewhat out of fashion given today's political environment, the nation's increasingly segregated schools, and the call from even some black leaders to voluntarily segregate their school systems into racially identifiable districts (e.g., Omaha, Nebraska public schools).

REFERENCES

Ascher, Charles. 1992. "School Programs for African-American Males and Females." *Phi Delta Kappan* 73(10): 777-782.

Armor, David. 1995. *Forced Justice: School Desegregation and the Law*, New York: Oxford University Press.

Bankston, Carl L. III, and Steven J. Caldas. 1996. "Majority African American Schools and Social Injustice: The Influence of De Facto Segregation on Academic Achievement." *Social Forces* 75:535-555.

Bankston, Charles L. III, Steven J. Caldas, and Min Zhou. 1997. "The Academic Achievement of Vietnamese American Students: Ethnicity as Social Capital." *Sociological Focus* 30:1-16.

Bankston, Carl L. III, and Steven J. Caldas. 1998. "The Inequality of Separation: Racial Composition of Schools and Academic Achievement." *Educational Administration Quarterly* 34:533-557.

Bankston, Carl L. III, and Steven J. Caldas. 2002. *A Troubled Dream: The Promise and Failure of School Desegregation in Louisiana.* Vanderbilt University Press.

Bean, Frank D., and Gillian Stevens. 2003. *America's Newcomers and the Dynamics of Diversity.* New York: Russell Sage Foundation.

Berndt, Thomas J., and Keunho Keefe. 1995. "Friends' Influence on Adolescents' Adjustment to School." *Child Development* 66:1312-1329.

Berndt, Thomas J., Ann E. Laychak, and Keunho Park. 1990. "Friends' Influence on Adolescents' Academic Achievement and Motivation: An Experimental Study." *Journal of Educational Psychology* 82:664-670.

Blau, Peter M. 1977. *Inequality and Heterogeneity: A Primitive Theory of Social Structure.* New York: Free Press.

Blau, Peter M. 1994. *Structural Contexts of Opportunities.* Chicago: University of Chicago Press.

Blau, Peter M., and Otis Dudley Duncan. 1967. *The American Occupational Structure.* New York: Wiley.

Blau, Peter M. and Joseph E. Schwartz. 1984. *Cross Cutting Social Circles: Testing a Macrostructural Theory of Intergroup Relations.* Academic Press.

Blum, Robert W., and Peggy Mann Rinehart. 1997. *Reducing the Risk: Connections that Make a Difference in the Lives of Youth.* Minneapolis, MN: Division of General Pediatrics and Adolescent Health, University of Minnesota.

Borjas, George. 1992. "Ethnic Capital and Intergenerational Mobility." *Quarterly Journal of Economics* 85:365–90.

Borjas, George. 1995. "Ethnicity, Neighborhoods, and Human Capital Externalities." *American Economic Review* 85:365-390.

Box, George E.P., and David R. Cox. 1964. "An Analysis of Transformations." *Journal of the Royal Statistical Society* 26:211-243.

Bridge, R. Gary, Charles M. Judd, and Peter R. Moock. 1979. *The Determinants of Educational Outcomes.* Cambridge, MA: Ballinger Publishing Company.

Bryk, Anthony, and Stephen W. Raudenbush. 1992. *Hierarchical Linear Models for Social and Behavioral Research: Applications and Data Analysis Methods.* Newbury Park, CA: Sage Publications.

Caldas, Steven J., and Carl L. Bankston 1998. "The Inequality of Separation: Racial Composition of Schools and Academic Achievement." *Educational Administration Quarterly* 34:533-557.

Carnevale, Anthony P. 1999. *Education = Success: Empowering Hispanic Youth and Adults.* Princeton, NJ: Educational Testing Service.

Carter, Prudence L. 2003 "'Black' Cultural Capital, Status Positioning, and Schooling Conflicts for Low-Income African American Youth." *Social Problems* 50:136-55.

Chubb, John E. and Terry M. Moe. 1990. *Politics, Markets, and America's Schools.* The Brookings Institution.

Clotfelter, Charles T. 2001. "Are Whites Still Fleeing? Racial Patterns and Enrollment Shifts in Urban Public Schools, 1987-1996." *Journal of Policy Analysis and Management* 20(2):199-221.

Cohen, Elizabeth G. 1975. "The Effects of Desegregation on Race Relations." *Law and Contemporary Problems* 39(2):271-299.

Coleman, James S. 1988. "Social Capital in the Creation of Human Capital." *American Journal of Sociology* 94 (Supplement):95-120.

Coleman, James S. 1990. *The Foundations of Social Theory.* Cambridge, MA: Harvard University Press.

Coleman, James S., Ernest Q. Campbell, Carol J. Hobson, James McPartland, Alexander M. Mood, Frederic D. Weinfeld, and Robert L. York. 1966. *Equality of Educational Opportunity.* Washington, D.C.: U.S. Government Printing Office.

Conger, Rand D., Katherine Jewsbury Conger, and Glen E. Elder. 1997. "Family Economic Hardship and Adolescent Adjustment: Mediating and Moderating Processes." Pp. 288–310 in *Consequences of Growing up Poor,* edited by Greg J. Duncan and Jeanne Brooks-Gunn. New York: Russell Sage Foundation.

Conger, Rand D., Xiaojia Ge, Glen H. Elder, Jr., Frederick O. Lorenz, and Ronald L. Simons. 1994. "Economic Stress, Coercive Family Process, and Developmental Problems of Adolescents." *Child Development,* 65: 541–561.

Cox, Martha J., Blair Paley, and Krisitina Harter. 2001. Interparental Conflict and Parent-Child Relationships. Pp. 249 – 273 in *Interparental Conflict and Child Development: Theory, Research, and Applications,* edited by John H. Grych and Frank D. Fincham. Cambridge, England: Cambridge University Press.

Crain, Robert L., and Rita E. Mahard. 1978. "School Racial Compositions and Black College Attendance and Achievement Test Performance." *Sociology of Education* 51, 81–101.

Dornbusch, Sanford M., Philip L Ritter, P. Herbert Leiderman, Donald F. Roberts, and Michael J. Fraleigh. 1987. "Adolescent School Performance." *Child Development* 58: 1244-1257.

Dornbusch, Sanford M., Philip L. Ritter, Randy Mont-Reynaud and Zeng-yin Chen. 1990. "Family Decision Making and Academic Performance in a Diverse High School Population." *Journal of Adolescent Research* 5(2): 143-160.

Entwisle, Doris R. and Karl L. Alexander. 1992. "Summer Setback: Race, Poverty, School Composition, and Mathematics Achievement in the First Two Years of School." *American Sociological Review* 57: 72–84.

Epstein, Joyce L. 1983. "The Influence of Friends on Achievement and Affective Outcomes. Pp. 177-200 in *Friends in School: Patterns of Selection and Influence in Secondary Schools,* edited by J.L. Epstein and N. Karweit. New York: Academic Press.

Epstein, Joyce L. 1985. "After the Bus Arrives: Resegregation in Desegregated Schools." *Journal of Social Issues* 41:23-43.

Fordham, Signithia and John Ogbu. 1986. "Black Students' School Success: Coping with the 'Burden of Acting White'." *The Urban Review,* 18(3): 176-206.

Frankenberg, Erica, Chungmei Lee, and Gary Orfield. 2003. *A Multiracial Society with Segregated Schools: Are We Losing the Dream?* Cambridge, MA: The Civil Rights Project at Harvard University.

Galambos, Nancy L., Erin T. Barker, and David M. Almeida. 2003. "Parents Do Matter: Trajectories of Change in Externalizing and Internalizing Problems in Early Adolescence." *Child Development* 74(2): 578-594.

Gerard, Harold B. 1988. "School Desegregation: The Social Science Role." Pp. 225-236 in *Eliminating Racism: Profiles in Controversy,* edited by Phyllis A. Katz and Dalmas A. Taylor. New York: Plenum Press.

Hallinan, Maureen T. 1982. "Classroom Racial Composition and Children's Friendships." *Social Forces* 59 (1): 225-245.

Hallinan, Maureen, and Aage B. Sørensen. 1985. "Class Size, Ability Group Size, and Student Achievement." *American Journal of Education* 94(1):71-89.

Harris, Kathleen Mullan, Greg Duncan, and Johanne Boisjoly. 2002. "Evaluating the Role of "Nothing to Lose" Attitudes on Risky Behavior in Adolescence." *Social Forces* 80:1005-1039.

Hawley, Willis D., and Mark A. Smylie. 1988. The Contribution of School Desegregation to Academic Achievement and Racial Integration." Pp. 281-97 in *Eliminating Racism: Profiles in Controversy*, edited by Phyllis A. Katz and Dalmas A. Taylor. New York: Plenum Press.

Haynie, Dana L. 2001. "Delinquent Peers Revisited: Does Network Structure Matter?" *American Journal of Sociology* 106 (4): 1013-1057.

Haynie, Dana L. 2002. "Friendship Networks and Adolescent Delinquency: The Relative Nature of Peer Delinquency." *Journal of Quantitative Criminology* 18(2):99-134. 66(1):43-68.

Hetherington, E. Mavis. 1998. "Social Capital and the Development of Youth from Nondivorced, Divorced and Remarried Families." Pp. 177–209 in *Relationships as Developmental Contexts,* edited by W. Andrew Collins and Brett Laursen. Mahwah, NJ: Erlbaum.

Hirschman, Charles. 2001. "The Educational Attainment of Immigrant Youth: A Test of the Segmented-Assimilation Hypothesis." *Demography* 38: 317-336. Hoxby, Caroline M. 2000. "The Effects of Class Size on Student Achievement: New Evidence from Population Variation." *Quarterly Journal of Economics* 115(4):1239-1285.

Israel, Glenn D., Lionel J. Beaulieu and Glen Hartless. 2001. "The Influence of Family and Community Social Capital on Educational Achievement." *Rural Sociology*

Jencks, Christopher. 1972. "The Coleman Report the Conventional Wisdom." Pp. 87-105 in *On Equality of Educational Opportunity: Papers Deriving From the Harvard Faculty Seminar on the Coleman Report,* edited by Frederick Mosteller and Daniel P. Moynihan. New York: Random House.

Jencks, Christopher and Meredith Phillips. 1998. The Black-White Test Score Gap: An Introduction. Pp. 1-51 in *The Black-White Test Score Gap,* edited by C. Jencks and M. Phillips. Washington, DC: Brookings Institution.

Joyner, Kara, and Grace Kao. 2000. "School Racial Composition and Adolescent Racial Homophily." *Social Science Quarterly* 81(3):810-825.

Kahlenberg, Richard D. 1996. *The Remedy: Class, Race, and Affirmative Action.* New York: Basic Books.

Kahlenberg, Richard D. 2001. *All Together Now: Creating Middle-Class Schools through Public School Choice.* Washington, DC: Brookings Institution Press.

Kao, Grace, and Martha Tienda. 1995. "Optimism and Achievement: The Educational Performance of Immigrant Youth." *Social Science Quarterly* 76:1–19.

Kubitschek, Warren N., and Maureen T. Hallinan. 1998. "Tracking and Students' Friendships." *Social Psychology Quarterly* 61:1-15.

Laosa, Luis M. 1982. "School, Occupation, Culture, and Family: The Impact of Parental Schooling on the Parent-Child Relationship." *Journal of Educational Psychology* 74: 791-827.

Lareau, Annette. 1989. *Home Advantage: Social Class and Parent Intervention in Elementary Education*. New York: The Falmer Press.

Leake, Donald, and Brenda Leake 1992. "African-American Immersion Schools in Milwaukee: A View from the Inside." *Phi Delta Kappan* 73: 783-785.

Lee, Seh-Ahn. 1993. "Family Structure Effects on Student Outcomes." Pp. 43-75 in *Parents, Their Children, and Schools*, edited by Barbara Schneider and James S. Coleman. Boulder, CO: Westview Press.

Lin, Nan. 1990. "Social Resources and Instrumental Action." Pp. 247-271 in *Social Mobility and Social Structure*, edited by Ronald L. Breiger. Cambridge, U.K.: Cambridge University Press.

Longshore, Douglas, and Jeffrey Prager. 1985. "The Impact of School Desegregation: A Situational Analysis." *American Review of Sociology* 11:75-91.

Madaus, George F., Thomas Kellaghan, Ernest A. Rakow, and Denis J. King. 1979. The Sensitivity of Measures of School Effectiveness, *Harvard Educational Review* 49: 207-230.

Mahard, Rita E. and Robert L. Crain. 1983. "Research on Minority Achievement in Desegregated Schools." Pp. 103-125 in *The Consequences of School Desegregation*, edited by Christine H. Rossell and Willis D. Hawley. Philadelphia: Temple University Press.

Maran, Meredith. 2000. *Class Dismissed: A Year in the Life of an American High School: A Glimpse Into the Heart of a Nation*. New York: St. Martin's Press.

McCarthy, Bill and John Hagan. 1995. "Getting into Crime: The Structure and Process of Criminal Embeddedness." *Social Science Research* 24:63-95.

McLanahan, Sara, and Gary Sandefur. 1994. *Growing up with a Single Parent: What Hurts, What Helps*. Cambridge, MA: Harvard University Press.

McLoyd, Vonnie C. 1998. "Socioeconomic Disadvantage and Child Development." *American Psychologist* 53:185–204.

McNeal, Ralph B., Jr. 2001. "Differential Effects of Parental Involvement on Cognitive and Behavioral Outcomes by Socioeconomic Status. *The Journal of Socio-Economics* 30(2): 171-144.

Moody, James. 2001. "Race, School Integration, and Friendship Segregation in America." *American Journal of Sociology* 107(3):679-716.

Morgan, Stephen L., and Aage B. Sørensen. 1999. "Parental Networks, Social Closure, and Mathematics Learning: A Test of Coleman's Social Capital Explanation of School Effects." *American Sociological Review* 64:661–681.

Muller, Chandra. 1995. "Maternal Employment, Parent Involvement, and Mathematics Achievement." *Journal of Marriage and the Family* 57(1): 85-100.

Nelson, Sandi, Rebecca Clark, and Gregory Acs. 2001. "Beyond the Two-Parent Family: How Teenagers Fare in Cohabiting Couple and Blended Families." Pp. 1-6 in *Assessing the New Federalism*. Policy Brief B-31. Washington, DC: The Urban Institute.

Ogbu, John. 1974. *The Next Generation: An Ethnography of Education in an Urban Neighborhood*. New York: Academic Press.

Ogbu, John. 1978. *Minority Education and Caste: The American System in Cross-Cultural Perspective*. New York: Academic Press.

Ogbu, John. 1981. "Origins of Human Competence: A Cultural-Ecological Perspective." *Child Development* 52: 413–429.

Ogbu, John. 1991. "Low Performance as an Adaptation: The Case of Blacks in Stockton, California." Pp. 249-85 in *Minority Status and Schooling*, edited by Margaret A. Gibson and John Ogbu. New York: Grand.

Orfield, Gary, and John T. Yun. 1999. *Resegregation in American Schools*. Cambridge, MA: The Civil Rights Project at Harvard University.

Orfield, Gary, Susan E. Eaton, and Elaine R. Jones, 1997. *Dismantling Desegregation: The Quiet Reversal of Brown V. Board of Education*. New York: The New Press.

Orfield, Gary. 1978. *Must We Bus? Segregated Schools and National Policy*. Washington, DC: Brookings Institution.

Patterson, Gerald R., John B. Reid, and Thomas J. Dishion. 1992. *Antisocial Boys*. Eugene, OR: Castalia.

Portes, Alejandro and Ruben G. Rumbaut. 2001. *Legacies: The Story of the Immigrant Second Generation*. Berkeley: University of California Press.

Portes, Alejandro, and Min Zhou. 1993. "The New Second Generation: Segmented Assimilation and Its Variants." *The Annals of the American Academy of Political and Social Sciences,* 530: 74-96.

Portes, Alejandro. 1998. "Social Capital: Its Origins and Applications in Modern Sociology." *Annual Review of Sociology* 24:1-24.

Raudenbush, Stephen and Anthony Bryk. 2002. Hierarchical Linear Models: Applications and Data Analysis Methods. 2d ed. Thousand Oaks, CA: Sage.

Raudenbush, Stephen and J.Douglas Willms. 1995. "The Estimation of School Effects." *Journal of Educational and Behavioral Statistics,* 20(4): 307-335.

Rivkin, Steven G. 2000. "School Desegregation, Academic Attainment, and Earnings." *The Journal of Human Resources* 35:333-346.

Roscigno, Vincent J. 1998. "Race and the Reproduction of Educational Disadvantage." *Social Forces* 76(3):1033–60.

Schneider, Barbara and James S. Coleman. 1993. *Parents, Their Children, and Schools*. Boulder, CO: Westview Press.

Schofield, Janet. 1993. "Promoting Positive Peer Relations in Desegregated Schools." *Educational Policy* 7: 297-317.

Sewell, William H. and Robert M. Hauser. 1975. *Education, Occupation, and Earnings: Achievement in the Early Career*. New York: Academic Press.

Smith, Mark H., Lionel J. Beaulieu and Glenn D. Israel. 1992. "Effects of Human Capital and Social Capital on Dropping out of High School in the South." *Journal of Research in Rural Education* 8(1):75-88.

Stanton-Salazar, Ricardo D. 1997. "A Social Capital Framework for Understanding the Socialization of Racial Minority Children and Youth." *Harvard Educational Review* 67:1-40.

Steinberg, Laurence D., Sanford M. Dornbusch, and B. Bradford. 1992. "Ethnic Differences in Adolescent Achievement: An Ecological Perspective." *American Psychologist* 47(6):723-729.

Stevens, James. 1996. *Applied Multivariate Statistics for the Social Sciences* (3rd ed.). Mahwah, NJ: Lawrence Erlbaum Associates.

Stevenson, David L. and David P. Baker. 1987. "The Family-School Relation and the Child's School Performance." *Child Development* 58:1348-1357.

Tatum, Beverly Daniel. 1999. *Why Are All the Black Kids Sitting Together in the Cafeteria?* New York: Basic Books.

Teachman, Jay, Kathleen Paasch, and Karen Carver. 1996. "Social Capital and Dropping out of School Early." *Journal of Marriage and the Family* 58(9):773-784.

Thomson, Elizabeth, Thomas L. Hanson, Sara S. McLanahan. 1994. "Family Structure and Child Well-Being: Economic Resources vs. Parental Behaviors." *Social Forces* 73(1):221–242.

Tienda, Marta, and Ronald J. Angel. 1982. "Headship and Household Composition Among Blacks, Hispanics and Other Whites." *Social Forces* 61:508-531.

U.S. Census Bureau. 2000. *Demographic Profiles: 1990 and 2000 Comparison Tables.* URL: http://www.census.gov/Press-Release/www/2002/dp_comptables.html.

U.S. Department of Education. 1999. *Trends in Academic Progress.* National Center for Education Statistics, National Assessment of Educational Progress (NAEP).

U.S. Department of Education, NCES. 2002. *Digest of Education Statistics 2001.* Washington, DC: U.S. Government Printing Office.

Vernez, Georges, Allan Abrahamse, with Denise Quigley. 1996. *How Immigrants Fare in U.S. Education.* Santa Monica, CA: RAND.

Wentzel, Kathryn, and Kathryn Caldwell. 1997. "Friendships, Peer Acceptance, Group Membership: Relations to Academic Achievement in Middle School," *Child Development* 68:1198–1209.

Willms, J., and Stephen W. Raudenbusch. 1989. "A Longitudinal Hierarchical Linear Model for Estimating School Effects and Their Stability" *Journal of Educational Measurement* 26(3):209-32.

Zhou, Min, and Carl L. Bankston. 1998. "Social Capital and Immigrant Children's Achievement." *Research in Sociology of Education* 13:13-29.

In: Educational Theory
Editor: Jaleh Hassaskhah, pp. 39-61

ISBN 978-1-61324-580-4
© 2011 Nova Science Publishers, Inc.

Chapter 2

CONSTRUCTIVISM AS EDUCATIONAL THEORY: CONTINGENCY IN LEARNING, AND OPTIMALLY GUIDED INSTRUCTION

Keith S. Taber
Faculty of Education, University of Cambridge, UK

ABSTRACT

Constructivism is a major referent in education, although it has been understood in various ways, including as a learning theory; a philosophical stance on human knowledge; and an approach to social enquiry. In terms of informing teaching, constructivism has variously been seen by different commentators as a basis for progressive, mainstream or failed approaches to pedagogy. This is unfortunate, as the different ways the term has been interpreted have confused debate about the potential of constructivism to contribute to planning effective teaching. This chapter sets out the basis of one version of constructivism: that which is informed by findings from both cognitive science, and from educational studies exploring learners' thinking about curriculum topics and about classroom processes. A key concept here is the way in which new learning is contingent on features of the learner, the learning context and the teaching. This version of constructivism (which has been widely embraced) offers a theoretical basis for designing effective pedagogy that is accessible to classroom teachers.

The chapter will explain that although constructivism understood this way certainly offers the basis for learner-centred teaching, it is far from 'minimally-guided' instruction, as caricatured by some critics. Rather, a feature of this approach is that it does not adopt doctrinaire allegiance to particular levels of teacher input (as can be the case with teaching through discovery learning, or direct instruction) but rather the level of teacher guidance (a) is determined for particular learning activities by considering the learners and the material to be learnt; (b) shifts across sequences of teaching and learning episodes, and includes potential for highly structured guidance, as well as more exploratory activities. When understood in these terms, constructivism provides a sound theoretical basis for informing teaching at all levels, and in all disciplines.

Keywords: Constructivism; learning theory; contingency in learning; designing instruction; evidence-based pedagogy.

INTRODUCTION

This chapter presents the basic tenets of constructivism as a learning theory, and so as a basis for developing pedagogy and designing curriculum and instruction. It is argued that constructivist pedagogy draws upon educational theory informed by research and broad scholarship, and so provides a sound foundation for evidence-based practice.

Unfortunately constructivism has become a widely adopted slogan that has been applied in different ways in various contexts. It is, *inter alia*, used to label qualitative approaches to research, various ways of thinking about learning and cultural reproduction, and approaches to pedagogy. The different associations of constructivism are so diverse, that constructivism in education has been variously seen as progressive, as the basis of current good practice, and as *passé*. Within science education, for example, constructivism has been considered as the accepted paradigm for thinking about learning, as a well-stabished principle now widely taken for granted, and as a philosophically dangerous tendency that undermines science through relativism. Some of those who consider constructivism in education to be progressive describe it as a student-centred approach, and some critics characterise constructivist teaching as 'minimally guided instruction' – although this is certainly not how most educators who consider themselves constructivists would understand their approach.

Given the wide range of different understandings of the term, it would be folly to make a claim for what 'constructivism' actually is: constructivism is clearly many things to many people. However, the present chapter is concerned with *constructivism as the basis of educational theory*, as it is generally understood by those educators who have developed constructivist approaches to thinking about teaching and learning. Constructivism as educational theory comprises of ideas about how human learning occurs, and the factors that tend to channel learning; and ideas about how curriculum and instruction should be designed to best respond to educational purposes, given what is understood about learning.

A CONSTRUCTIVIST PERSPECTIVE ON LEARNING

The constructivist perspective on the nature of learning (Bodner, 1986; Glasersfeld, 1989; Larochelle, Bednarz, and Garrison, 1998; Novak, 1993; Phillips, 2000; Sjøberg, 2010; Taber, 2009b) can be seen as part of a long tradition in educational thought (Egan, 1984), but in its modern form has as its basis how people make sense of their experience. It might be understood in terms of a shift in the location of the meaning of what is found in our environment.

A traditional, commonsense, way of thinking about this is represented in figure 1. This assumes that the learner comes to knowledge by recognising the meaning of what is found in the environment. So the object or event in the environment – this could be anything: a chair, a chemical reaction, a utility bill on the doormat, a sentence read from a novel, the utterance of a teacher in a classroom – is assumed to have some inherent meaning, which the learner is able to identify, and so add to their store of knowledge about the world. Perception is about recognising the inherent meaning of what is experienced.

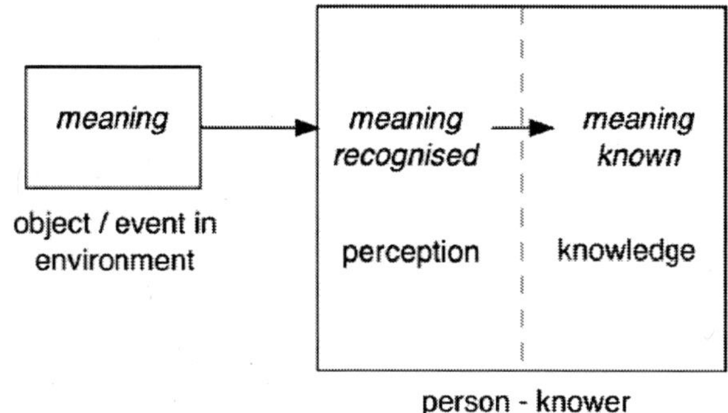

Figure 1. A traditional view of how we come to knowledge.

This perspective makes sense in many situations. After all a chair does have an inherent 'meaning', at least in the sense that it is created with a particular function in mind. Similarly, when the teacher tells the class that 'Paris is the capital of France', the utterance is motivated by the intention to communicate a specific meaning, and pupils need to recognise *that* meaning if they are to acquire the knowledge that is represented in the teacher's words.

In human societies most of the knowledge we acquire is based on what is already part of the pool of available cultural knowledge. A primary rationale for formal education, then, is to allow 'reproduction' of this knowledge. The commonsense view of how schooling works is based on a folk model of learning as based on knowledge transfer, or more accurately knowledge copying from one mind to another (figure 2).

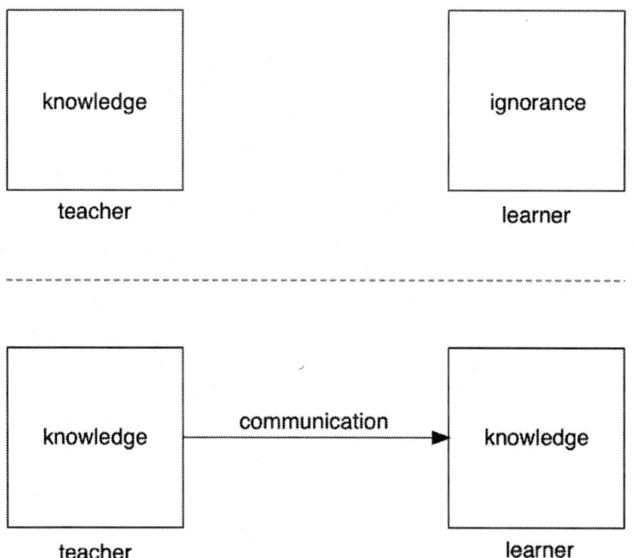

Figure 2. The folk model of teaching is that somehow the teacher's knowledge is copied into the mind of the learner.

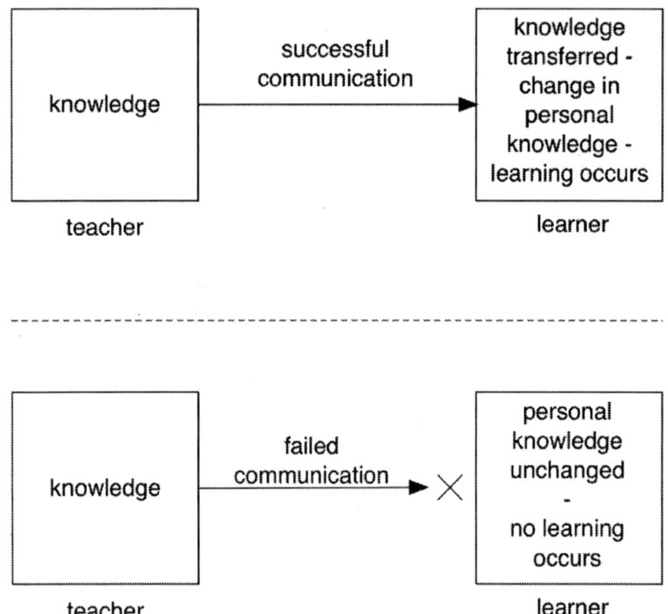

Figure 3. A binary view of teaching – either the teacher's knowledge is copied to the learner's mind, or there is no learning.

At one level this model works well. At one time, a good deal of effort was spent in many classrooms on the teacher drilling learners in repeating information considered to be worth knowing. In this way, pupils can learn multiplication tables, spellings, the dates of major wars, the main economic activities of South American countries, how to say good morning in various foreign languages, and very much more. Humans can learn a wide range of material by rote, at least with sufficient practice and appropriately spaced opportunities to practice. Rote learning has its place. In a performance of a play, where the particular language used is considered an inherent part of the art, it is appropriate for each actor to say the lines as written, rather than to offer the gist in their own vernacular. We say, the actor must 'learn the lines', not that the actor must learn the essence of their meaning. In poetry the precise choice of words is as important as the ideas they represent.

If education was solely concerned with this kind of 'facsimile' reproduction of information, then we could consider teaching effectiveness in binary terms (figure 3): sometimes learning occurs, and sometimes not. Complex (rote) learning can be analysed as a sequence of specific items to be communicated, each of which is either learnt or not.

Meaningful Learning

Yet rote learning is very limited. Learning 'word-perfectly' that the square of the hypotenuse of a right-angled triangle is equal to the sum of the squares of the other two sides, or that when a body A exerts a force on a body B, then the body B exerts a force, equal in magnitude, opposite in direction, and along the same line of action, on body A, is generally considered to be of little value if the ideas represented in the form of words can not be applied, because they have been learnt without understanding. Indeed one of the real issues in assessing students through formal tests and examinations is that it is far easier to judge when to award marks if the criterion is remembering a specific canonical formulation for a law, rule, theorem etc, than to judge whether the students' 'own words' can be considered to reflect an understanding sufficiently close to the canonical meaning (Taber, Forthcoming). Yet if understanding is the aim of much teaching, ability to reproduce given statements and definitions is of limited interest. So although learning by rote is an important phenomenon, much of formal education (and informal learning, for that matter) is about a different kind of learning: what Ausubel (1968, 2000) termed 'meaningful' learning. This brings us back to figure 1, because it soon becomes very clear that even when it may be justified to assume there to be inherent meaning in the objects and events we perceive in the environment (a teacher's explanation; a paragraph in a text book), there is no automatic process of acquiring that meaning.

Rather, we have available what might be termed 'cognitive apparatus' that allows us to interpret what we see in meaningful ways, because we can call upon existing cognitive resources (knowledge elements, interpretative frameworks, discussed further below) from which to make sense of experience (figure 4, cf. figure 1). This cognitive apparatus usually allows us to, for example, recognise a chair, even if it is not quite like any chair we have experienced before. Someone who had never seen a chair might well decide to use it to sit on, just as they might decide to use a convenient boulder as a seat. In general, however, people recognise a chair because they have developed cognitive resources for recognising chairs, based on previous experiences relating to chairs.

Personal Meaning-Making

The nature of human cognition – that we have to actively make sense of our experiences in terms of existing internal analytical resources – helps make our thinking flexible (so we can make sense of a design of chair never seen before), but mitigates against teaching being a binary process where an intended meaning is either communicated unchanged or not at all. Experiences of working in classrooms reinforces this conclusion: sometimes learners seem to acquire intended meanings; sometimes they seem to fail to learn anything; but often something else happens – students learn something which is *different* from that intended. Students often acquire a partial and/or distorted version of what was intended (Gilbert, Osborne, and Fensham, 1982).

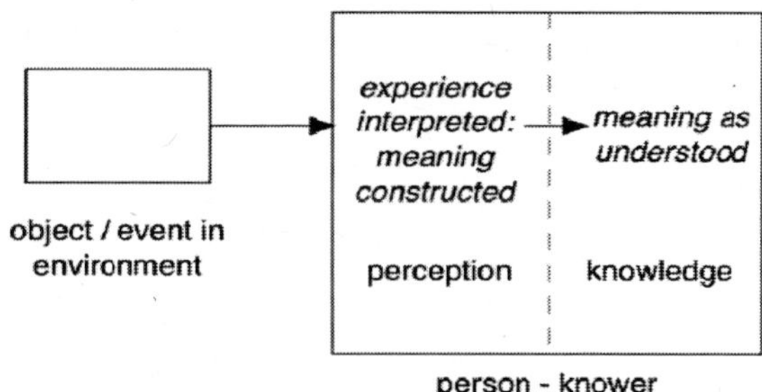

Figure 4. Knowledge constructed by interpreting new experiences in their light of existing conceptual frameworks.

Figure 2 does not describe the general process, at least when what we mean by knowledge requires more than learning by imitation. We know this because it so often becomes clear that learners have acquired a different meaning to that intended by the curriculum developers, the textbook author, or the classroom teacher. If matters were as simple as figure 2 suggests, then learning processes would be binary: successful or null, as in figure 3.

The constructivist view suggests this is because the processes by which we come to experience our surroundings are processes of *interpretation*. So the individual has to actively construct a meaningful interpretation of what is being seen and heard. That is, all meaningful learning is a process of personal meaning making through that individual's current knowledge and understanding. Consequently, each person in a classroom will construct a personal version of what is being taught (see figure 5).

Sometimes most students in a class will construct a similar meaning, and it will closely reflect the teacher's intended meaning. However, often this is far from being the case. This makes sense from a constructivist viewpoint, and indeed the popular uptake among educators of constructivist approaches to thinking about teaching and learning was in part because it made sense of the common finding that in many topics where students experienced learning difficulties, it was not a matter of students not understanding teaching, but rather of them understanding differently to what was intended (Taber, 2009b).

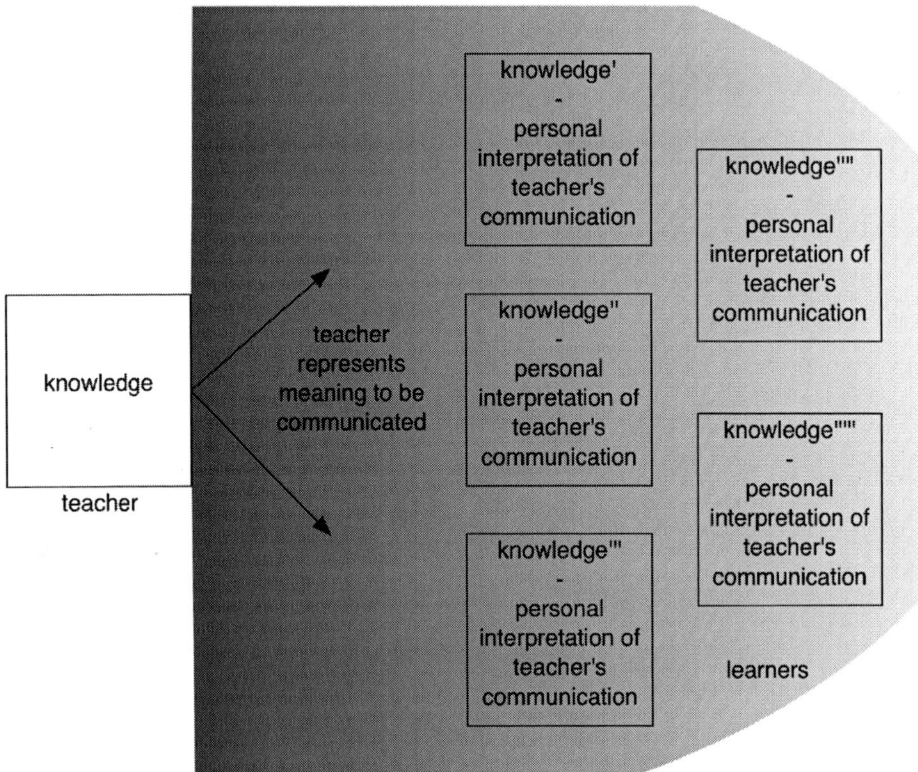

Figure 5. Each learner develops personal knowledge that is a unique reconstruction of the teacher's knowledge, by interpreting the public representation of the teacher's knowledge through available interpretive resources.

ELEMENTS OF A CONSTRUCTIVIST THEORY OF LEARNING

To draw a distinction between the apparatus of human cognition, the 'hardware' if we adopt a familiar metaphor, and the resources available to support cognition (the software and data files if we keep with the metaphor) is not entirely appropriate (Taber, Forthcoming). The substrate supporting cognition is the brain, a highly interconnected network of neurons that can act as tiny switches and signal boosters. Current thinking suggests that there is probably not a strong demarcation between brain processes involved in thinking and storing (memory) – that is, the structures which represent knowledge are active in, *and modified by*, the processing of new information, as well as acting as the basis for recalling information (Fuster, 1995). Often our memories of events (a lesson, a conversation, a concert, etc) are much less *records* of those events, than reconstructions of the experience based on our impressions of all those experiences which we categorise in a similar way. Myriad discrepant witness accounts and strained marital conversations show how often different people's memories of the 'same' event, even when offered totally honestly, show fundamental inconsistencies that illustrate different observers or participants cannot all hold accurate memories. Partly this is about how something is interpreted and experienced at the time, and partly this is about the way human memory works. When we remember something, our consciousness is provided (by the preconscious processing we are not aware of) with the best attempt at a coherent account. Unless the original event was highly salient and 'impressed' itself upon us (i.e. usually this means we were especially alert as a surge of adrenalin was triggered), memory is likely to be at least in part a re*construction*.

Key Constructivist Premises

Constructivism as learning theory can be considered to make claims about the nature of human learning. Two such claims would be:

- Human learning is constrained and channeled by the nature of the cognitive apparatus that inevitably has built-in biases;
- Human learning is contingent upon the cognitive resources that are available to any particular individual to interpret (make sense of) information.

'Information' here can simply mean the electrical signals that enter the brain from the senses: these signals are representations of the external environment (patterns of light falling on the retina; vibrations in the air leading to a resonance with certain sensory neurons in the cochlea) in the form of electrical pulses. From the biological perspective, this seems to be the physical basis of perception and cognition.

The hypothetical example earlier of the individual who was able to recognise a chair that had never been seen before, needs to be understood in these terms. Somehow information from the senses, in the form of electrical pulses, is processed in the brain and interpreted as representing a chair, by drawing on existing cognitive resources developed through prior experiences of (other) chairs.

This however begs the question of how we learnt about chairs in the first place: for *re-cognition* depends, by definition, on having previously had that cognition. So there is an issue of how we can come to know something new. Socrates had an answer to this, in that he assumed that we were born into the world with this knowledge, which just needed to be activated (e.g. by appropriate questions that might help us remember it). Modern constructivists take a different view, which is that knowledge is developed in an iterative process, and built up slowly through life's experiences. This leaves a key question of what the starting point for construction is – what the original building materials are.

The Genetic Element

Clearly this is not the place to explore this issue in any depth, but it is important to understand that human beings are never a complete *tabula rasa*: a blank slate upon which anything can be written. By the time a human being is born, she is already the outcome of an extensive development process. This is not just the individual's pre-natal period, but rather includes a much more extensive evolutionary history. For at conception the new organism carries genetic information that will inform cognitive development, and that information has been shaped by the outcomes of millions of learning experiences of that person's ancestors. Of course, this does not mean that if great Grandmother learnt to play Chopin on the piano, our neonate will come into the world as a pianist. But it does mean that the newborn has biases built into the basic structure of the brain that channel how sensory information will be interpreted. We are all somewhat unique. Throughout human (and pre-human) history our ancestors' brains varied, and so their perceptions of the world varied; as did the extent to which their interpretations of their world supported their ability to have families; and not to starve, or get eaten, or drown, or fall off cliffs and so forth (or at least, not until they had produced some offspring).

The brain of the new born child is already biased to perceive the world in particular ways (Goswami, 2008): not 'the way' the world is; and perhaps not in an optimum way to understand the world; but usually in ways much like the ways that generations of forebears found supported a productive life.

For most of that extensive development period, those forebears were living in a world that is quite significantly different to the cultural, physical and technological environment that our newborn will find: so the new human being might well be better adapted to making sense of a hunter-gather's life on the savannah as part of a community of a few dozen, rather than that of an accounts clerk working in a corporate office in a vast metropolis. One appropriate metaphor might be to suggest that we are the products of extensive market research, but unfortunately carried out in a rather different market place to that in which we are expected to sell our wares!

Pre-Wiring and Pre-Dispositions

Babies come into the world with the apparatus in place to almost immediately recognise faces. That does not mean there is a single gene for face recognition, but rather that the genetic code common to all normal humans leads (due the interaction of various genes and the environment of the embryo) during gestation to the development of a pattern recognition system that very readily recognises faces. The bias is so strong that even as adults we readily 'recognise' faces from the most basic symbols, and indeed in many accidental configurations (craters on the moon, butter melting on toast, etc).

Our genetic inheritance is also thought to predispose us to learning human language (Chomsky, 1999): that is, all human languages follow certain aspects of a common template (a 'universal grammar') that has evolved with us so that we readily pick up the basis of spoken language in the community we experience during a particularly sensitive period. We are not genetically predisposed to learn English, or Mandarin, or Esparanto – but we are genetically predisposed to learn a human language rather than bird or whale song or Klingon.

Similarly, very early in child development, babies appear to show surprise at physically impossible events (e.g. an object that was seen to be placed behind an obstruction not being revealed when the obstruction is moved), and to have a notion of agency: that some types of regularities in their environment are able to deliberately act to bring about events. These types of findings suggest that the human brain has evolved to readily appreciate certain types of pattern in the world, and so to readily interpret what is sensed in particular ways. These biases give the youngster a head (sic) start in making sense of the "great blooming, buzzing confusion" (James, 1890) of early experience, but – being biases – also lead to false positives, that is, the tendency to over-interpret experiences in certain ways.

One example of this might be the tendency of young children to anthropomorphise inanimate objects: to see the sun and moon, and wind and clouds, etc to be sentient actors in the world, acting because of their own reasons. Piaget (1929/1973), for example, reported much of this type of thinking in children. These biases are not readily overcome as we mature – just as adults still tend to see faces when the cues are quite minimal and ambiguous, ☺. The present author has reported how high ability, college students, quite readily assigned wants and needs (and sometimes even emotions like jealousy) to individual atoms as the basis of their attempts to explain chemical phenomena (Taber, 1998; Taber and Watts, 1996).

Cognitive Development

Piaget's (1970/1972) great project (his 'genetic epistemology') was intended to investigate how humans could possibly come to knowledge of the world, given the starting point (in effect a single cell containing only genetic information from the parents). His stage theory is still highly respected in some parts of the world, although many of the details of his model and claims have been widely critiqued (Donaldson, 1978; Sutherland, 1992). Despite the varying credence given to the specifics of his work, Piaget's vision offered an approach to appreciating conceptual development that was viable given philosophical considerations and biological constraints. Piaget saw (i) that the baby was not in a position to construct formal, abstract knowledge of the world, but was able to act in the world, in an intelligent way, because it was able to use its sensori-motor experience to model the world, and then modify that model in the light of further experience; and (ii) that by iterative processes it was possible to move through qualitatively different levels of understanding: Einstein the man was constructed from and *by* Einstein the neonate, through the iterative processes of making sense of the world (constructing internal mental models), acting in the world according to expectations (predictions based upon those models), and comparing new experiences with predictions, so to develop understanding (by modifying the models on the basis of feedback). This is clearly what happens in cognitive development, and Piaget developed the evidence-base to start to understand how and why this development occurs.

Piaget therefore contributed to the viability of a constructivist view of learning, something that had much earlier origins (Glasersfeld, 1989), showing that the individual who enters the world with no knowledge of calculus, or of the causes of the industrial revolution, can construct such abstract formal knowledge of the world because we are genetically endowed with *the potential to construct the apparatus needed for formal thought* by iterative action on the environment. We are not born with innate knowledge of the world in the sense of Socrates, but rather we are endowed with innate knowledge of how to construct a system of personal knowledge about the world, and one which if not exactly 'pre-tuned' by evolution, certainly has some design features that have been extensively pre-tested for us.

Of course, the flip side of this amazing process is that all of our knowledge is *personal construction*, and so work-in-process: the current iterations of our models that best make sense of our experience so far, when interpreted in terms of the inherent biases which got the process underway, and the constant cycling of new perceptions (*interpreted through the current state of knowledge*) being matched against what the current state of knowledge would lead us to expect. No wonder that as humans, we are subject to 'confirmation bias' – we tend to recognise the evidence that supports, rather than challenges, our current thinking. Accepting this means accepting that human knowledge cannot be seen as absolute, in some positivistic sense, but rather our current best fit model to experience (Glasersfeld, 1990), in the pragmatic tradition of thinkers such as John Dewey (Biesta and Burbules, 2003).

Implications for Teaching: Intuitive Theories, and Alternative Conceptual Frameworks

A key point that arises from this perspective, is that teaching is seldom about helping learners build up knowledge from nothing: indeed the constructivist approach suggest that would not be possible, as learning always builds upon, and with, the cognitive and conceptual resources already available. This leads to a number of key constructivist principles for teachers:

- Teaching involves activating relevant ideas already available to learners to help construct new knowledge;
- Students will build their new knowledge upon partial, incorrect, or apparently irrelevant existing knowledge unless carefully guided.

Students often have their own ideas about a topic that they have developed spontaneously (see below), or have acquired from other sources (family, friends, media), and which are seldom a very good match to the canonical version of knowledge presented in a curriculum. This has been explored extensively in the context of science learning, where hundred of examples of 'alternative conceptions', 'preconceptions', 'intuitive theories', and 'alternative conceptual frameworks' that students acquire, and which are inconsistent with school science, have been reported (Duit, 2009; Taber, 2009b).

As what a student will understand of teaching will be contingent upon their existing ideas and ways of thinking about a topic, teachers therefore have to diagnose student thinking effectively, so that they can channel that thinking towards the target knowledge presented in the curriculum (Brock, 2007). Where teaching is not designed to closely build upon a learner's current state of knowledge, a range of things can go wrong – misinterpretations, failures to make expected links, making inappropriate links (Taber, 2001).

When teaching abstract concepts that cannot be directly shown or demonstrated to learners, the teacher needs to find ways to help students make connections with knowledge that could be relevant: using models, analogies and metaphors for example. As this suggests, effective constructivist teaching, whilst 'student centred' in terms of its focus on how knowledge building takes place in the mind of the learner, is very much 'hands-on' teaching where the teacher seeks to guide learning by supporting the knowledge-construction process.

CONCEPT DEVELOPMENT AND TEACHING

Piaget's work has faced various criticisms, and one is that he focused largely (though not exclusively) on the lone epistemic subject interacting with the environment, whereas much human learning is social in nature. Piaget was himself very aware of this, and clearly very few of us rediscover the theorems of geometry, or the causes of the rise and fall of the Roman Empire, from first principles. We learn from family, from peers, from media, from educational experiences such as schooling (for pupils), or professional development opportunities (for their teachers). Piaget's approach may be seen as a sensible move in a research project, what Lakatos might have called following a 'positive heuristic' (Lakatos, 1970): perhaps something along the lines, 'consider the epistemic subject in his environment as the unit of analysis, and leave aside complications of social interactions as detail to be considered at a later stage'.

Piaget's contemporary Vygotsky, however, looked at some of the same basic questions about how humans come to knowledge in a complementary way. If a 'hard core' assumption (i.e. in Lakatosian terms, a central commitment which is taken for granted in the research programme) of the Piagetian programme was the centrality of a individual epistemic subject, then Vygotsky's socio-historical programme included a 'hard core' assumption that the knowledge of a person living in a human community will to a large extent derive from social interactions, through which aspects of the culture are acquired (Vygotsky, 1978).

This perspective goes beyond consideration of the 'content' of thinking, and also relates to the forms of thinking available. Whereas Piaget suggested a model with an invariant sequence of stages of cognitive development that all individuals normally passed through, Vygotsky's socio-cultural perspective suggested that more 'advanced' forms of thinking were themselves culturally mediated. Certainly when his colleague Luria led an expedition to the Soviet Asian republics, he found that illiterate peasants did not engage with standard modes of thought common among those who have been through the formal education system: for example they seemed unable or willing to complete syllogisms, and tended to group objects according to those which could be understood within an imagined narrative, rather than those with similar functions (Luria, 1976). This is somewhat different from suggesting that these individuals did not attain what Piaget would call formal operations, but certainly suggests that modes of thought which people within a specific culture take for granted are not universal human norms. Reading Luria's examples of informants refusing (for example) to infer the colour of a hypothetical bear, that had reportedly been seen in the North, where the investigator claims all the bears are white, the sense is not of an inability of appreciate logic, but more a failure to appreciate the point of offering a conclusion, based on hear-say evidence, that the investigator could draw for themselves (cf., Smagorinsky, 1995). Commonly the peasants took the reasonable stance that, as they had never been to the North themselves, they had no good grounds for guessing the colour of a bear they had never seen. Schooling, it seems, encultures us into certain 'language games' that might seem quite bizarre to the uninitiated.

Two Types of Concepts

Vygotsky suggested that there were two origins for concepts (Vygotsky, 1934/1986), that we construct our own informal concepts spontaneously, without initially being able to operate with them effectively, or having language to talk about them; and that we also learn about 'scientific', or 'academic' (Vygotsky, 1934/1994), concepts from others. We might think of the former type of concepts as those acquired through the types of action in/on the environment discussed by Piaget, based on the inherent pattern-recognition qualities of the human cognitive apparatus. Piaget's model would suggest that these spontaneous concepts would have the potential to be developed into formal tools for conscious thought through the iterative processes of cognitive development he studied.

Vygotsky, however, focused on how in normal circumstances the individual exists in a social and cultural context, where the personal concepts of individuals are modified by interactions with others, to allow the development of a somewhat common language, and to some extent at least a sharing of concepts. That is, although each individual has to construct their own conceptual frameworks, these are 'moderated' by interactions with others.

Vygotsky had the insight to appreciate that academic concepts presented in formal teaching, for example, whilst pre-packaged in linguistic and logical forms, would not automatically be available to the learner. In other words he seems to have appreciated the notion of rote learning, and realised that concepts cannot be unproblemtatically copied from one mind to another, as meaningful concepts are those that are integrated into existing frameworks of understanding. In Vygotsky's model, the process of cognitive development is one of the gradual linking of the personal, largely implicit, spontaneous concepts with the formal, but initially isolated and non-functioning academic concept.

Modern Ideas about Concept Development

Vygotsky's model has much in common with modern thinking about learning. It has been argued that much of our knowledge is built from primitive knowledge elements, that act at preconscious levels of thinking, and which are acquired spontaneously through the inherent pattern recognition mechanisms of the cognitive apparatus (diSessa, 1993; Smith, diSessa, and Roschelle, 1993). During conceptual development it has been suggested that such implicit knowledge elements can pass through several stages of re-representation at successively more explicit levels (i.e. becoming more directly accessible to conscious thought and operation), to the highest level where such concepts can be thought about and manipulated linguistically (Karmiloff-Smith, 1996). This process can be somewhat accelerated when the individual learns about concepts (i.e. Vygotsky's 'academic' concepts) from others through language.

The Zone of Next Development

One of Vygotsky's (1978) best know ideas is the zone of proximal, or next, development (ZPD), which referred to what a learner could not yet do unaided, but could do with support from a more knowledgeable individual (see figure 6).

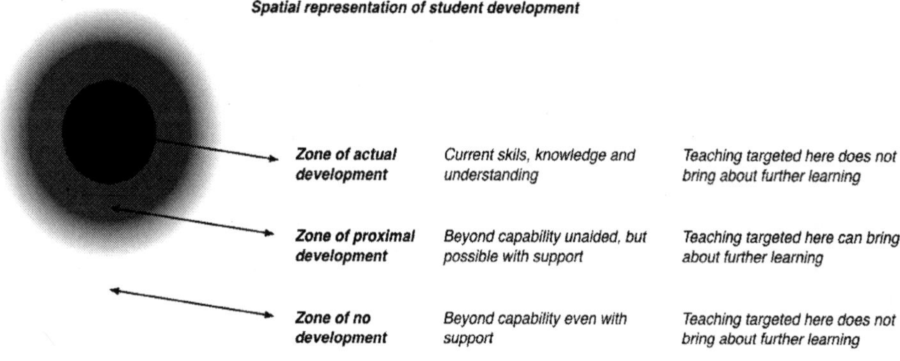

Figure 6. The Zone of proximal development.

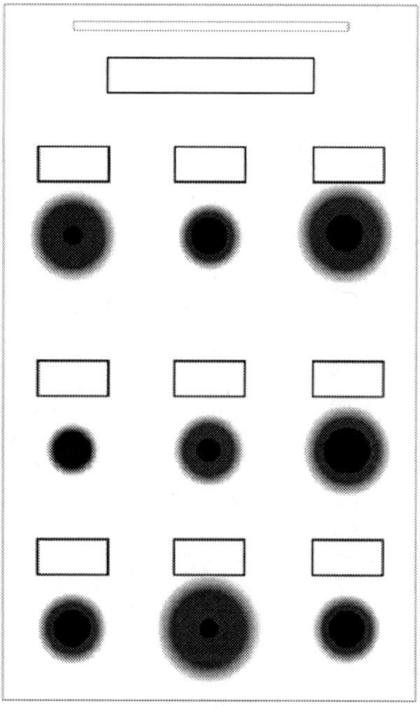

Figure 7. In any class, the teacher is faced by learners with different current levels of development, and different potentials (ZPD) for making progress.

Vygotsky's point went beyond the obvious (it is easier to do something difficult if we are helped by someone who can do it better than us!) to highlight two issues of relevance to teachers, that might provide the basis for two more constructivist claims:

- Meaningful learning only takes place when teaching is pitched beyond what is currently known and understood, but 'within reach' of existing knowledge and understanding;
- Different learners, although apparently having the same starting points, may differ in how far they can 'reach' beyond existing knowledge and understanding, to meaningfully learn new material.

In other words, the ZPD is not a standard-sized 'space' around existing learning, but is an individual characteristic (see figure 7): Vygotsky suggested that given the social context of formal education, it was more useful for a teacher to know about an individual's ZPD than their current state of knowledge, as learning took place in the ZPD.

Scaffolding Learning

This leads to the notion of teaching as scaffolding (Wood, 1988), informed by Vygotsky's work. This is the principle of setting a learner a task that is currently beyond their expertise, but within the ZPD; and then providing support – modelling, guidance, hints, etc., so that the learner can achieve with support. In Vygotsky's thinking, what is achieved first on the inter-personal level can become assimilated into the zone of actual development (ZAD), becoming internalised so that it can then be achieved unaided (Scott, 1998). The teacher's role is to offer support, and then gradually fade this as the learner masters the task, until the ZAD (and so the ZPD around it) has shifted (see figure 8).

Vygotsky's work has clear implication for differentiation of teaching. The same task may be routine for one member of a class, suitable to challenge and potentially develop another, and well beyond what another classmate can achieve even with support. In practice, in the latter case, the outcome is either explicit failure, or an apparent achievement that is so heavily based on input by the teacher or the learner's classmates that it has no value as a learning experience.

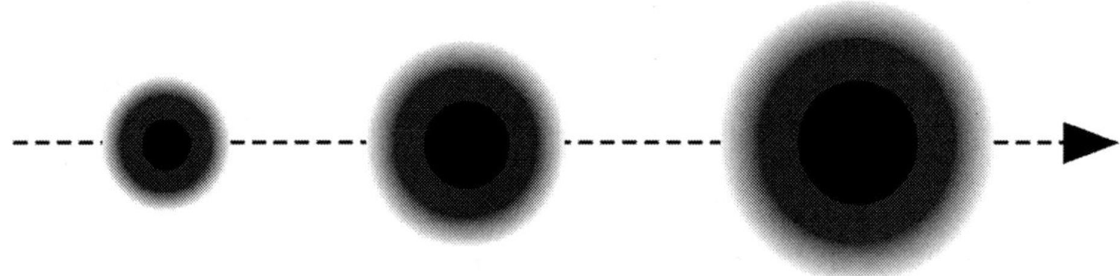

Figure 8. Learner progression involves the expansions of the ZAD, which supports growth in the ZPD around it.

It was also a feature of Vygotsky's work, that the relevance of other learners, and not just the teacher, is recognised as important in the learning process. Students often learn a great deal by working with, and having discussion with peers, who because of the generally similar level of development may inherently pitch their inputs within each other's ZPD.

Conceptual Trajectories and Student-Centred Teaching

A constructivist model of learning as construction of personal knowledge suggests that every student in a class will bring unique conceptual and cognitive resources to bear on a lesson (as well as different levels of motivation, interest, confidence, metacognition etc). A lesson taught as a lecture, presented to a class, will be understood and interpreted in as many different ways as there are students in a class. This is inevitable, but the target knowledge set out in the curriculum applies to all the students. Even if it is recognised as unreasonable that all students should reach the same final knowledge state, it is usually expected that the teacher facilitates all the learners to develop in the same 'direction'.

Yet with each individual pupil's ideas being channeled by the unique current state of their knowledge, each is likely to take a somewhat different trajectory in their learning. The teacher's job is then, to some extent, like that of an educational sheepdog, running between different members of the flock, to help marshal them towards the same end-point.

CONSTRUCTIVISM AND APPROACHES TO TEACHING

This outline, of key thinking about constructivist principles of learning, sets the scene for considering the nature of teaching that might be considered constructivist. This has been a major issue of debate, to the extent that constructivist approaches to teaching have been denounced (Kirschner, Sweller, and Clark, 2006), and metaphorically put on trial (Tobias and Duffy, 2009).

Whilst approaches to pedagogy have always been the subject of much interest, the debate came alive after a paper by Kirschner, Sweller and Clark (2006) arguing that constructivist, discovery, problem-based, experiential, and inquiry-based teaching had all failed. For these authors, these different labels all related to iterations of the same fundamental approach to pedagogy, which had been shown to be ineffective. However, the key phrase used to collectively describe these different teaching approaches adopted by the Kirschner and colleagues was 'minimally guided' instruction. In considering their arguments then, there would seem to be two questions: whether what can reasonably be considered 'minimally guided' instruction is an effective means to support learning; and whether constructivist approaches to teaching can reasonably be considered 'minimally guided'.

The Myth of Minimally Guided Instruction?

Certainly when Kirschner, Sweller and Clark's paper led first to a public debate at the American Educational Research Association (in 2007) and then a book asking whether constructivist instruction was indeed successful or not (Tobias and Duffy, 2009), a key issue was what was meant by minimally guided instruction, and whether recommended approaches to pedagogy could be considered to fit this description. In some of the rhetoric, pedagogy became presented as a choice between 'direct instruction' and 'minimally guided instruction' (Taber, 2010b).

Direct instruction is at heart a specific, well-tested, approach to designing instruction, and has found to be effective in a number of fields. 'Minimally guided' instruction, is a blanket term which has been used to describe a range of approaches that deliberately do not explicitly teach all the content to be learnt to the student. At first sight this looks very much like a 'no contest'. If the curriculum required student to learn, for example, the capitals of European Union (EU) states: France-Paris; Eire-Dublin; Italy-Rome, and so forth; then we could caricature the two options as: (a) the teacher who has this knowledge, to make it available to the learners by presenting a table, and perhaps a large map with the state and capital city names clearly shown; (b) the teacher to tell pupils that they need to know the names of the EU states and their capital cities, and then retire to a quiet corner of the classroom to enjoy a much-earned cup of coffee.

It seems obvious that students are more likely to learn accurately and quickly in the former situation, than in the latter situation. However, even in this apparently clear-cut example, it may be that the teacher wishes to combine the learning of these simple facts, with some higher level educational aims: learning research skills on the internet; developing skills of self-directed learning and greater metacognitive awareness; ability to cooperate effectively in small group, etc. From this perspective it may not matter if the learning of state capitals is less efficient, especially if the teacher views this as less important than the other goals.

It also becomes clear that if the teacher is looking to develop this broader range of skills, she may not be prepared to 'tell the answers', but she is likely to be very busy in the classroom in monitorial and supporting the processes of learning. Her coffee may have to wait. It is also clear that although it would have been much easier for all concerned if the teacher had simply presented the students with the information about states and capitals, it is rather harder to see how she could have explicitly taught them to have greater metacognitive awareness, or to work better in groups, without setting up activities where they had to try things out for themselves.

Of course this example is just a caricature of direct instruction, which is a developed approach that goes beyond just telling learners the answers. Baumann (1984) refers to how the teacher tells/shows/models/demonstrates/teaches skills, and contrasts this with learning from resources such as books or worksheets, where the teacher primarily facilitates the use of the resources rather than directly controls the sequence and pace of focus of the learning. That 'direct teaching' in this sense should be more effective than the alternatives is perhaps not surprising: at least, it should not be surprising from a constructivist perspective. Given the individual differences in any class (see figure 7), effective learning is only likely to be possible when there is a constant matching of current learning to learning needs in order to scaffold the next learning activity: and this requires careful monitoring and regulation of the learner at an individual level.

The monitoring or regulation is unlikely to be something that can be programmed into learning resources directly (Taber, 2010a), and will almost certainly need to be carried out by a person with appropriate levels of knowledge and skills. For the most advanced students - academic scholars, autodidacts – this regulation and monitoring will be carried out by the learners themselves, and effective learning from interaction with resources is quite possible. For most students, certainly at school level, considerable input is needed by the teacher to direct learners. Undoubtedly, the greater the learners' motivation, self-efficacy, and - above all – existing metacognitive skills, the easier the teacher's job becomes: thus the development of the learners' metacognition (and such proxies as 'study skills') should have high priority as an educational aim (Taber, 2009a).

The skills and knowledge of the effective classroom teacher should not be underestimated, for effective teaching means operating a series of parallel interactions with individual learners and groups, 'on-line', in real-time. This is the case whether the main mode of instruction is teacher-talk, or the teacher acting as the manager for group or individual activities. Whether 'direct instruction' is more effective here, is surely going to be in part dependent upon the quality of the learning resources, and the teacher's knowledge and understanding of their rationale and design, as well as whether they find teaching as an activity more or less rewarding when teaching in this mode. The point here, though, is not to question the superiority of direct instruction over resource-led teaching, but rather to point out that from a constructivist perspective, effective teaching will depend upon the teacher making on-line decisions informed by their knowledge of subject matter, subject pedagogy, and of the particular learners in the class. So from this constructivist perspective effective learning cannot be considered as 'minimally guided', regardless of whether it is primarily the teacher standing at the front of the class talking to the whole group, or whether the teacher is flitting around a busy room supervising different learners engaged in a range of learning activities.

Discovery Learning and Constructivist Perspectives

The notion of minimally guided teaching fits better with approaches to 'discovery' learning that are open-ended. Here the learner is provided with the potential tools for making discoveries and then left to make those discoveries. Of course, discovery learning takes place within a curriculum context (so there are specific learning goals), and the provision of specific apparatus or resources act as some form of structuring of activity, even if the teacher takes an extreme view about learners needing to find out for themselves. (And in my experience, most teachers' instincts make them more likely to intervene too quickly during activities where students need to take time to think things through, rather than to leave students to their own devices for too long.)

Such an approach might be considered informed by a constructivist perspective drawing uncritically on a Piagetian model, i.e. that people naturally build up increasing complex models of the world by interacting with their environment, so the provision of a specific environment may facilitate the construction of desired knowledge. This would of course, on the Piagetian scheme, require the learner to be at a current level of cognitive development that supports the specific desired learning. So this is not an approach that is likely to allow individuals to make for themselves the discoveries underpinning modern culture, to which a great many gifted individuals contributed over many centuries.

That is not to suggest there is no place for discovery. Indeed the term 'discovery' appears in steps in versions of the learning cycle (Marek, 2009). In one early version the 'preliminary exploration' (which was actually the open-ended familiarisation stage) is followed by 'invention' (where the teacher introduced the concept to be learnt, and its name, drawing upon student familiarity deriving from the previous stage), and then 'discovery' which was actually the stage where students discovered *how to apply* the new concept to new examples. The term 'guided discovery' was used for processes that were considered analogous to (but not strictly identical with) the processes of discovery in science. Later the discovery phase became renamed as 'conceptual expansion' or 'concept application'.

At some level, constructivism implies that the individual has to create knowledge themselves, and clearly the feeling of discovering a pattern oneself rather than just being told, can have considerable motivational value. However, often such discoveries are only going to come about when the environment is carefully set up to make the important patterns discoverable: in other words, the teacher needs to scaffold learning within the learner's ZPD. Certainly in science education it is well recognised that getting students to undertake classroom experiments intended to reveal patterns in nature is a very haphazard way of helping students to discover scientific laws and principles (Driver, 1983).

Often the pattern that seems obvious to the science teacher is completely missed by the student, who instead imposes quite a different pattern on the observations. This is not surprising from a constructivist perspective, as perceptions are channelled through existing conceptual frameworks, and many of the ideas in science are quite counter-intuitive (which is why great scientists like Newton, Curie, Darwin and Einstein are fêted). So, given the iterative nature of learning, discovery approaches are likely to lead to students discovering patterns, but those that are contingent upon *their* existing ways of thinking, rather than those which have currency in the culture, and are privileged in the curriculum. Whilst some genuinely open-ended 'discovery' learning way well be useful to allow students to follow interests and to encourage creativity, effective discovery learning will - from the constructivist perspective - need to occur in carefully engineered situations designed to scaffold desired learning. Discovery learning can be either minimally guided; or it can be supported by constructivist teaching; but *not both*.

Constructivism And Enquiry Learning

Where 'discovery learning' tends to be a phrase that is less commonly used today, as Kirschner and colleagues (Kirschner et al., 2006) recognised, similar thinking has informed the idea of learning by enquiry (or inquiry, sometimes used interchangeably), which is very popular, especially in subjects such as maths and science (Lawson, 2010). As with 'constructivism', the term is widely used without a clear, agreed meaning (Bencze and Alsop, 2009), but it is generally associated with teaching that is based around setting-up student enquiries that mimic the academic research process. This type of teaching is widely advocated in the United States (Alsop and Bowen, 2009). The same considerations apply here as for discovery learning, but it is important to note that the focus on enquiry often means that the rationale for using this approach is somewhat different. It way well be accepted that enquiry learning – setting up enquiries for pupils to undertake, sometimes over extended periods – is not the most effective way of teaching the focal concepts, but this is still preferred because the primary rationale is to teach students the skills and processes of enquiry.

Where this is the aim, it may well be considered acceptable if students do not come to the 'right' answers by themselves, as long as they are learning to pose good questions, and to develop their skills in the methods of enquiry: data collection, analysis, argumentation etc.

Given this, the general point made above still applies. A constructivist teacher might, given these educational goals, allow considerable leeway in how students undertake their enquiries, but will not be allowing students to develop their own methodologies of enquiry in a laissez-faire manner. So effective, constructivist, enquiry teaching will carefully guide the learning about the logic and methods of enquiry, ideally so that each student is working within their ZPD as regards their developing conceptualisation and skills for undertaking enquiry. So there may appear to be minimal guidance in terms of the actual enquiry directions and decisions taken by students, but at a meta-level, the learning is being carefully monitored and scaffolded in terms of the understanding of inquiry processes, and the tools made available to make and execute those decisions. So again, learning by enquiry *could* be minimally guided, but genuinely constructivist enquiry-teaching will need to be carefully scaffolded by the teacher.

CONSTRUCTIVISM AS OPTIMALLY GUIDED INSTRUCTION

The aim of this chapter is to give readers a flavour of constructivist thinking about learning, and of how this can inform pedagogy. The central challenge of the personal constructivist perspective on teaching is to balance two central features of learning:

- Learning is a process of changing the potential for behaviour, by the iterative interaction between an individual's internal mental models and their interpretation of experience;
- As new learning is contingent on current knowledge and understanding, the iterative nature of the process is (in the absence of external guidance) likely to lead to an increasingly idiosyncratic way of understanding the world.

Within a society, the latter tendency is moderated by constant interactions with others, providing specific feedback on our own interpretations of the world that tend to keep them largely in line where there is general consensus – as Piaget himself recognised (Glasersfeld, 1997). Educational institutions formalise this process, by setting up bodies of canonical target knowledge, and charging teachers with the job of offering feedback to channel the student's development. However, the constructivist teacher knows that this channeling process must be designed to provide the 'database' for learning, and to guide, but not swamp the inherent internal processes of reflection upon experience. For only when, at some level, the learner recognises a misfit between expectations and experience, is the intrinsic process of modifying ideas triggered.

The aim of constructivist teaching then is not to provide 'direct' instruction, or 'minimal' instruction, but *optimum* levels of instruction. Constructivist pedagogy therefore involves shifts between periods of teacher presentation and exposition, and periods when students engage with a range of individual and particularly group-work, some of which may seem quite open-ended. However, even during these periods, the teacher's role in monitoring and supporting is fundamental. Constructivism as a learning theory suggests that effective teaching needs to be both student-centred *and* teacher-directed (see figure 9).

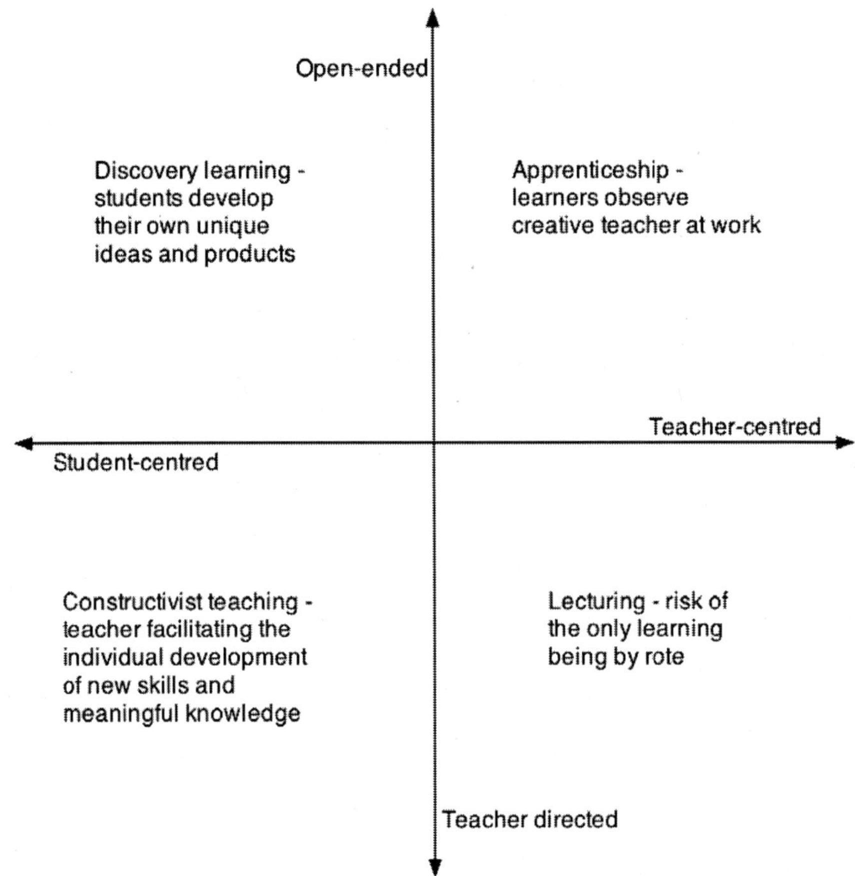

Figure 9. Teaching informed by constructivist theory will be both student-centred, and teacher directed.

So although constructivism is a learner-centred theory of teaching, the constructivist teacher works in the students' ZPD, to monitor and direct learning, from a perspective that understands how learning is contingent upon each individual's existing conceptual structures. Constructivist theory informs the teacher that each learner needs time, space, and suitable experiences, to support the learning processes; but also that minimal guidance during learning is unlikely to lead to the desired outcomes.

Such a teacher recognises that teaching designed to help students learn canonical knowledge is only possible where the teacher has a good understanding of both where the learner is now (the adage of Ausubel, 1968 about the teacher fidning out that the leaner already knows), and where the learner is expected to go to (the importance of the structure of the subject matter, Bruner, 1966; Gagné and Briggs, 1974) as well as of appropriate levels and form of guidance to bring this about (i.e. pedagogic subject knowledge, Gess-Newsome and Lederman, 1999). Constructivism, when understood in these terms, is recommended as the basis for designing pedagogy that is most likely to bring about high levels of desired learning.

REFERENCES

Alsop, S., and Bowen, M. G. (2009). Inquiry science as a language of possibility in troubled times. In W.-M. Roth and K. Tobin (Eds.), *Handbook of Research in North America* (pp. 49-60). Rotterdam, The Netherlands: Sense Publishers.

Ausubel, D. P. (1968). *Educational Psychology: A cognitive view.* New York: Holt, Rinehart and Winston.

Ausubel, D. P. (2000). *The Acquisition and Retention of Knowledge: a cognitive view.* Dordrecht: Kluwer Academic Publishers.

Baumann, J. F. (1984). The Effectiveness of a Direct Instruction Paradigm for Teaching Main Idea Comprehension. *Reading Research Quarterly, 20*(1), 93-115.

Bencze, J. L., and Alsop, S. (2009). A critical and creative enquiry into school science inquiry. In W.-M. Roth and K. Tobin (Eds.), *Handbook of Research in North America* (pp. 27-47). Rotterdam, The Netherlands: Sense Publishers.

Biesta, G. J. J., and Burbules, N. C. (2003). *Pragmatism and Educational Research.* Lanham, MD: Rowman and Littlefield Publishers.

Bodner, G. M. (1986). Constructivism: a theory of knowledge. *Journal of Chemical Education, 63*(10), 873-878.

Brock, R. (2007). Differentiation by alternative conception: Tailoring teaching to students' thinking - A review of an attempt to target teaching according to the alternative conceptions of electricity held by year 7 students. *School Science Review, 88*(325), 97-104.

Bruner, J. S. (1966). *Towards a Theory of Instruction.* New York: W W Norton and Company.

Chomsky, N. (1999). Form and meaning in natural languages. In M. Baghramian (Ed.), *Modern Philosophy of Language* (pp. 294-308). Washington D C: Counterpoint.

diSessa, A. A. (1993). Towards an epistemology of physics. *Cognition and Instruction, 10*(2and3), 105-225.

Donaldson, M. (1978). *Children's Minds.* London: Fontana.

Driver, R. (1983). *The Pupil as Scientist?* Milton Keynes: Open University Press.

Duit, R. (2009). *Bibliography - Students' and Teachers' Conceptions and Science Education.* Kiel: http://www.ipn.uni-kiel.de/aktuell/stcse/stcse.html.

Egan, K. (1984). *Education and Psychology: Plato, Piaget and Scientific Psychology.* London: Methuen.

Fuster, J. M. (1995). *Memory in the Cerebral Cortex: An Empirical Approach to Neural Networks in the Human and Nonhuman Primate.* Cambridge, Massachusetts: The MIT Press.

Gagné, R. M., and Briggs, L., J. (1974). *Principles of Instructional Design.* New York: Holt, Rinehart and Winston.

Gess-Newsome, J., and Lederman, N. G. (1999). *Examining pedagogical content knowledge.* Dordrecht: Kluwer.

Gilbert, J. K., Osborne, R. J., and Fensham, P. J. (1982). Children's science and its consequences for teaching. *Science Education, 66*(4), 623-633.

Glasersfeld, E. v. (1989). Cognition, Construction of Knowledge, and Teaching. *Synthese, 80*(1), 121–140.

Glasersfeld, E. v. (1990). An Exposition of Constructivism: Why some like it radical *Monographs of the Journal for Research in Mathematics Education, 4*, 19-29. Retrieved from http://www.univie.ac.at/constructivism/EvG/papers/125.pdf

Glasersfeld, E. v. (1997). Amplification of a constructivist perspective. *Issues in Education, 3*(2), 203-209. Retrieved from http://www.univie.ac.at/constructivism/EvG/papers/202.pdf

Goswami, U. (2008). *Cognitive Development: The Learning Brain*. Hove, East Sussex: Psychology Press.

James, W. (1890). The Principles of Psychology Available from http://psychclassics.yorku.ca/James/Principles/index.htm

Karmiloff-Smith, A. (1996). *Beyond Modularity: A developmental perspective on cognitive science*. Cambridge, Massachusetts: MIT Press.

Kirschner, P. A., Sweller, J., and Clark, R. E. (2006). Why minimal guidance during instruction does not work: An analysis of the failure of constructivist, discovery, problem-based, experiential, and inquiry-based teaching. *Educational Psychologist, 41*(2), 75-86.

Lakatos, I. (1970). Falsification and the methodology of scientific research programmes. In I. Lakatos and A. Musgrove (Eds.), *Criticism and the Growth of Knowledge* (pp. 91-196). Cambridge: Cambridge University Press.

Larochelle, M., Bednarz, N., and Garrison, J. (Eds.). (1998). *Constructivism and Education*. Cambridge: Cambridge University Press.

Lawson, A. E. (2010). *Teaching Inquiry Science in Middle and Secondary Schools*. Thousand Oaks, California: Sage Publications.

Luria, A. R. (1976). *Cognitive Development: Its cultural and social foundations*. Cambridge, Massachusetts: Harvard University Press.

Marek, E. A. (2009). Genesis and evolution of the leanring cycle. In W.-M. Roth and K. Tobin (Eds.), *Handbook of Research in North America* (pp. 141-156). Rotterdam, The Netherlands: Sense Publishers.

Novak, J. D. (1993). Human constructivism: A unification of psychological and epistemological phenomena in meaning making. *Journal of Constructivist Psychology, 6*(2), 167-193.

Phillips, D. C. (Ed.). (2000). *Constructivism in Education: Opinions and second opinions on controverisal issues*. Chicago, Illinois: National Society for the Study of Education.

Piaget, J. (1929/1973). *The Child's Conception of The World* (J. Tomlinson and A. Tomlinson, Trans.). St. Albans: Granada.

Piaget, J. (1970/1972). *The Principles of Genetic Epistemology* (W. Mays, Trans.). London: Routledge and Kegan Paul.

Scott, P. (1998). Teacher talk and meaning making in science classrooms: a review of studies from a Vygotskian perspective. *Studies in Science Education, 32*, 45-80.

Sjøberg, S. (2010). Constructivism and learning. In E. Baker, B. McGaw and P. Peterson (Eds.), *International Encyclopaedia of Education* (3rd ed., pp. 485-490). Oxford: Elsevier.

Smagorinsky, P. (1995). The social construction of data: methodological problems of investigating learning in the zone of proximal development. *Review of Educational Research, 65*(3), 191-212.

Smith, J. P., diSessa, A. A., and Roschelle, J. (1993). Misconceptions reconceived: a constructivist analysis of knowledge in transition. *The Journal of the Learning Sciences, 3*(2), 115-163.

Sutherland, P. (1992). *Cognitive Development Today: Piaget and his critics*. London: Paul Chapman Publishing.

Taber, K. S. (1998). An alternative conceptual framework from chemistry education. *International Journal of Science Education, 20*(5), 597-608.

Taber, K. S. (2001). The mismatch between assumed prior knowledge and the learner's conceptions: a typology of learning impediments. *Educational Studies, 27*(2), 159-171.

Taber, K. S. (2009a). Learning from experience and teaching by example: reflecting upon personal learning experience to inform teaching practice. *Journal of Cambridge Studies, 4*(1), 82-91.

Taber, K. S. (2009b). *Progressing Science Education: Constructing the scientific research programme into the contingent nature of learning science*. Dordrecht: Springer.

Taber, K. S. (2010a). Computer-assisted teaching and concept learning in science: the importance of designing resources from a pedagogic model. In B. A. Morris and G. M. Ferguson (Eds.), *Computer-Assisted Teaching: New Developments* (pp. 37-61). New York: Nova.

Taber, K. S. (2010b). Constructivism and Direct Instruction as Competing Instructional Paradigms: An Essay Review of Tobias and Duffy's Constructivist Instruction: Success or Failure? *Education Review, 13*(8), 1-44. Retrieved from http://www.edrev. info/essays/v13n8index.html

Taber, K. S. (Forthcoming). *Modelling learners and learning in science education: Developing representations of concepts, conceptual structure and conceptual change to inform teaching and research*: Springer.

Taber, K. S., and Watts, M. (1996). The secret life of the chemical bond: students' anthropomorphic and animistic references to bonding. *International Journal of Science Education, 18*(5), 557-568.

Tobias, S., and Duffy, T. M. (Eds.). (2009). *Constructivist Instruction: Success or failure?* New York: Routledge.

Vygotsky, L. S. (1934/1986). *Thought and Language*. London: MIT Press.

Vygotsky, L. S. (1934/1994). The development of academic concepts in school aged children. In R. van der Veer and J. Valsiner (Eds.), *The Vygotsky Reader* (pp. 355-370). Oxford: Blackwell.

Vygotsky, L. S. (1978). *Mind in Society: The development of higher psychological processes*. Cambridge, Massachusetts: Harvard University Press.

Wood, D. (1988). *How Children Think and Learn: the social contexts of cognitive development*. Oxford: Blackwell.

In: Educational Theory
Editor: Jaleh Hassaskhah, pp. 63-82

ISBN 978-1-61324-580-4
© 2011 Nova Science Publishers, Inc.

Chapter 3

BRIDGING EDUCATIONAL TECHNOLOGIES AND SCHOOL ENVIRONMENT: IMPLEMENTATIONS AND FINDINGS FROM RESEARCH STUDIES

Francesca Bertacchini[*], *Lorella Gabriele*
and Assunta Tavernise
Università della Calabria, Italy

ABSTRACT

The aim of this chapter is to present educational technology experiments with school students, organized as laboratories. Among these laboratories, we introduce arrangement and findings of the Virtual Theatre and the Edutainment Robotics Laboratories, also presenting that based on the construction of Chua's circuits. Regarding the first one, the objective has been the manipulation of virtual contents, as well as the measure of both acceptation of technology and learning. In particular, we have tested a Virtual Theatre software as an educational tool in grammar classes of different schools in Cosenza (Italy). The system has been presented and a list of tasks has been provided, including the manipulation of: - the content "script of the story" in a group writing laboratory; - sounds for the recording of dialogues; - virtual agent to model/animate on the basis of the script to perform; - the performance in the virtual theatre.

As regards the Edutainment Robotics Laboratory, the objective has been the investigation of the cognitive strategies showed by students in building and programming a Lego MindStorms Robot, adopting a systematic methodology in data collection. The aim has been the leading of subjects in the acquisition of new knowledge as well as the development of advanced cognitive skills in problem solving, in thinking strategies and in the acquisition of new concepts. The Robotics Laboratory has consisted in two parts: the first phase has foreseen some key theoretical lessons about Robotics and the programming language; in the second phase, the task "to build and program a robot able to cross an arena in order to take part in a race" has been assigned to each group. At the end of the educational activities, subjects have tested the robot behaviour and presented a project report (a documentation on each phase of the work). Reports have showed the

---

[*] E-mail: francesca.bertacchini@unical.it

work strategies, the modalities of problem solution, as well as the cognitive strategies adopted by students in programming the robot.

Regarding the laboratory devoted to the construction of Chua's circuits, its aim has been the dissemination of new science concepts among young students during the project "Chaos at School: building a Chua's circuit, simulating its behaviour and using it to create sound and music". The purpose of the project was to familiarize high school students with chaos and complexity related concepts, motivating them to build the physical circuit, simulate its behaviour and then to create patterns and music by software applications. Results have showed that the direct contact with the circuit has encouraged students to think, to formulate hypotheses and to test their hypothesis through experiments. Hence, results of all experiences have shown that an active learning can remarkably enhance students' learning efficiency; moreover, a rich interaction can provide fruitful feelings of participation in the educational process. In this view, the tension between new forms of learning and old forms of schooling could not be solved with the victory of one on the other, but through a bridge between the two.

1. INTRODUCTION

Nowadays, in knowledge society, the possibility of accessing, searching and manipulating information has acquired a key-role, becoming a critical factor for the success of new generations. Regarding educational process, the necessity of learning complex scientific contents as well as the opportunity to use innovative media at school, have originated questions as the following: what will the process of cognitive, behavioural, and social development of the "digitally born" students' generation, be? Will the future of educational institutions be to provide an easy access to knowledge? How will schools be able to reinvent themselves? In fact, in recent years, in some educational contexts, a specific space has been reserved to the utilize of educational technologies, and in particular to the manipulation of real and virtual contents [Papert and Harel, 1991; Kafai and Resnick, 1996; Bednar et al., 1995; Bertacchini P.A. et al., 2008], implementing the process of skills development [Collins, 2008; Bilotta and Tavernise, in press]. In particular, it has been demonstrated that building, programming, and simulating the evolution of an artefact (i.e. robot behaviour) have enabled students to develop advanced cognitive skills in problem solving, in thinking strategies and in the acquisition of new concepts [Lund and Pagliarini, 2002; Gabriele et al., 2005; Bilotta, Gabriele, Servidio et al., 2007; Bilotta et al., 2008; Herold, 2010]. Furthermore, manipulation and exploration of virtual contents have given a great chance to carry on unique and personalized experiences through the placement of activities and tasks supporting learners' own interests [de Freitas and Neumann, 2009; Naccarato et al., 2011; Bilotta and Tavernise, in press]. From this perspective, the use of didactic technologies is strictly linked to the constructivist approach [Piaget, 1967, 1971; Papert, 1980, 1986; Martin, 1994; Resnick, 1989, 1994; Harel and Papert, 1990; Gärdenfors and Johansson, 2005; Gabriele, 2006; Bilotta et al., 2001; Moshe and Yair, 2009; Bertacchini F., Bilotta, Gabriele et al., 2010].

Regarding the virtual educational experiences, several studies have aimed at exploiting the potentiality and acceptance of videogames as learning tools [Kiili, 2005; Ke, 2008; Hamalainen, 2008; Owston et al., 2009; Paraskeva et al., 2010] and have showed a positive educational perception, thanks to specific characteristics such as ease of use and usefulness

[Bourgonjon et al., 2010; Pantano and Tavernise, 2009]. Also the research for the realization of educational virtual worlds has shown a considerable growth [van Raaij and Schepers, 2008; Pantano and Tavernise, in press]: for example, web-based communication platforms have been implemented in order to allow students, without limitation of time and place, to access educational tools, such as program information, course content, teaching assistance, discussion boards, document sharing systems, and learning resources [Bertacchini P.A. et al., 2008; Febbraro et al., 2008; Chen, 2009]. In addition, learners can virtually "manipulate" significant 3D objects, and 3D imagery can be used to create immersive experiences by integrating a range of different tools via a single user interface [de Freitas, 2006], such as texts, images, audios, videos, pictures, and animations. In this view, users in educational virtual worlds are actively enabled to search and identify, learn about and evaluate an artefact on the basis of its specific dimensional and typological characteristics, as well as it spatial and temporal relations in order to "construct" their own knowledge [Bilotta and Tavernise, in press].

Regarding the use of virtual agents to promote learning in virtual worlds, educational technologies have become more attractive, because of their strong positive affective impact on students' perception of their experience [Lester et al., 1997], thus revealing the persona effect [Elliott et al., 1999]. Pedagogical advantages that have been proposed in the literature concern increased motivation, stimulation of particular learning activities, and an enhanced flow of communication [Wang et al., 2008]. In fact, agents "show and elicit emotion as a central factor behind the hypothesized increased motivation" [Gulz, 2004], and students have felt learning as more entertaining [van Mulken et al., 1998] or likeable [Sproull et al., 1997]. These benefits have caused the design of lifelike characters also in many other fields, linked to different factors [Corvello et al., in press].

However, even if students learn both enjoying the enriched learning environment and have an active role exploring and/or manipulating the content [Kafai, 2006; Bertacchini P.A., Bilotta, Gabriele, et al., 2006; Bilotta et al., 2010], further research has still to be done [Macnish and Trinidad, 2005; Kolyda and Bouki, 2005]. In fact, laboratories have to be systematically integrated with traditional lessons and cognitive data have to be quantitatively measured and used for improving new teaching/learning methods.

The aim of this chapter is to present three educational technology laboratories in order to demonstrate that they have a great potential for teaching practices and that can be easily integrated into the traditional school context. In fact, results have demonstrated an active engagement in the process of skills development and showed a high score of satisfaction and a good learning of contents. Section 2 introduces the Virtual Theatre, the Edutainment Robotics, and "Chaos at school" Laboratories. Section 3 draws conclusions.

2. EDUCATIONAL TECHNOLOGY LABORATORIES

2.1. Virtual Theatre

In this chapter we introduce the results of an experimental laboratory with the Face3D software, by which parameterized Talking Heads can perform in a Virtual Theatre (VT). The software has been designed and implemented by Evolutionary Systems Group (ESG, http://galileo.cincom.unical.it/) at University of Calabria and consists of three Graphical User Interfaces (GUIs): Face3DEditor for modelling the heads of virtual actors, Face3DRecorder for animating them, and Virtual Theatre for the performance of these synthetic agents, which are expressive faces of famous personalities in different fields (i.e. History, Science, Philosophy) (Figure 1).

Figure 1. An example of virtual actors performing in Face3D Virtual Theatre: Confucius and Buddha.

Talking Heads can also be characters of novels or theatrical works, or the reconstruction of Greek masks. For example, in order to represent the characters of Greek comedies, we have selected six masks among the pictures of the terracotta miniatures that had been found in Lipari (one of the Aeolian Islands, in Sicily - Italy), a Magno-Greek settlement [Bernabò Brea, 2001]. The ancient masks created by the scholar Menander (342-290 a.C.) have been modelled.

For the realization of the performance in the VT, the script is usually elaborated in the laboratory as the manipulation of a basic text. In fact, users can choose the subject because the scripts can be related to a wide range of themes, which can be learnt in an effortless and gratifying way. Voice recording is carried on by learners, too.

2.1.1. Subjects

Since the aim of the first research phase has been the gathering of information on learners' acceptation of technology, in relation to the use of VT with Talking Heads in classroom context, the subject of the focus group consisted of 20 Science teachers and 30 high school students between 15 and 18 years of age.

In the second phase of the research, another sample (constituted by 40 children - 20 male and 20 male) tested the VT in a grammar school laboratory, in order to know users' opinions on software utility, easiness of use and learning satisfaction. In particular, the subject belonged to two different classes, were between 9 and 10 years old, and had a basic knowledge on personal computers.

2.1.2. Materials

For the focus group, the following materials have been used:

- the Face3D software;
- a performance realized by using the Face3D Virtual Theatre.

For the grammar school students, the following materials have been used:

- a pre-test, consisting of 4 questions about students' data (age, sex, class) and familiarity with the use of personal computers;
- pens/papers in the writing laboratory;
- the Face3D software;
- the Questionnaire for User Interface Satisfaction by Lund [2001].

Regarding the software, a generic parametric basic model constituted by a low number of vertices (131) is the starting point for the generation of all virtual heads. The Face3DEditor interface (Figure 2) allows inserting a background image (photo or drawing) as a reference image and changing the position of the vertices, in order to model the virtual face. Textures realized with other Computer Graphics software can be imported in order to complete the Talking Head.

Users can synchronize standard facial expressions (neutral, anger, surprise, sadness, fear, joy, disgust, attention) with pre-recorded files of speech using the Face3DRecorder (Figure 3). Facial expressions have been standardized using the Facial Action Coding System (FACS) [Ekman and Friesen, 1978; Ekman et al., 2002]. In fact, FACS categorizes all possible movements of the facial musculature producing a visible change in the face. Each discrete movement is called Action Unit (AU) and the activation of different AUs results in a combination that makes up a facial expression [Vanger et al., 1998]. The recognition of the eight standard facial expressions has been tested with good results [Bertacchini P.A. et al., 2006b]. However, since human faces are able to show minute changes in a very fast way [Bertacchini P.A. et al., 2007], rapid alterations of virtual emotional expressions can be realized. Moreover, a random movement of head and eyes inspired by Perlin's "noise" [Perlin, 1997] can be adopted in order to provide the animated heads with a more realistic blinking.

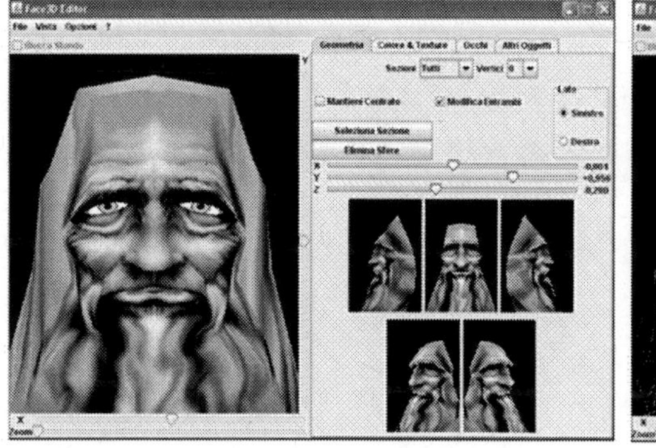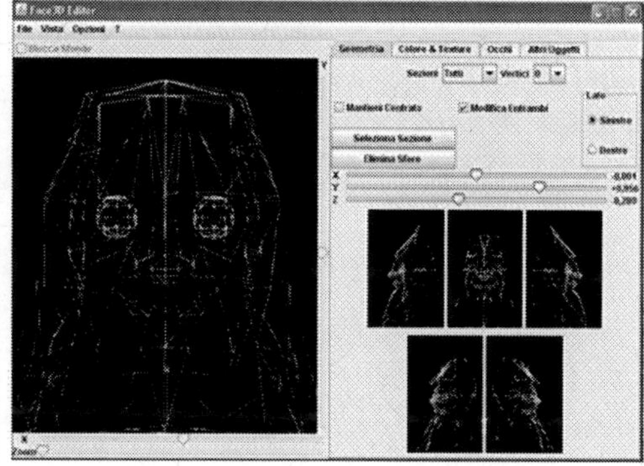

Figure 2. The Face3DEditor interface.

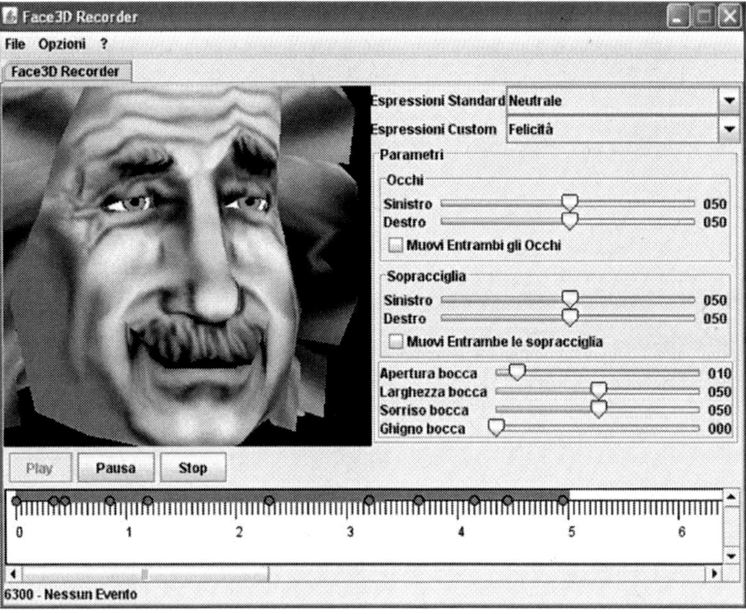

Figure 3. The Face3DRecorder interface.

In particular, the user opens the file of the recorded text and, thanks to a time-line panel, chooses the facial expressions of the 3D head on the basis of the speech. In this case the richness of characterisation and intonation is very important, giving a human feature to the virtual objects [Bilotta et al., 2010]. Finally, the "Virtual Theatre" (Figure 4) imports the animations of the talking heads created with the Face3DRecorder, managing the performance of many virtual agents.

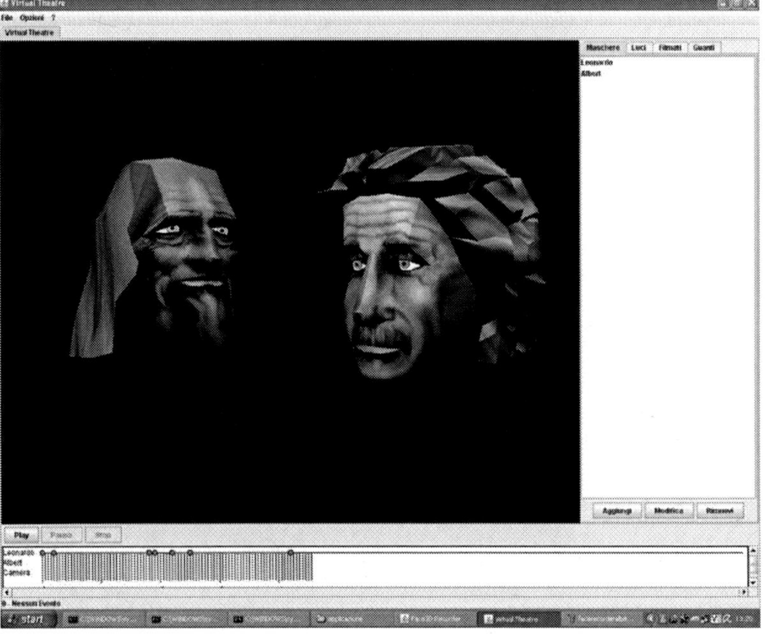

Figure 4. The "Virtual Theatre" interface.

2.1.3. Methodology

We have showed Face3D software and a final performance to a focus group with the aim of detecting learners' acceptation of VT technology in classroom context [Adamo et al., 2010]. Thus, a qualitative questionnaire has been administrated to teachers and high school students. Data derived from focus group questionnaires have been analyzed by a content analysis software (MAXQDA, <www.maxqda .com>), and the results have been very positive.

This encouraging acceptation of technology has determined the carrying out of another experiment, with the aim of testing learners' satisfaction regarding the use of Face3D VT as an educational tool [Bilotta et al., 2010]. For this reason, after a pre-questionnaire on the knowledge of computers, in two grammar classes students had to:

1. choose the topic to be represented;
2. arrange the script of the story in a group writing laboratory;
3. record the dialogues;
4. model the characters on the basis of the content to perform, using Face3DEditor;
5. synchronize the recorded files with the facial expressions, using Face3DRecorder;
6. create the performance, using Face3DVT.

Afterwards, each subject has compiled the Questionnaire for User Interface Satisfaction [Lund, 2001], which measures users' opinions on software utility, easiness of use and learning, satisfaction.

2.1.4. Results

Regarding results from focus group questionnaires, students have been enthusiastic about being part of the audience and also about the possibility of further participation in the educational path of a future performance (character modelling, creative writing and so on). For this reason, a second part of the experiment to model the talking heads and to manage the dialogues has been planned and realized.

Since the starting of the laboratory on Face3D, grammar school children have been passionate for the possibility of a participation in the creation of a virtual performance. Thus, the 98% has shown great satisfaction in the use of Face3D software, the 94% has affirmed that the Virtual Theatre created is useful, and the 99% that it is easy to learn. Finally, the 97% has declared that it is also easy to use. Thus, it has been demonstrated that, through the writing of texts and the construction/manipulation of talking heads, it is possible to engage students in an immersive and entertaining learning. Moreover, the possibility of using this tool with a very young sample is also been displayed.

2.2. Educational Robotics Laboratory

The Robotics Laboratory has been activated with a twofold aim: to investigate the applicability of robotics in educational context and to adopt a systematic methodology in data collection in order to investigate the cognitive skills of the subject linked to the manipulation of software and hardware tools [Bilotta et al., 2009]. The approach has foreseen the development of concrete experiences in which subjects have designed, built and programmed a robotic artefact, using a commercial robot set: Lego MindStorms kit.

2.2.1. Subjects

The sample consisted in twenty-eight students, with an average age of 20. Subjects were divided in 6 workgroups, composed by 4/5 persons, in order to promote a cooperative and collaborative approach.

2.2.2. Materials

We have provided each workgroup with a Lego MindStorms kit, one of the most used commercial systems to build and program a robot without specific knowledge. The kit includes more than 700 traditional Lego pieces, the RCX (Robotics Command System), an infrared transmitter, different types of sensors (such as light and touch sensors), motors, gears, and a guide called Constructopedia™. The building guide helps students to build working robots, as well as it is a source of inspiration for more complex robotic inventions models. The RCX is a microcomputer that allows the robot programming; it receives input from the environment through sensors, processes data and then transfers the output to the motors. Each user can program the robot using a specific programming language and then download the program into the RCX using an infrared transmitter.

2.2.3. Methodology

The Robotics Laboratory has consisted of two parts:

a) a theoretical part to present some basic concepts of robotics, the functioning mechanism of a robot (actuators, sensors, gears), and the characteristics of an agent build with the Lego Mindstorms kit. At the same time, the programming language and some simple behaviour on the robots have been introduced;

b) a practical part, in which each group has had "to build and program a robot able to cross an arena in order to take part in a race".

Moreover, at the end of the Laboratory, each workgroup has presented a project, a full report to describe the robot planning, the resolution of the problems encountered in the construction of the robots, the programming methodologies adopted, the number of tests and the dividing up of work within the group. In particular, they have documented each phase of the work through reports, schemes, photos and videos. At the end of the laboratory activities, a race divided into two rounds has taken place (in each round robots had two minutes to complete the race).

The projects reports made by students during their laboratory activities have allowed the acquiring of valuable information regarding:

- the work strategies adopted by each workgroup;
- the modalities of solution of the problems;
- the cognitive strategies adopted by students in programming the robot.

2.2.4. Analysis of the Results

Some important and useful information has been obtained analyzing the reports. Firstly, we have found that groups have used three different work modalities, each of them characterized by a different approach in problem solving. In particular, the first modality, adopted by three groups, has foreseen the assumption of a precise role of each group member (for example, a person read the instructions, and another chose the appropriate piece), while all the members have collaboratively programmed the robot. In the second modality, adopted by two groups, members have not had a fixed rule in building and programming the robot, but they have adopted a collaborative and cooperative work approach during all the phases of the robot constructions. A third modality has been adopted only by a group, with the presence of a leader monitoring the work (hierarchic approach).

Regarding the programming and planning modalities, each group has carried out different tests to modify the behaviour of the robot, before the obtaining of a robot able to carry out the assigned task. Each group has correctly programmed the behaviour of the robot. The robots of the first and fourth group have also obtained a good time in the first round of the race, reducing the maximum time in the second one. The robots of the first and fourth groups have not completed the race because they have exceeded the maximum time in the second stage.

From these results and from the report analysis, we have identified two kinds of strategies of problem solving: 1) task-oriented strategies, and 2) solution-oriented strategies.

The groups using the first strategy have tested the behaviour of the robot only few times, focusing their attention on the comprehension of the task (groups 3 and 4) (in Figure 2 the robot built from Group 4). In the second strategy, subjects have not analyzed the problem but have immediately tested possible solutions. Groups using this strategy have tested the behaviour of the robot many times and have focused their attention on the goal (groups 1, 2, 5 and 6). The robot that completed the two rounds and obtained the best time has been the robot of group 5 that has used the solution-oriented strategy.

The best times in the final race were obtained by groups 3 and 5, which had adopted the second typology of work subdivision (without fixed roles, collaborating for every task). These groups carried out a small number of tests in building and programming the robot. Although the hardware structure of the robot was very complex (see the large amount of gears and very particular of final actuators used), this robot did not complete the race, as it was very slow.

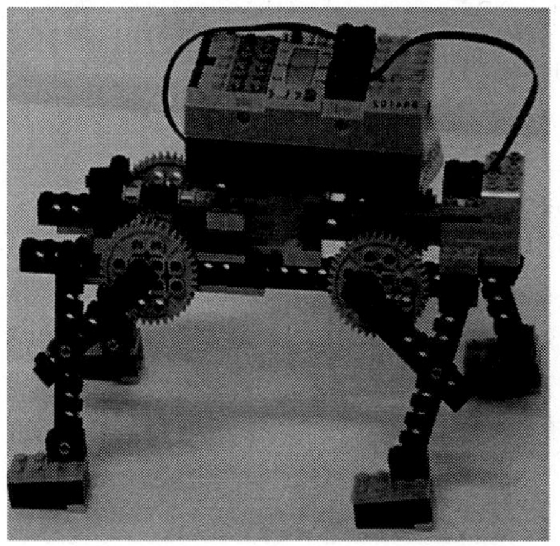

Figure 5. An example of robot built by students (group 4).

2.2.5. Some Remarks on Educational Robotics Laboratory

During the building phase, students have learned how to assemble the robot by using basic pieces, sensors, motors and microcomputer. In the programming phase, they have developed the program on a computer taking into account the task that to be performed (for example to avoid obstacles). If the model did not work, they had to change either the structure of the robot, or the program, or both. In this context, robots have became a "mental cognitive artefacts", since they have been capable to support, guide and extend the user's thinking processes. Robots have helped students to use their mental efforts in a fruitful and effective way, facilitating learning and the building of meanings; moreover, they have supported the development of critical thinking, actively involving subjects in the creation of knowledge reflecting a real understanding of the information presented by the teacher, rather than a replica of the contents. Hence, the use of robotic tools in educational contexts has allowed students to learn in a practical way through the artefacts they create and the phenomena they simulate through the tangible observation and the interaction with them [Bertacchini P.A., Bilotta, Gabriele, Pantano et al., 2006].

2.3. Chua's Circuit Laboratory

Other laboratories have been focused on virtual environments, the generation of sounds and music from Chaos, and the physical construction of Chua's circuits [Bertacchini F., Bilotta, and Pantano, 2009; Bertacchini F., Bilotta, Bossio et al., 2009; Bertacchini F., Bilotta, Bossio, and Pantano, 2010], in order to disseminate advanced scientific concepts among young people. In particular, Chaos Theory considers non-linear dynamical systems with deterministic behavior, that evolves in a apparently random sensibility to initial conditions. Unlike random series, these systems always evolve in the same way for a given set of initial conditions and parameters values; hence, chaotic systems can create a number of unpredictable form and shapes, known as strange attractors. It is impossible to witness this kind of evolution in real-world settings, but it is possible in digital simulations. In fact, Chua's circuit, a physical device able to reproduce chaotic behavior, can produce a large number of chaotic structures of many different patterns and size [Bilotta et al., 2007a, 2007b; Bilotta and Pantano, 2008]. Changing the set of the control parameters, the system can converge to a fixed point, show a limit cycle, or result in a strange attractor (Figure 6). It is also possible to listen to the representations of the circuit's behavior transformed into sound and music. However, some sets of control parameters are physically impossible, so the system becomes unstable and the numeric simulation diverges to infinity. As the control parameters and the initial values change, the dimensionless equations produce a large variety of strange attractors of different shapes and sizes. The dynamical system's applications are really a great number and for this reason are used like a creative source. Many of these applications are illustrated in the website. So dynamical systems are a source in using and exercise creativity. An example of such applications has been used in primary and high schools.

Students can manipulate sounds, music and images from chaos choosing shape, colour creating a never ending numbers of artworks. Another example is music creation: associating notes to point in parameter space creating the attractor from the dynamical system, every point touched by the attractor sounds, then choosing MIDI instrument and playing with post-production software, Chua's circuit is another time a creative source.

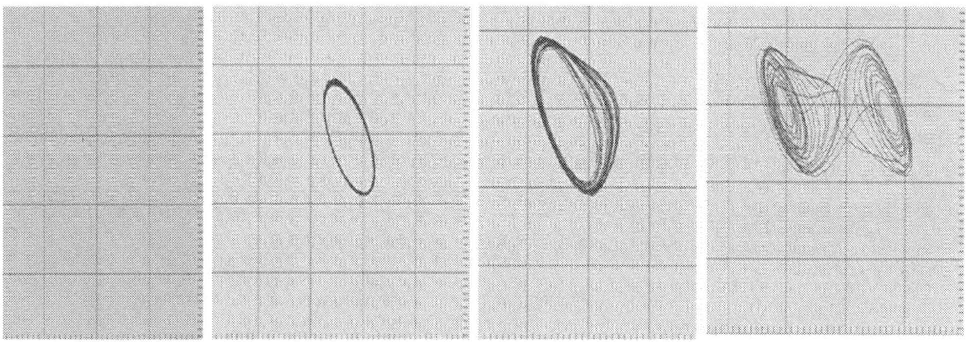

Figure 6. First route to chaos in Chua's circuit.

Two experimental sessions on these topics have been carried out in the project "Chaos at School: building a Chua's circuit, simulating its behaviour and using it to create sound and music" [Bilotta et al., 2010]. The purpose of the project is to familiarize junior and senior high school students with chaos and complexity related concepts, motivating them to build the physical circuit, simulate its behaviour and then to create patterns and music by software applications. Even for learners without a strong mathematical training, the experience has been exciting and accessible. Direct contact with objects encourages students to think, to formulate hypotheses and to test their hypothesis through experiments. So students that have been engaged in this constructivist hands-on activities remembered the material better, felt a sense of success when the task was completed and found it easier to transfer their experience to other learning situations. The proposed method allows students to become a very important part of the learning process. From these two experiments, we have implemented a web site (http://galileo.cincom.unical.it/Chua/index.html) in which students can learn to:

a) build the Chua circuit and visualize its chaotic behaviour with a simulated oscilloscope;
b) simulate chaos by using the specific visualization environment on the site;
c) understand the beauty, simplicity and creativity of chaotic behaviour by using some software applications the site contains, in order to allow students to create digital art products related to sound, music and image digital art production.

The website on Chua's circuit shows many routes to chaos, three dimensional models of the Chua's attractors and finally some artistic metaphor of chaotic trajectories, that become flowers or building into an imaginary world (see Figure 7). The home page shows a menu where all the sections are linked with evocative icons contained in a circle. An intuitive and engaging graphical user interface has been implemented using Adobe Flash Player functionalities. The aim of the home page website is to present information about the Chaos Theory to explain the most advanced technologies related to the educational activities.

The first section presents Chaos Theory and the Chua's Circuit. This section starts with a theoretical introduction to the basic concepts of chaotic phenomena. Then, it includes a didactic activity called "Building the Chua's Circuit".

A specific characteristic that has made the outstanding Chua's invention is the possibility to reconstruct the circuit supporting a very lowest cost and succeed to compose the circuit correctly following the instructions [Bilotta and Pantano, 2008]. The interface (Figure 8) includes a slide show on the left so that a final user can see the components and the steps needed to build the circuit.

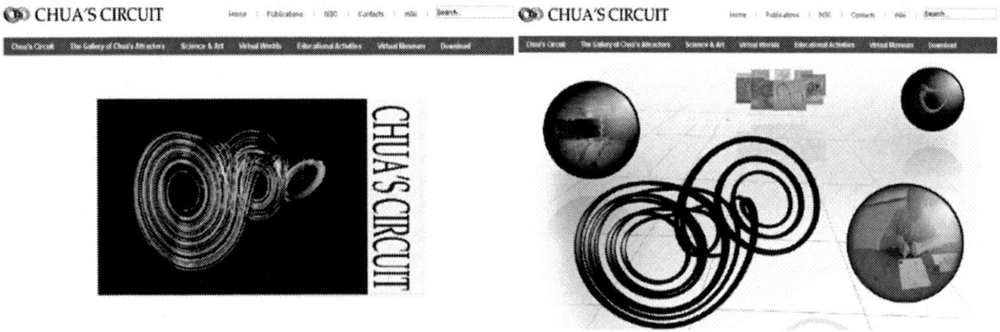

Figure 7. The introductory page to the web site and the home page interface.

On the right side of the screen, there is a short video where young people build Chua's circuit and use it as a source to create images and music. This experiment was realized in order to investigate whether it is possible for young students to acquire concepts as difficult as chaos, usually obtained in engineering or physical university courses.

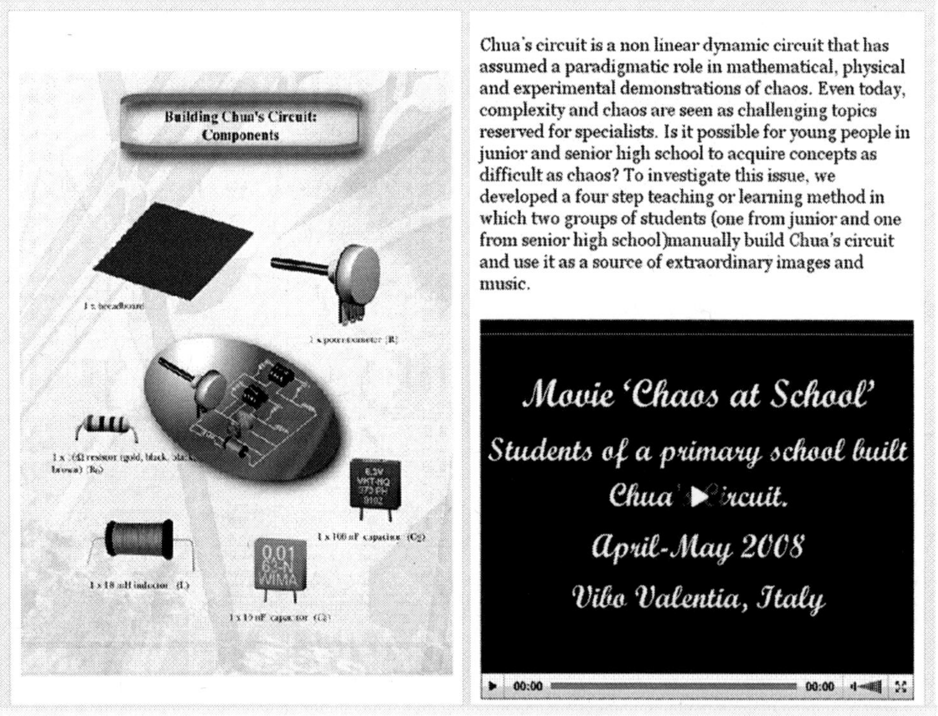

Figure 8. Building Chua's circuit page.

The physical construction of the Chua's circuit promotes the growth of a practical intelligence, stimulating the productive dimension of thinking by manipulation. In this approach, knowledge is not transmitted as organized pieces, but every student can construct it under the expert mediation of a guide, in a context that supports learning by manipulation. This environment could facilitate an active and meaningful learning process of the concepts, especially if they are scientific. Constructivist method shows that people who have used manually experiences remember the material better, feel a sense of success when the task is completed, and find it easier to transfer their experience to other learning situations. With these methods, users become part of the learning process and not just viewers.

The second section shows the "Gallery of Chua's attractors" that represents a classification of the wide number of patterns coming from the scientific visualization of chaotic behaviors in Chua's circuit. Here a collection of images and interactive 3D models (Figure 9), created by the numerical simulation of the circuit, is presented. Users can manipulate the 3D attractors to observe their highly evocative forms from different points of view and then can modify the initial shapes and create new and unpredictable attractors, by changing the system's parameters.

The mathematical models of the Chua's circuit have also been used to produce artistic objects. In accordance with the new architectonic tendencies which use dynamical systems to propose new architectonic vanguards, the third section of the site presents a short movie on the "City of Imagination", where Mathematics and Art are strictly linked (Figure 10).

In this movie users can admire new attractive buildings created by exploiting the forms of chaotic attractors. The fourth section named "Virtual Worlds" presents 3D futuristic spaces. Here, the movies show synthetic scenarios based on chaotic forms, where mathematics is the basis for the artificial worlds and chaos becomes a fantastic representation of the real world.

Since the circuit and its generalizations can create a broad range of acoustic signals and melodies, the fifth section is dedicated to music and sounds from chaos. Furthermore, through the use of MIDI instruments, many musical pieces have been already generated. Much sound architectures created in Pure Data allow users to produce sound and music from chaos.

The sixth section presents some educational activities previously implemented. In the first section we explain a didactical methodology that has been already experimented in primary and high schools, in order to introduce Chaos theory to students,

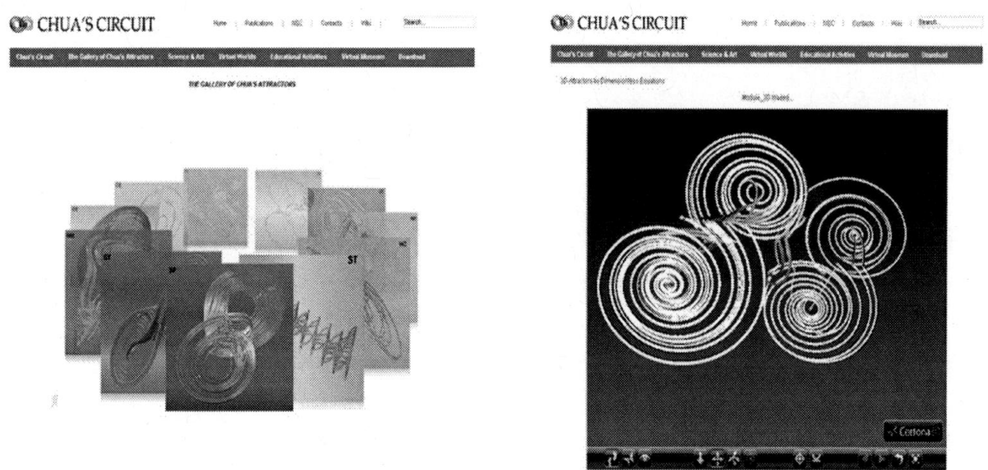

Figure 9. Images from 'Gallery of Chua's attractors and 3D models gallery page.

In this page we present different metaphors and suggestions used for journey in virtual worlds, here Mathematics and Art are strictly linked. The videos derive from the images, are used as cover of various issues of International Journal of Bifurcation and Chaos.

Figure 10. The City of Imagination.

This part presents a four step teaching/learning method through activity reports, pictures, videos, and test results (Figure 11). The originality and beauty of the circuit attractors gave the idea for an exhibit, presented in the web site. Different virtual environments, as shown in the website, try to realize a concrete idea of edutainment tool that combines the educational and entertainment purposes.

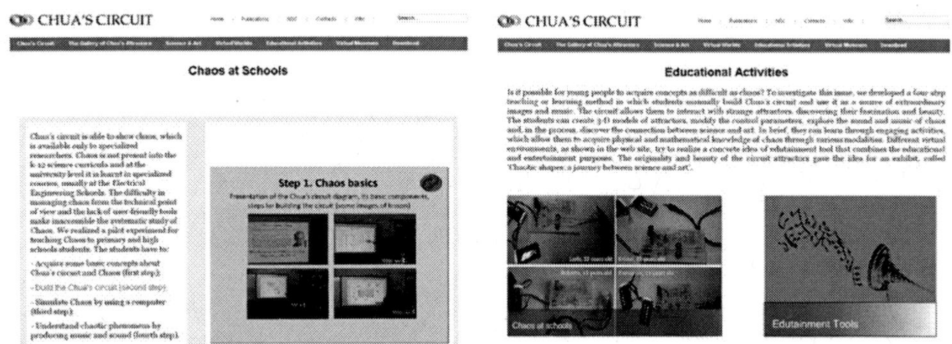

Figure 11. Educational activities page and educational activities page.

A session dedicated to Art and Science is also linked to the educational activities pages (Figure 12). Here many creative interpretations of chaotic shapes are presented. The artistic creativity has allowed the realization of flowers, evocative images, painting with spots of color, Pollock like, that have departure forms of attractors.

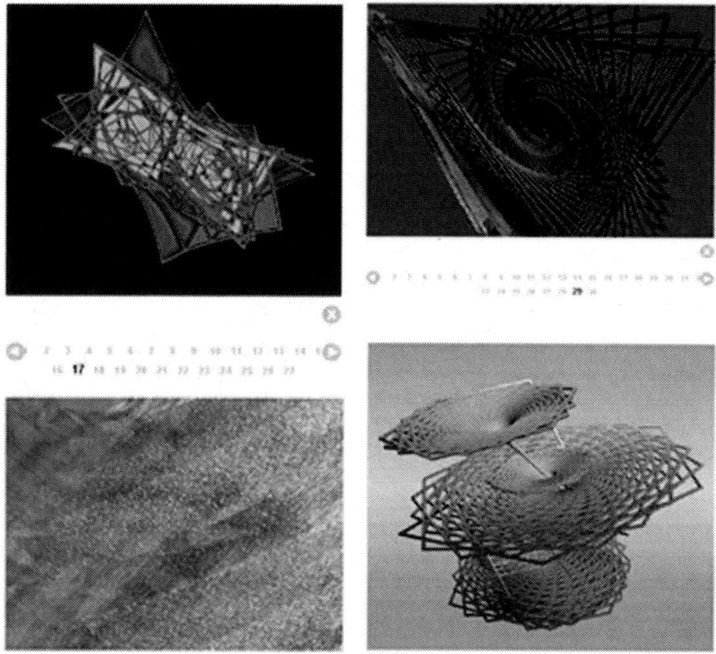

Figure 12. Some pictures from ArtandScience page.

The seventh section presents the "Virtual Museum", which introduces a video of a 3D interactive application in which users can explore more than thousand attractors as if they were in a museum (see Figure 13).

Figure 13. The Virtual Museum web page.

The Virtual Museum of Chua's Attractors presents the collection of all the patterns produced by Chua's circuit, making them available to the students. It's an interactive environment, in which the learner can explore the extraordinary shapes Chua systems are capable of generating. The Museum consists of a single navigable space containing the Gallery's pictures. The setting consists of a navigable area divided by panels showing pictures of attractors and chaotic evolution. The visitor can control his or her position by using the general map of museum, located on the right bottom site of the screen. The museum symbolically contains five sections, representing five different typologies of artistic productions coming out from chaotic system simulations. An avatar works as a guide during the exploration.

Two final sections allow the download of software applications related to attractors, music and sound creation and the exchange/sharing of artistic productions using a wiki system.

CONCLUSION

There are many factors that can influence learning experience, such as the infrastructure, the quality of content and assessment, the quality of learner support systems, the assumptions made by learners and facilitators about the learning experience itself, peer support networks for learners and facilitators, and the educational design (Macnish and Trinidad, 2005). Regarding this latter, laboratories can be foreseen and planned in the school context, explicating their educational potentiality. Thus, it will be possible to know the impact of new technologies on new generations' learning, as well as to realize a model of a school of the future. Moreover, the bridging of educational experiences based on advanced technologies with old forms of schooling will cause a learning that is not only very attractive, but also particularly successful (Bilotta and Tavernise, in press).

REFERENCES

Adamo, A., Bertacchini, P.A., Bilotta, E., Pantano, P., and Tavernise, A. (2010). Connecting Art and Science for Education: Learning by an Advanced Theatrical Environment with "Talking Heads". *Leonardo Journal*, MIT press, 43(5), 442-448.

Bednar, A.K., Cunningham, D., Duffy, T. M., and Perry, J. D. (1995). Theory into Practice: How Do We Link?. In T.M. Duffy, and D.H. Jonassen (Eds.), *Constructivism and the technology of instruction: A conversation*. Hillsdale, NJ: Lawrence Erlbaum Associates, 17—34.

Bernabò Brea, L. (2001). *Maschere e personaggi del teatro greco nelle terracotte liparesi*. Roma: L'Erma di Bretschneider.

Bertacchini, F., Bilotta, E., and Pantano, P. (2008). Educational Virtual Scenario for Learning Chaos and Complex Theories. *The International Journal of Virtual Reality*, 7(2), 19-26.

Bertacchini, F., Bilotta, E., and Pantano, P. (2009). *Il Caos è semplice*. Padova: Gruppo Editoriale Muzzio.

Bertacchini, F., Bilotta, E., Bossio, E. L., and Pantano, P. (2010). Making scientific topics simpler: a website for learning chaos. In L. Gmez Chova, D. Mart Belenguer, and I. Candel Torres (Eds.), *International Technology, Education and Development Conference - INTED* (pp. 5845-5853). Valencia – Spain.

Bertacchini, F., Bilotta, E., Bossio, E. L., Pantano, P., and Vena, S. (2009). Learning Chaos in an Interactive Virtual Museum. *Paper presented at the International Conference on Web-based Learning – ICWL: Vol. VIII* (pp. 1-16).

Bertacchini, F., Bilotta, E., Gabriele, L., and Servidio, R. (2010). Using Lego Mindstorms in Higher Education: Cognitive strategies in programming a quadruped robot. In T. Hirashima et al. (Eds.). *Workshop Proceedings of the 18th International Conference on Computers in Education* (pp. 356-360). Putrajaya, Malaysia: Asia-Pacific Society for Computers in Education.

Bertacchini, P. A., Bilotta, E., Gabriele, L., Pantano, P. and Servidio, R. (2006). *Apprendere con le mani. Strategie cognitive per la realizzazione di ambienti di apprendimento-insegnamento con i nuovi strumenti tecnologici.* Milano: Franco Angeli.

Bertacchini, P. A., Bilotta, E., Gabriele, L., Servidio, R., and Tavernise, A. (2006). La modellazione 3D di espressioni facciali per il riconoscimento delle emozioni. *Paper presented at the National Congress f Experimental Psychology – AIP*, Trento, Italy.

Bertacchini, P. A., Bilotta, E., Pantano, P., Battiato, S., Cronin, M., Di Blasi, G., Talarico, A., and Tavernise, A. (2007). Modelling and Animation of Theatrical Greek Masks in an Authoring System. In R. De Amicis, and G. Conti (Eds.), *Eurographics Italian Chapter 2007 Conference* (pp. 191-197). Germany: Eurographics Assovciation.

Bertacchini, P. A., Feraco, A., Pantano, E., Reitano, A., and Tavernise, A. (2008). Cultural Heritage 2.0 – "Prosumers" and a new collaborative environment related to Cultural Heritage. *International Journal of Management Cases*, 10(3), 543-550.

Bilotta, E., Gabriele, L. and Servidio, R. (2001). Robotica e Creatività: una ricerca empirica in bambini di scuola elementare. *Quaderni del Centro Interdipartimentale della Comunicazione*, 10, UNICAL: Cosenza.

Bilotta, E., Gabriele, L., Servidio, R., and Tavernise, A. (2009). Edutainment Robotics as Learning Tool. In Z. Pan, A.D. Cheok, W. Müller, and M. Chang (Eds.), *Transactions on Edutainment III*, 2(2). Springer Berlin: Heidelberg, 25 - 35.

Bilotta, E., Gabriele, L., Servidio, R., and Tavernise, A. (2007). Investigating Mental Models in Children interacting with Small Mobile Robots. *Paper presented at the Interactive Computer Aided Learning Conference – ICL2007.* Villach, Austria.

Bilotta, E., Gabriele, L., Servidio, R., and Tavernise, A. (2008). Moto-Manipulatory Behaviours and Learning: an Observational Study. *European Journal of Online Engineering*, 4(3), 13-17.

Bilotta, E., Pantano, P., and Tavernise A. (2010). Using an Edutainment Virtual Theatre for a Constructivist Learning. In T. Hirashima et al. (Eds.). *Workshop Proceedings of the 18th International Conference on Computers in Education* (pp. 356-360). Putrajaya, Malaysia: Asia-Pacific Society for Computers in Education.

Bilotta, E., Pantano, P. and Stranges, F. (2007a). A Gallery of Chua Attractors. Part I, *International Journal of Bifurcation and Chaos*, 17(1), 1-60.

Bilotta, E., Pantano, P. and Stranges, F. (2007b). A Gallery of Chua Attractors. Part II, *International Journal of Bifurcation and Chaos*, 17(2), 293-380.

Bilotta, E., and Pantano, P. (2008). *A Gallery of Chua Attractors*. Singapore: World Scientific Publishing Co Pte Ltd.

Bilotta, E., and Tavernise, A. (in press). Designing educational paths in virtual worlds for a successful hands-on learning: cultural scenarios in NetConnect project. In S. D'Agustino (Ed.), *Immersive Environments, Augmented Realities and Virtual Worlds: Assessing Future Trends in Education*. USA: IGI Global.

Bourgonjon, J., Valcke, M., Soetaert, R., and Schellens, T. (2010). Students' perceptions about the use of video games in the classroom. *Computers and Education*, 54, 1145-1156.

Chen, C.M. (2009). Personalized E-learning system with self-regulated learning assisted mechanism for promoting learning performance. *Expert Systems with Applications*, 36(5), 8816-8829.

Collins, A. M. (2008). Rethinking Education in the Age of Technology. In Woolf B.P., Aïmeur E., Nkambou R., and Lajoie S. (Eds.), *Intelligent Tutoring Systems*. Lecture Notes in Computer Science, 5091/2008, 1-2.

Corvello, V., Pantano, E., and Tavernise, A. (in press). The design of an advanced Virtual Shopping Assistant for improving consumer experience. *Advanced Technologies Management for Retailing: Frameworks and Cases*. Hershey, PA - USA: IGI Global.

De Freitas, S. (2006). Using games and simulations for supporting learning. *Learning, media and technology*, 31(4), 343–358.

Lester, J. C., Converse, S. A., Kahler, S. E., Barlow, S. T., Stone, B. A., and Bhogal, R. S. (1997). The persona effect: affective impact of animated pedagogical agents. *Paper presented at the SIGCHI conference on Human factors in computing systems CHI '97*. New York, USA.

De Freitas, S., and Neumann, T. (2009). The use of 'exploratory learning' for supporting immersive learning in virtual environments. *Computers and Education*, 52(2), 343-352.

Elliott, C., Rickel, J., and Lester, J. (1999). Lifelike Pedagogical Agents and Affective Computing: An Exploratory Synthesis. *Artificial Intelligence Today*, 195-211.

Ekman, P., Friesen, W. V. (1978). *Facial action coding system: A method for the measurement of facial movement*. Palo Alto, CA: Psychologist Press.

Ekman, P., Friesen, W. V., and Hagen, J. C. (2002). *The Facial Action Coding System*. London: Weidenfeld and Nicolson.

Febbraro, A., Naccarato, G., Pantano, E., Tavernise, A., Vena, S. (2008). The fruition of digital cultural heritage in a web community: the plug-in "Hermes"". In P. Kommers (Ed.), *IADIS Multi Conference on Computer Science and Information Systems (MCCSIS'08) - WBC 2008* (93-99). Amsterdam: IADIS Press.

Gärdenfors, P., and Johansson, P. (2005). Cognition, education, and communication technology. Mahwha. New Jersey: Lawrence Erlbaum Associates.

Gabriele, L. (2006). APPRENDERE CON LE MANI. Aspetti cognitivi dei processi di manipolazione e interazione con strumenti. Studi empirici con soggetti universitari. *PhD. Thesis*.

Gabriele, L., Servidio, R., and Tavernise, A. (2005). Acquisire concetti complessi attraverso l'uso di strumenti: un'indagine empirica. *Paper presented at the National Congress f Experimental Psychology – AIP*, Cagliari, Italy.

Gulz, A. (2004). Benefits of virtual characters in computer based learning environments: claims and evidence. *International Journal of Artificial Intelligence in Education*, 14, 313-334.

Hamalainen, R. (2008). Designing and evaluating collaboration in a virtual game environment for vocational learning. *Computers and Education*, 50(1), 98-109.

Harel, I., and Papert, S. (1990). Software design as a learning environment. *Interactive Learning Environment*, 1(1), 1-32.

Herold, D. K. (2010). Mediating Media Studies – Stimulating critical awareness in a virtual environment. *Computers and Education*, 54, 791–798.

Kafai, Y. (2006). Playing and making games for learning: Instructionist and constructionist perspectives for game studies. *Games and Culture*, 1(1), 36-40.

Kafai, Y., and Resnick, M. (1996). *Constructionism in practice – designing, thinking and learning in a digital world.* Mahwha, New Jersey: Lawrence Erlbaum Associates.

Ke, F. (2008). A case study of computer gaming for math: Engaged learning from gameplay? *Computers and Education*, 51, 1609-1620.

Kiili, K. (2005). Digital game-based learning: Towards an experiential gaming model. *The Internet and Higher Education*, 8(1), 13–24.

Kolyda, F., and Bouki, V. (2005). The effectiveness of educational technology on children's learning in a school environment. In C. Crawford et al. (Eds.), *Proceedings of Society for Information Technology and Teacher Education International Conference 2005* (898-905). Chesapeake, VA: AACE.

Lund, A.M. (2001). Measuring Usability with the USE Questionnaire. *STC Usability SIG Newsletter*, 8(2). Retrieved from http://www.stcsig.org/usability/newsletter/home-0110.html.

Lund, H. H., and Pagliarini, L. (2002). Edutainment an Robotic games for children. *Paper presented at the 2nd IFAC Conference on Mechnatronic System*, Elsevier.

Macnish, J., and Trinidad, S. (2005). Technology and education - implementation in an Australian context. In P. Kommers and G. Richards (Eds.), *Proceedings of World Conference on Educational Multimedia, Hypermedia and Telecommunications 2005* (2282-2285). Chesapeake, VA: AACE.

Martin, F. (1994). Circuits to Control: Learning Engineering by Designing LEGO Robots, *Ph. D. Thesis*. Boston: MIT.

Moshe, B., and Yair, Z. (2009). Robotics projects and learning concepts in science, technology and problem solving. *International Journal of Technology and Design Education*, 19(3), 289-307.

Naccarato, G., Pantano, E., Tavernise, A. (2011). Educational personalized contents in a Web environment: Virtual Museum Net of Magna Graecia. In G. Styliaras, D. Koukopoulos, and F. Lazarinis. (Eds.), *Handbook of Research on Technologies and Cultural Heritage: Applications and Environments*. Hershey, PA - USA: IGI Global.

Owston, R., Widerman, H., Sinitskaya R. N., and Brown, C. (2009). Computer game development as a literacy activity. *Computers and Education*, 53(3), 977-989.

Pantano, E., and Tavernise A. (in press), Enhancing the educational experience of Calabrian Cultural Heritage: a technology-based approach. *International Journal of Information Communications Technologies and Human Development - Human Development and Global Advancements through Information Communication Technologies: New Initiatives*. Hershey, PA - USA: IGI Global.

Pantano, E., and Tavernise, A. (2009). Learning Cultural Heritage through Information and Communication Technologies: a case study. *International Journal of Information Communication Technologies and Human Development*, 1 (3), 68-87.

Papert, S. (1980). *Mindstorms: Children, Computers, and Powerful Ideas*. New York: Basic Books.

Papert, S. (1986). *Constructionism: A New Opportunity for Elementary Science Education*. A MIT proposal to the National Science Foundation.

Papert, S., and Harel, I. (1991). *Constructionism*. Norwood: Ablex Publishing.

Paraskeva, F., Mysirlaki, S. and Papagianni, A. (2010). Multiplayer online games as educational tools: Facing new challenges in learning. *Computers and Education*, 54, 498-505.

Perlin, K. (1997). Layered compositing of facial expression. In *ACM/SIGGRAPH Technical Sketch*. Retrieved at http://mrl.nyu.edu/ perlin/experiments/facedemo.

Piaget, J. (1967). *Lo sviluppo mentale del bambino*. Torino: Einaudi.

Piaget, J. (1971). *L'epistemologia genetica*. Roma-Bari: Laterza.

Resnick, M. (1989). LEGO, Logo, and Life. In Langton C. (Ed.), *Artificial Life. Redwood City*, CA: Addison-Wesley.

Resnick, M. (1994). *Turtles, Termites, and Traffic Jams: Explorations in Massively Parallel Microworlds*. Cambridge, MA: MIT Press.

Sproull, L., Subramani, M., Kiesler, S., Walker, J., and Waters, K. (1997). When the Interface is a Face. In B. Friedman (Ed.), *Human Values and the Design of Computer Technology*. New York, NY: Cambridge University Press, 163-190.

van Mulken, S., André, E., and Müller, J. (1998). The persona effect: how substantial is it?. In H. Johnson, L. Nigay, L., and C. Roast (Eds.), *Proceedings of HCI'98: People and Computers: XIII* (pp. 53-66). Berlin: Springer.

van Raaij, E.M., and Schepers, J. J. L. (2008). The acceptance and use of a virtual learning environment in China. *Computers and Education*, 50, 838–852.

Vanger, P., Hoenlinger, R., and Hakeny, H. (1998). Computer aided generation of prototypical facial expressions of emotion. *Methods of Psychological Research Online*, Vol.3, No.1 Retrieved from: http://www.pabst-publishers.de/mpr/

Wang, N., Johnson, W.L., Mayer, R.E., Rizzo, P., Shaw, E., Collins, H. (2008). The politeness effect: Pedagogical agents and learning outcomes. *International Journal of Human - Computer Studies*, 66(2), 98-112.

Reviewed by
Maria Teresa Linaza
Visual Communication and Interaction Technologies Centre –
VICOMTech, www.vicomtech.es, Spain

In: Educational Theory
Editor: Jaleh Hassaskhah, pp. 83-95

ISBN 978-1-61324-580-4
© 2011 Nova Science Publishers, Inc.

Chapter 4

ONE NIGHT IN NIGHT SCHOOL TO HIGH SCHOOL IN BRAZIL: SOME IMPRESSIONS

Heslley Machado Silva
University of Itauna and Unversity of Formiga, MG, Brazil

ABSTRACT

Introduction: This study aims to follow a typical night of high school night in a public school, trying to demonstrate its characteristics from the perspective of students and especially from the classroom. Intends to analyze to the relevant literature.

Method: We used the observation as the main instrument of research. The issues findings were used in guided interviews with students, intending to develop a qualitative analysis.

Results and Conclusions: Students, counselors and teachers resent the educational policies that sought to reduce repetition and suit the age, such as accelerated classes. The students revealed a desire by teachers who meet with their proposals, which are severe and prepare their lessons, although occasionally give signals that take advantage of the loopholes of the lack of limit to have fun. It is necessary that the high school to review their roles and allow the issues revealed by his young students, such as the necessity for compliance with basic objectives can be analyzed and answered promptly.

INTRODUCTION

The high school, and especially the night, has often been neglected in educational research. Maybe by finding themselves in a limbo of institutional responsibility. Elementary education is the responsibility of the municipality and the state and higher education is related to federal law. Who is to support and monitor the school? Review and discuss issues of high school becomes therefore imperative for the field of educational research in Brazil. Who's the student is in school, and especially the night? What's your new guy? Constitutes a new group? Homogeneous or heterogeneous? What new proposals for the educational field? Castro, 2008, pg. 115, discusses these questions:

Receives an increasing diversity of students and do not know what to do with them. Too many roles. Without much fear of contradiction, we can say that is one level in constant crisis. Year in, year out, somewhere in the world there are protests, or motions for turning everything upside down.

This article is the analysis of a part of a broader research project entitled "Youth in high school night: Demand for school." Which culminates in a dissertation. This breakdown is shown a typical night in a school classroom, with its virtues and flaws. This review will focus on the environment of the classroom, trying to discern how to build a relationship between students and teachers, students and school supervision. It is intended to discuss what the impressions left by the students during the five school hours, including breaks and recess.

Squeezed between the school and upper secondary education is pointed out by several authors as a period with limited identification. Castro, 2008, pg. 116, considers that the high school:

> ... Is at a crossroads, is cornered. Below is the key which is the minimum education for a modern society. It has a very simple agenda of teaching the rudiments of education. The top recruit who is professional and, more or less knows what she wants.

This same school suffers from an identity crisis, trying to figure out their role in society. The same Castro, 2008, pg. 116 discusses this dilemma: "The major problem is the medium between preparing for work or prepare for higher education. Things are well mixed and, if anything, compete seriously for the student's time.. " It is this sector which is expected to launch a distinct look. It aims to present a typical night of high school night in a large public school, highlighting its characteristics, ailments and attempted solutions of their urgency.

This work emerges from the researcher's perception about the peculiarities arising from the coexistence of two years of research within the school in question. The interest also comes from years of teaching in the educational field, by observation as a teacher and researcher, trying to establish dialogue between what happens in the everyday life of this school, classroom and what they have discussed the school night.

To try to understand the routine of this student, broke two research instruments: observation and interview. The first allowed an overview, an overview of day-to-day that school, the classroom, teachers and their students. Subsequent interviews with students possible to deepen the questions that arise in the observation.

Development

The mark of contempt In mid-March, we perceive a climate of school started, which caused us surprise, given that classes had started in February, already a week late. Lacked teachers to complete the teaching staff. After a month and a half classes begin, some classes had not yet had, for example, no class of chemicals. "(...) Face increasing difficulties in filling their tables with expert teachers "(Franco and Novak, 2001, pp. 170). Krawczyk (2003) indicates the severity of the shortage of professionals to teach in secondary education as a critical issue for the operation of the school term. The leadership tried to find all types of replacement, but the office seemed to be financially unattractive. As quoted by authors such as George and Carnielli, 2003, pg. 52, the surge in high school at night is the last option of work of teachers, who even does not allow the establishment of an identity with the reality of school.

The imposing appearance of the school building masked the situation of abandonment of the inner area. Portfolios mostly spoiled, some apparently vandalized, some dirty walls etc.. We noticed some movement toward conservation, but the results are meager. Interestingly some rooms looked better, but the room who were following the first series had a very critical aspect.

There was a remarkable fact: over the chalk in school. It became necessary to ask students to take the chalk. Complained about the lack of any type of material. Paper for photocopying? Only if students buy. All materials had to be written on the board or dictated. The specifications call were not ready, the attendance lists confusing, missing cleaning products. All this sets the framework a reality far from what is expected of an educational institution. Students are far from the minimum conditions, what about advanced educational resources that promote inclusion? The new technologies seem a utopia for the school night. Sousa and Oliveira, 2008, pg. 69, discusses the impact of these conditions:

> The scarcity of resources available at school, plus the speed and volume of information in circulation, further aggravates the situation of isolation, reducing the opportunities for social inclusion of young people and adults served by the school at night.

Despite this chaotic picture, there was a waiting list for enrollment and the waves were good plays. He asked if the rooms on who has missed much, suggesting that the vacancy could be filled. Finally the direction asked the students who contribute two dollars for basic expenses, mainly so that the school could offer meals. Krawczik (2003) addresses the issue of directors and supervisors are often worried because they have to resort to a certain charity community to maintain the proper functioning of the school, regarding the operation of the school meals and cleaning up the building.

The state government which is responsible for maintaining the operating conditions of the public school seems distant. Authors such as Sousa and Oliveira, 2008, pg. 66, suggest this: "(...) demand growth exacerbates the problem of lack of specific source of funding for secondary education, with its resources pills, statewide, (...)". This assignment, if ever, have long found abandoned. The feeling is that once paid the salaries of teachers and staff in general and the building being built, end here the role of government. According to Gomes and Morgado, 2007, p. 236, when discussing the funding of school "... it is the first quantity, ensure the vacancies, taking into consideration the demand for education in general and meeting-skilled election to the demands. "You do not notice any movement of claim, passivity seemed to be general, also did not realize any channel for that possibility.

The course of one night in any public school in high school ...

Presents relevant events occurring during a round school, which has facilitated its analysis.

The Arrival

Before 18:00, some students begin to cluster in the vicinity of the school, sitting on the stairs. The groups will be setting at the school gate, some more animated than the others. As it approaches the time to enter, the buzz becomes quite a stir. Hits the mark. Several students who were already at the door of the school do not come, either to wait for the second time, or perhaps taking advantage of the tolerance of the minutes of the first schedule to spend a moment longer and meet to talk freely. It can be suggested that there is an obligation to go to school, far from a willingness to be there. Some seem to show any aptitude for school life, must suffer great pressure to at least have the degree. Castro, 2008, pg. 116, makes an analysis of this issue:

> A problem that is worsening is the presence in the middle of students who preferred not be in school. (...) Therefore, the average receives many students who have no affinity with their school or with their studies, but they are required to attend classes . And that, at the age of increased personnel turbulence, driven by surging hormones. Obviously, the existential revolution and hormonal create even more problems for the school.

It is striking predominance of young-looking teens. Hardly sees adults. The idea of night school as that focused only on adults is not supported here. This assertion can be supported by Gonçaves and others, in a survey of a middle school in Rio de Janeiro, "Factor is interesting that the night school is being attended by young people, because 48% of students are between 15 and 19 years. (2005, pg. 350). This new component can be a complicating factor in a school apparently designed for the the young and adult workers, the appearance and behavior of students at the school gate point in another direction. New challenges are put to the same school, both in the forms of teaching as the issue of discipline.

He drew attention to a certain type of young students that we have seen, since before the beginning of class, and throughout the first time at the school gate. They stood alone, absorbed in themselves, introverts, not talking, and only occasionally greet someone. You can not define whether they are tired or are grumpy, but do remember, even remotely, the image of youth who have, or be an energetic, eager for contact with their peers, so agitated. It seems that the attitude seen fleeing the reality of a majority and would merit further investigation.

It's time for the second entry, the agitation is restarted, it takes five minutes of schedule, some students complained, asking why the door is closed. One student says it is "stupid (sic) school of the poor", showing a contempt for the public institution. The impassive, as mentioned earlier, continue in the same condition. Finally hits the mark. Those who enter do so in a relatively orderly manner. Some decide to stay out, why, if they waited so long? There is no coherent answer.

The First Time

It's a relatively quiet time, the delay in getting the teachers' room to match the delay of the students. Many students were outside, which is reflected in the climate of the classroom. This is considered a warm time, which gives little respect, because she knows that she will have to be repeated. In some classes, this seems to be viewed as a time lost, in others, the teachers think is best, with regard to discipline, because the number of students is lower. There is a wide disparity in the way of looking at this moment in night school, some find it useless, utterly disposable, others feel that teachers should give the matter normally, because the "problem" of those who missed it and, ultimately, so many missed no apparent reason. There is no consensus, and opinions vary, even from series to series.

The feeling is that for many classes, for a large portion of students, and even some teachers and people connected to the administration, the class will only start effectively from the second zone. It's almost institutional.

Analyzing the whole situation in the first time at the entrance, and those who are outside, we come to some possible conclusions. First, when young people find a loophole, a way of breaking with the rigid schedule, try to enjoy it, even at the expense of lessons. In conflict, some students who feel more free and have fun, enjoying the space for living and recreation at the school gate, as seen by Dayrell, 1992, sometimes resting inside the room are the ones who harshly criticized the lack limits and rules, complain of night school, comparing the "mess" of the turn with an alleged ordination morning shift. They do not like this situation but it seems that there are possibilities to claim and eventually conforming on the grounds that at night is like that, because "most of them work, then the course has to be weaker. You can find authors who understand the same question "the institutional culture that at night everything is easier, the lack of time as a basis and justification" (Gomes and others, 2005, pág.353). Possibly for not meeting benchmarks of resistance, are resigned to the expectation of low future.

The Second Time

The schedule begins with a few minutes late, the young students take advantage of this for quite a bit of room, sharing the excitement of the arrival of large numbers that only comes in the room at that time. In some classes the class actually begins now.

A fact draws attention at this time: the entry supervisor to give a few warnings. The person occupying the position is feared, because it enters an immediate impact, the environment is another, the group changes its behavior. But what will interest us is that the supervisor has to say and how will the assimilation and representation made by the students.

The first issue addressed was the discipline. Warns that repression is severe, and the heavy punishment. To reinforce the message, are given examples of actions that ended in suspension: a student who killed behind a class photo; other four who hid in the bathroom, climbed on the toilet to escape the "search", but to no avail, the supervisor found them all and punished with suspension. The threat is hard if they are caught in the corridor. Indeed, the presence of students in school hallways, during class time are practically nonexistent, there is no movement, no noise, but at times it seems that the conflict moved into the classroom. Later, after the departure of the supervisor, the class remains silent. Soon after, you hear a student imitating bird, another student in another class, sneaks into the room to escape surveillance in hallways, seems to be what concerns them most, are perceived movements that attempt to break the routine, it can be a joke, a noise, a laugh, a confrontation.

The supervisor believes that a subject gets serious: the return of the reproof. She says that years of mess over, that there is a new order coming with the new government. Says "that" the students were accustomed over, that while other schools are still under the previous system, this school will be different. To enhance your speech, she asks if anyone is repeating the year, seven answer yes, to which she replies: "see?". The class as a whole apparently assimilates the speech well, and clearly supports the ideas presented.

The "accelerated classes" in all its forms (elementary and middle school) are severely attacked. The supervisor and the students themselves argue that students from those programs know nothing, having been pushed, reaching as far as to identify them among those present and, resigned, they all confirmed that they are charged.

It can be noticed in the school context a new category of students. Considered without knowledge of past, not future possibilities, are orphans of an adequate government policy, does not deserve to occupy the place they occupy, being outcasts. Within the school environment, provided the direction to the students, all agree with the predicament of this group. Silva (2000) sees the critical view of students in relation to this condition.

Students show an awareness of the situation of backwardness in relation to a school that is not considered ideal. This reflection is part of those who experienced both these processes of acceleration and the ones who live with them. Table of alienation often described for these is not supported here as the perception of the consequences of the process they experienced. It discusses the effectiveness of the accelerated classes. There are those who were unable to study at the right time and they could not do it (repetition on repetition), also exceeding the legal age. Either way, there is a dilemma: either return to the system set up to retrieve them and failed to do so or try a regular school and could face the cycle of failure, coping with prejudice and ending at the end, giving up everything. One is left with the questions of the educators of this school: What to do with these students? As the school will deal with students who feel unable to keep up with others? The return of the "bomb" will exclude the opportunity again this group of mainstream education? How to deal with pupils with low self-esteem and so they then have reinforced this condition daily at school? It is worth reflecting on the consequences of changing public policies and guidelines for these policies and, more importantly, on how the education sector has been engaged in ideas that at first glance might even be positive, without however having thought well in its implementation and its possible outcomes. Silva (2000) discusses this issue, the order of disapproval, or at least reduce it at all costs, when he says that in view of the students this kind of measure is a great deception, but only part of the government's electoral propaganda, only to deceive the popular classes, because no one can say that the government offered no education, while of dubious quality. The same author, 2003, pg. 75, shows convincingly that question from the students themselves:

> Young people complain that this process tends to keep students who are weak at the same level, and that does not encourage others to strive. Good or bad, the mechanism historically devoted to "study to pass the year" was killed abruptly, giving students the impression of a void, an abandonment. They believe that the everyday classroom was impaired, attention has become more difficult. There is more concern with the evidence. You miss it once was.

Scraps of supervisor close with an application for each student to think well on your situation, they may be occupying seats contested by others, and for those who do not want to fulfill their "obligations" and disciplinary study, which will be better leave for other places, because the turn "night" at school where they are is much disputed.

Despite all this competition for places, there is a clear negative image of high school at night. Students feel inferior, are compared and compare themselves with students in day shift, private schools, comparing the structure of teachers and their school, consider themselves victims of misguided educational policies such as accelerated classes and reducing disapproval. Perceive themselves as left out of the possibility of aiming for the realization of the university, because they would have the basic requirements. Sousa and Oliveira, 2008, pg. 58, makes a similar analysis:

> There are also the students a sense of inferiority (there is constant compared to the day shift) and the notion that everything conspires against its goals: school worse, less motivated teacher, public policy wrong or missing. Severely criticized the lack of disapproval, claiming, among other reasons, which is part of the implicit objectives of the government that they complete the course without proper preparation and able to pass the entrance exam.

The Third Time

Students distinguish basically two types of lessons, with the argument that is in the hands of teachers to conduct one or another model, and they define the model closer to the ideal. We will try to make everyday moments, highlighted by the students, to expose the two conditions. Call "class A" that which represents the groups that had discipline problems and, "class B", the representative of those in the classes passed without major hassles. It became clear in conversations with students during class, they considered the best model B and know what qualities they thought the teacher would need to achieve it. On the other hand, also showed what would be the profile and attitudes of the teacher who would lead the situation A.

In the third schedule of the "class A", we were alerted by students at that time there was no class because the teacher can not impose. It highlights the entire class to mold a new behavior. For starters, most left the room at halftime, going to the runner or even the patio. Ten minutes after the signal, the teacher arrives, few realize its arrival. Several minutes later, when it comes to matters in the context, that copy are rare, noting that some content that was already saying in any previous class. It starts a noise that tends to turn din. The teacher warns them not to confuse friendship with the mess, making threats of expulsion and point out, among others. There is a brief lull to soon thereafter, back bustle. She asks a student to dictate the subject, apparently in the hope that they get some control, as he goes to his desk to do something, maybe proofread. Ironic mistake. The student can not dictate anything again and turmoil settles. In a last attempt, the teacher suggested to correct the exercises because the proof will be in the next class, and the proposal has the tone of menace. In principle the idea works, but to the extent that most do not understand, installs new turmoil. One can not judge what bothers her most, the confusion caused by "unruly" or the claim of "geeks" who are not following the correction. Amid all this, is the image of the teacher, lost, without any control, seeming to hope for that class finally come to an end, but the little time remaining for that time seems an eternity. The teacher says that it does not occur in the private school where she teaches during the day, and the revolt of students is greater. Finally hit the sign and the torture ends. The teacher comes out quickly, some students had gone for a long time before the recess.

Obviously there is a lecture presented, it is a patchwork quilt made of moments that led to the discipline slip and were witnessed by the researcher. All of this will help us respond to questions asked at school entry? It may be interesting to find out who hates to find out what is sought. These moments were expressed by students themselves as situations that led to chaos. Disrespect for students, lack of authority, something that was explained as "lack of posture," meaning the inability to cope with the daily classroom; inexperience (though not generally as there are newbies who get a good relationship and sometimes experienced that does not happen), lack of knowledge of the subject taught. These are the main characteristics of the teacher in question and hence the class. Silva (2000) points out that the new policy to avoid the disapproval of the maximum was eliminated, a reference to shape behavior. In the voice of young people themselves, they were not a barrier to disruptive behaviors, fear of repeating a grade. As for the lack of preparation in relation to content, Franco and Novak, 2001, pg. 170 shed light on the issue:

> (...) We can deduce that the universities are not structured to train teachers in Physics, Mathematics, Biology, Languages, Sociology etc.. Capable of mastering the specific content of their disciplines and the skills and skills necessary to face the challenge of having to prepare their classes in an interdisciplinary perspective.

He drew attention to students' insistence that such situations were perceived. They said: "... see what the problem is not our own." "We have no chance to compete for college and the labor market." "To attend a class like this?", "Is ... bad public school, there's no way to get the teacher. "" ... they (the teachers) get nervous about their problems and cash on us. "They even reveal who would like to have good classes because, although think of the fun moments of indiscipline, realized they were wasting precious time and believed to be in the hands of teachers to change that reality. They argued, then, about the possibility of being different, referring to the case of the groups that we characterize as "class B". There seems to be by some teachers an additional disregard for the night shift. Anchored in the perspective of those students who are weak or tired, or rogues (moved to night because it's easier), introject all these prejudices and repeat them in their daily classroom. The fatigue may be trying to minimize the teachers for this kind of vision, less class, so less effort. Gomes and Carnielli, 2003, pg. 64, corroborate this analysis:

> For teachers, discrimination (in relation to the night shift) begins to exist when the lower level of education. Make it too easy, arguing that students work and get tired. There is much paternalism. It seems that teachers of night disguised his weariness with the students, because most work in other jobs.

We come now to the third schedule of the "class B". Even before the beginning of class, students will warn: "now you see what is and what is classroom teacher." It creates an expectation of what would prove an ideal classroom. I am astonished us by the simplicity of the criteria used by students for this classification. The teacher has not arrived yet, but we are already seeing a different behavior of the class, most remain in their places, a few welcome Professor at the door and are quite sympathetic to their presence, therefore they are all in their wallets and the climate is very favorable. Is dictating, passing under the matter, explaining, correcting quizzes or group activity, class flows very nice. Interestingly, no innovation teaching is presented, only the attitude of respect. When requested, the teacher is very responsive and shows know the subject well, these attributes are recognized by students. She manages to maintain discipline, nullifying any sign of trouble, sometimes it's ironic, even harsh, but those moments reveals himself as someone who knows how to draw the line, which is of great value to students. And so the lesson goes to the end without problems in an orderly manner without disruption, with optimum student participation, with games that never go beyond, as the rules are clear, and seem to satisfy both parties. Hit the sign for the playground, mostly leaves, some are still talking to the teacher.

Again, we are describing a prototype of the class B to class as a whole has not occurred as it was presented, with all these events simultaneously, but it was composed of fragments of what the students were citing, indicating during classes, and that ordained as a close to ideal. The discipline, the 'moral' seems to be the great merit, followed by a relationship of "friendship," a rapport that there are limits, and, combined with these qualities: knowledge. Impressed by the simplicity of what students want. Interestingly not require different classes, with innovative teaching methods; just want the lesson to be given effect, and she can spend as usual. Do not want to give here all responsibility for teachers. Logically, students end up creating many difficulties, but I have noticed is that, from some basic features of the teacher, it creates an empathy that provides a good development of the lesson. There is a clear line of work, the students know what to expect with this teacher, your requirement, their approaches to the content. KRAWCZYK (2003, p. 197) records a similar analysis:

> The student's intellectual interest in the various disciplines is closely linked to his relationship with the teachers and their school results. In general, students approve demanding teachers, who use different resources to explain, they facilitate the understanding of content and have availability to answer your questions, willing to be consulted outside the room, etc.

This great value attributed by students to that teacher who can develop your content is perceived by Zagury (1999) when reporting the authority as a key point of the discipline. You realize the rigor and definition of rules as the characteristics of a trader. Silva (2000) indicates that the discipline in the students' vision does not mean lack of freedom, they want to negotiate its borders and thus build a healthy relationship. Since the rules were defined, should be respected by both sides. Believe that the maintenance of discipline could be a prerequisite for professional teachers, and that this matter be involved in their formation. Compare the times and claim that some are not worth watching with such confusion, therefore, their continued absences would be fair. What students crave can be seen in Gomes and others (2005, pg. 353) where they show. The love is reflected in how the teacher "gives" to his class, and dislike, disinterest in teaching classes to provide more dynamic than the faults (which are few), which causes the motivation of students. Despite the lack of academic background and lack of time to study undertaken by most respondents, is the magical figure of the great differential teacher to student learning.

The Playground

The groups get together, buy some snacks, the school does not receive free lunch from the government, only in mid-year through a competition managed to buy something that nobody knows how long it will last. At this point turns to notice certain students to remain isolated, without interaction with others, looking tired, with little motivation to gel.

In the conversations become more lively, we highlight some of the dialogue among students. One of the teachers complain that they lacked, saying that although they had arrived tired, the students wanted to take lessons and have had no calls then, lazy teachers. Paradoxically, this same student is buzzing with the imminence of leaving early. Another student celebrating the same thing. One asks, then why not stay home? He replies that he is not funny to miss class, the fun is in cutting class, to circumvent the rules and cheat the school authority.

Another group said the end of almost automatic approval and possible return of repetition. The opinions are conflicting, some regard the return of "bomb" to moralize the school, others fear it because they realize they "know nothing" and that eventually repeating several times the same series. Anyway, say they are not sure what will happen, because every day that "they" say one thing and that nothing is set.

A student has an advantage over fact. She said: "She (teacher) asked: What is dualism? Then I said, I do not know. "Considers its response as a great victory, and concludes:" It was too much weight."

The dialogues mentioned seem to have no link, but, overall, provide us some reflections. In the first and second dialogue, reveals the conflict between what one wants and what one is conscious of being needed. Looking for the easy laugh, the overcoming of the adult world, are young, some teenagers, want to enjoy. In parallel, they realize that there is a charge on one side, and a great competition for the labor market, on the other side. They want to be treated like adults but sometimes behave like children. Want accuracy, but fear it.

The last speech can reveal the rebellion, immediacy, maybe a certain hedonism. That momentary pleasure of confrontation with the teacher worth the risks and consequences of this attitude. After all there was a break with the expectation of the adult world, it was expected that she knew the answer, but she did not. Even though the complete ignorance may seem like ignorance, and that this would have consequences for the student, his response was a non-conformist, an act of courage, even if ephemeral, but she boasts.

We must also realize the establishment of a precarious space for recreation and socialization of these students, perhaps one of the few that they encounter in their daily lives. They are mostly young, some even adolescents, in contrast with the expectation that they were working adults. They want to take this space in several ways. Sousa and Oliveira, 2008, pg. 57 perceive this issue:

> Either way, the school for all students, seems to be in addition to a teaching space, a cultural and social space. In most cases, is the sole and / or main public space of access to information and culture systematically.

Bed Time

A teacher has failed, either because it is a license and there is no substitute, or simply walked away without explanation to the students, or worse, the teacher is at school, but for various reasons will not give that lesson, finally, the reason is not always clear, showing disregard for the student. It was agreed that, with time vacant for any reason, you can move up the timetable. You get to witness certain situation in which a teacher sent the matter to advance their classroom through the teacher herself responsible for that zone, ie a time using the other, although both were in school. In conclusion, the students were dismissed early, all the teachers present. Krawczyk, 2003, pg. 193 addresses this issue:

> Another difficulty that schools must face daily is the systematic lack of teachers. There is a kind of naturalization of this situation, which causes no longer call the attention of the directors nor the students nor the fact that missing two or three teachers at every turn.

A typical example of rising time which witnessed: Since there was information that the teacher did not come. After about ten or fifteen minutes of waiting, the professor who was going up the schedule appears to mark an activity and warns that unless more that participate will not favor them. There are occasions when a student seeks an exercise with the teacher and pass on the board to fill the vacant hours.

It seems that this mechanism favors all night after everyone is tired and deserve to rest soon and that time is being fulfilled, but not quite. Few are interested in that activity was slow in coming, although most expect to copy. The uproar is inevitable. Often the students are drawing attention to each other, fearing that bad behavior can lead coordinator not to let it go over the schedule. The warning is always absolutely ignored. A teacher usually come to check the progress of the exercise, sometimes it does not appear, students pretend to be doing something. At times, the second student comment, the exercise that was sent had been done in previous classes. Some students complain that there are no evening classes. With ten minutes to do the time, virtually everyone had gone and hardly anyone made the proposed activity.

Despite the pleasant aspect of these procedures: the rise time, leave early, do not have class, can make a mess, students notice and point out the harm it causes them. Often times the rise in cascade, ie, the teacher missed the first time, then sends the second pass something to the table; the second time, the teacher asks you to do a third year and so on. The result is that came to witness instances of classes in which there was no class with the teacher's presence. In these cases, students said they consider useless to go to school to get through it. Another perverse effect of this mechanism is that it leaves behind only the class where the teacher lacked, but the group who should be the teacher who is also climbing the time a loss, because, being a large school, the teacher, in an attempt to controlling "the two classes, just spending time outside the two rooms. Result: the damage reaches a much larger number of students.

According Krawczik, 2003, pg. 193, is a frequent absenteeism of teachers, creating a climate of low production in the school with students outside the room and discouraged, directors and coordinators trying to compensate for the lack of teaching staff with recreational activities.

Fifth Time

You get to the last time. Some rooms are now empty, and those where there is still class, appear distinct realities. Drowsiness is visible among students. There is resistance to class by students in some classes, citing fatigue. Some teachers also seem tired. This weariness, discouragement that seems to radiate between faculty and students, an inertia settles in most classrooms, teachers, most of them do not want to venture into activities that require more of students at that time. Glimpses a consensus that enough for today and the sooner done, the better. It installs a climate of mutual understanding, that students understand the weariness of a teacher and vice versa. Both sides reveal this condition as detected by Krawczik, 2003, pg. 196:

> Young people recognize the adverse conditions in which the teacher works at night when they say they come to school tired because they had to work all day and have less patience. It is possible that teachers express, verbally or not this tired. This type of communication, undoubtedly creates a climate of apathy and low motivation, climate often denounced by teachers and students.

Again a surprise. A teacher normally teaches caring nothing for the time, quietly develop the content, gives exercises and collecting their execution. Students, in turn, respond promptly. Here we have a teacher with some virtues that have been highlighted in the "class B", described in the third zone. The commonplace according to which the last time something is lost is not supported in this room. Resorts to Sousa and Oliveira, 2008, pg. 58, to try to understand what happens in this environment:

> These young people, in turn, express the desire to avoid being seen as working students tired but wanted to clear rules and requirements. The fatigue is attributed by students over the monotony of classes and lack of space for participation than the fatigue resulting from work.

Finally we reached the end of class, the signal is received as a relief for most students. Some appear to be quite tired. We must rethink the end of shift and scale until putting this high school at night to fulfill their role. Gomes and others (2006) indicated that the same high school bypasses the professional and personal needs of students. But how is this failure? Many fragments of neglect have been raised that night. At the same time saw themselves some moments of success that need to be resized so that they capture these pathways and describe them so that, once understood, can cite other teachers and others interested in improving school night.

CONCLUSION

There are several lessons to be drawn from such monitoring. The high school night consisted of adult students or young workers typically did not match the actual situation, most students are on the threshold of adolescence and youth. The impact of new educational policies aimed at reducing repetition and commendable adequacy of age had a negative impact on all involved in this school, two aspects stand out: the first relates to self-esteem, poor and accentuated by the perception that they are facilitating academic life for its possible failure. The second aspect is the lack of discipline, because the near absence of disapproval extinguished a major disciplining mechanisms, fear of repeating a grade. Referring to this subject, indiscipline, the students clamoring for it, point the way to get it, have contradictory positions, but always signal bounds. Live with a school that has not figured out how to deal with them, but are teachers who oppose this slump. Students know the characteristics indicate that teacher that captivates as well as those of those who repudiate. Lack the training courses for teachers to consider these issues in a forceful way. No magic formulas applying sophisticated technologies or innovative teaching, teachers who want to comply with its basic role of leading the class with respect and safety, preferably with quality. The night school high school needs to find its balance point so you can meet their workload in a productive way, demonstrating that it is possible to alleviate their difficulties and to highlight their virtues, so that it can be a guide to a group of students who for various factors, including his precocious and lack of perspectives, needs a new direction.

REFERENCES

CASTRO, Claudio de Moura. Secondary education: an orphan of ideas, heir of misunderstandings. Ensaio: aval. pol. públ. *Educ., Rio de Janeiro*, v. 16, n. 58, p. 113-124, Jan. / Mar. 2008.

DAYRELL, Tarcisio Juarez. *Education of Student-Worker: An Alternative Approach. Educ.* Rev., Belo Horizonte (15): 21-29, jun. 1992.

FRANCO, Maria Laura P. Barbosa and Novaes, Glaucia Torres Franco. The young high school and their social representations. *Cadernos de Pesquisa*, n. 112, March-2001.

GOMES, Candido Alberto and Carnielli. Expansion of secondary education: concerns about the education of youth and adults. *Cadernos de Pesquisa*, n. 119, p. 47-69, July-2003.

______; CAPANEMA, Clelia de Freitas, CAMERA, Jacira da Silva; Cabanel, Lakné Campbell. Education and work: representations of teachers and high school students. Ensaio: aval. pol. públ. *Educ., Rio de Janeiro*, v. 16, n. 58, p. 113-124, Jan. / Mar. 2008.

______; MORGADO, Patrícia Cristina Rodrigues Chaves. Financing of secondary education: transparency or opacity? Ensaio: aval. pol. públ. *Educ., Rio de Janeiro*, v. 16, n. 58, p. 113-124, Jan. / Mar. 2008.

GONÇALVES, Lia Roberts, STEPS, Sara Moura Sá Martins Rozinda of STEPS and Alvaro Mariano of. New Directions for High School Night - how and why do? Ensaio: aval. pol. públ. *Educ., Rio de Janeiro,* v.13, n.48, p. 345-360, July / Sept. 2005

KRAWCZYK, Nora. The middle school: an area without consensus. Ensaio: aval. pol. públ. *Educ., Rio de Janeiro*, v. 16, n. 58, p. 113-124, Jan. / Mar. 2008.

SILVA, Heslley Machado. Young high school night: demands in relation to school. Thesis (MA in education). Federal University of Minas Gerais, 209 pags., Belo Horizonte, 2000.

SOUSA, Sandra Zákia and OLIVEIRA, Romualdo Portela. High school night: democratization and diversity. Ensaio: aval. pol. públ. *Educ., Rio de Janeiro*, v. 16, n. 58, p. 113-124, Jan. / Mar. 2008

Zagury, Tania. Teacher / student relationship, Discipline and Knowledge. In: Youth and Education. *Patio Educational Magazine*. Porto Alegre: Artes Médicas. No August, Year 2, p. 9-12. Feb / April 1999.

In: Educational Theory
Editor: Jaleh Hassaskhah, pp. 97-108

ISBN 978-1-61324-580-4
© 2011 Nova Science Publishers, Inc.

Chapter 5

PRE-SERVICE MATHEMATICS TEACHERS' PERCEPTIONS ABOUT MATHEMATICS PROBLEMS AND THE NATURE OF PROBLEM SOLVING

Fatma Kayan Fadlelmula and Erdinç Çakiroğlu
Department of Elementary Education,
Middle East technical University, Ankara, Turkey

ABSTRACT

Problem solving is an important component of mathematics education, mainly because it provides an environment for students to reflect on their conceptions about the nature of mathematics, and develop a relational mathematical understanding. Due to its powerful characteristics, problem solving has been given value in mathematics education as a skill to be taught, as a goal for mental development, and as a method for teaching. Especially, for the last three decades, there have been attempts all around the world to make problem solving the focus of school mathematics rather than being an isolated part of mathematics curriculum. This study aimed to investigate pre-service elementary mathematics teachers' beliefs about mathematics problems and the nature of problem solving. The sample of the study consisted of 244 senior undergraduate students studying in Elementary Mathematics Teacher Education programs at 5 different universities in Turkey. The data were collected during the spring semester of 2005-2006 academic years. Participants completed a survey composed of three parts as demographic information sheet, questionnaire items, and non-routine mathematics problems. The results of the study indicated that, in general, pre-service teachers held positive beliefs about mathematical problem solving. However, a number of pre-service teachers held several traditional beliefs about problem solving, such as following predetermined sequence of steps while solving mathematics problems and the importance of computational skills in mathematics education. In addition, it was found that a number of pre-service teachers did not value problems that do not cover any topic in the curriculum, problems that do not involve any number and problems that take a long time to solve.

Keywords: mathematical problem solving, pre-service teachers, teacher education.

INTRODUCTION

The term 'problem' may have different meanings depending on one's perspective. From a mathematical perspective, problem is defined as "a situation where something is to be found or shown and the way to find or show it is not immediately obvious" (Grouws, 1996, p.72). For a teacher of mathematics, problem is an engaging question for which students have no readily available set of procedures, but have the necessary factual and procedural knowledge to do so (Schoenfeld, 1989). For a task to be a problem for an individual, it should involve novel situations, and have a level of challenge (Martinez, 1998). In this aspect, a problem for an individual may not be a problem for another. Similarly, a problem for a particular individual today may not be a problem for him or her tomorrow (Henderson and Pingry, 1953).

It is important to know the difference between a mathematics problem and an exercise. Generally, an exercise is a simple question which is prepared to check whether a student can correctly use a recently introduced idea or symbol (Polya, 1953), and come up with a correct answer which is usually agreed beforehand (Lester, 1980). On the other hand, a mathematics problem is a complex question which requires students to use a variety of cognitive strategies and come up with a logical solution (Manuel, 1998). Sometimes, a mathematics problem may have no solution, or it may have more than one correct solution (Lester, 1980). Actually, while solving a mathematics problem the critical point is not reaching to a solution but trying to figure out a logical way to do so (Henderson and Pingry, 1953).

Problem solving is an important component of mathematics education, mainly because it provides an environment for students to reflect on their conceptions about the nature of mathematics, and develop a relational mathematical understanding (Lester, 1994). Due to its powerful characteristics, problem solving has been given value in mathematics education as a skill to be taught, as a goal for mental development, and as a method for teaching (Brown, 2003). Especially, for the last three decades, there have been attempts all around the world to make problem solving the focus of school mathematics (NCTM, 1980) rather than being an isolated part of mathematics curriculum. Similarly, in the new Turkish mathematics curriculum, problem solving is regarded as an integral part of mathematics learning and one of the vital common basic skills that students need to demonstrate for all subject matters (Ministry of National Education, 2005).

Problem solving is most effective when students sense two things; that the teacher regards problem solving as an important activity, and that the teacher actively engages in solving problems as a regular part of mathematics instruction (Lester, 1980). In this aspect, teachers play a crucial role in changing the ways that teaching takes place (Handal and Herrington, 2003). Especially, teachers' beliefs have a considerable effect on the nature of their classroom practices (Wilkins and Brand, 2004; Ball, 1998), and in turn, have a close relation with their students' beliefs, attitudes and performances (Grouws, 1996; Schoenfeld, 1992). For the changes in mathematics curriculum to take place in the real classrooms, it is very essential that both teachers and students believe in the importance and role of problem solving in mathematics instruction.

There are various findings in the literature regarding pre-service and in-service teachers' beliefs about the role of problem solving in mathematics education. A number of these studies indicate that teachers in different contexts hold positive beliefs about mathematical problem solving. For example, Brown (2003) found that teachers highly support the idea that students should spend time on problems, and try to understand why a solution to a mathematics problem works. Similarly, Futch, Stephens and James (1997) found that teachers believe that problem solving should be integrated into the entire mathematics curriculum, and students should share their problem solving approaches with each other. On the other hand, some other studies reveal that teachers hold traditional beliefs about mathematical problem solving. For example, Brosnan and Erickson (1996) found that teachers give more importance to students' answers rather than their problem solutions. In a similar vein, Schoenfeld (1992) found that teachers determine their judgments about successful problem solvers as the ones applying predetermined steps, and come up with an answer only in a few minutes.

In particular, studies conducted in Turkey revealed that, until recently, many aspects of the curriculum, especially the textbooks, displayed a traditional view where concepts and skills are considered as prerequisites for solving problems (Toluk and Olkun, 2002). Recent studies conducted with elementary school children indicated that, in general, students' abilities in problem solving need significant improvement (Soylu and Soylu, 2006; Karataş and Güven, 2004). Furthermore, a recent study conducted with mathematics and elementary pre-service teachers revealed that most of the pre-service teachers did not know the difference between a problem and an exercise (Korkmaz, Gür and Ersoy, 2006). The pre-service teachers thought that problems are exercises solved at the end of lesson in order to practice a recently introduced idea, and believed that there is only one solution to any problem, and that open-ended problems are not suitable for elementary classes.

The purpose of this study was to explore the kinds of beliefs pre-service elementary mathematics teachers have toward mathematical problem solving. More specifically, the present study attempted to investigate what pre-service elementary mathematics teachers believe about (1) the importance of understanding why a solution to a mathematics problem works, (2) problems that cannot be solved by following a predetermined sequence of steps, (3) time consuming problems, (4) problems that have more than one way of solution, (5) the kind of mathematics instruction emphasized in the new Turkish elementary curriculum, and (6) technology usage while solving mathematics problems. In addition, the present study attempted to examine how pre-service elementary mathematics teachers assess a number of mathematics problems regarding their appropriateness in elementary mathematics education, and then to conclude whether their assessments about mathematics problems are in line with their beliefs about problem solving.

METHOD

Participants

The target population of the present study was all pre-service teachers studying in elementary mathematics teacher education programs in Turkey. There were 23 universities offering this program in Turkey. Among them 5 universities were selected based on the convenience and permission of access. The sample of the present study consisted of 244 senior undergraduate students studying at universities located in Black Sea Region and Central Anatolia Region in Turkey. All of the participants were chosen to be senior pre-service elementary mathematics teachers so that they have reasonable background in their subject area and pedagogy.

Of the 244 pre-service teachers, 113 were males, and 131 were females. Likewise, in each university the number of pre-service teachers was nearly half males and half females. Approximately 40% of the pre-service teachers ($f= 99$) have taken courses related to problem solving prior to data collection. In general, participants' prior experiences with problem solving involved solving questions in textbooks ($f=26$), working on mathematical puzzles ($f= 8$), and getting prepared for post-graduate exams ($f= 6$).

Data Collection Instrument

In the present study, 'Belief Survey of Pre-service Mathematics Teachers on Mathematical Problem Solving' was administered as the data collection instrument. This survey was prepared by the researchers mainly by making use of four previously implemented instruments in the related field, with several modifications and additions in the light of literature review. The instrument consisted of two parts. In the first part, the pre-service teachers were asked to evaluate five mathematics problems as either poor, average or strong according to their educational value and appropriateness in elementary mathematics education, and then to explain the reasons of their evaluations. These problems were selected in a way that they are open to different interpretations.

In the second part, the pre-service teachers were asked to indicate their agreements or disagreements about 39 items on a five-point Likert scale ranging from 5 to 1; 5 indicating 'strongly agree' and 1 indicating 'strongly disagree.' Parallel with research questions, the items intended to measure the pre-service teachers' beliefs about (1) the importance of understanding why a solution to a mathematics problem works (sample item: "A person who does not understand why an answer to a mathematics problem is correct, has not really solved the problem"), (2) problems that cannot be solved by following a predetermined sequence of steps (sample item: "Any problem can be solved if you know the right steps to follow"), (3) time consuming problems (sample item: "Mathematics problems that take a long time to solve are not bothering"), (4) problems that have more than one way of solution (sample item: "It is possible to get the correct answer to a mathematics problem using methods other than the one the teacher or the textbook uses"), (5) the kind of problem solving instruction emphasized by the principles of new Turkish national curriculum (sample item: "Problem solving is a process that should permeate the entire curriculum"), and (6) the usage of technologic equipments while solving mathematics problems (sample item: "Appropriate technological equipments should be available to all students all times"). While preparing the data collection instrument, as a first step, a number of questionnaire items were selected and adapted from four previously implemented studies (Emenaker, 1996; Hart, 2002; Kloosterman and Stage, 1992; Zollman and Mason, 1992), on the basis of their relevance to the Turkish pre-service teacher education. Next, several items were developed by the researchers regarding the expectations mentioned in the new Turkish mathematics curriculum.

In the third part, the instrument includes five mathematics problems. It was not required for participants to solve them, but they were asked to indicate their opinions about the instructional value of each problem. They were first asked to judge each problem as either "poor," "average," or "strong," then to explain the reasons of their judgments in written form. This part was essential to better understand participants' conceptions of the nature of problems and problem solving, presuming that the mere application of the questionnaire items would not provide an adequate insight into the research questions. Moreover, it would be possible to examine whether pre-service teachers' assessments of mathematics problems fit in with their problem solving beliefs illustrated in the questionnaire items.

After the construction of the instrument, several revisions and corrections were made in order to develop and finalize the instrument. Feedbacks were taken from two experts, and two pilot studies were conducted by sophomore and junior pre-service elementary mathematics teachers, until the clarity and reliability of the instrument was found to be satisfactory. The overall alpha reliability of the second part of instrument was calculated as 0.87, indicating high consistency. Then, the final draft of the instrument was administered to 244 senior pre-service elementary mathematics teachers in their classroom settings during the spring semester of 2006. The pre-service teachers responded to the instrument on voluntary basis, and each administration took approximately 25 minutes.

RESULTS

The purpose of this study was to investigate the kinds of beliefs pre-service elementary mathematics teachers have about mathematical problem solving. In order to explore this research question, both the pre-service teachers' responses to the questionnaire items and their interpretations about several mathematics problems were analyzed. In general, the results were summarized using descriptive information.

Results Regarding the Questionnaire Items

When the pre-service teachers' beliefs were examined regarding the importance of understanding why a solution to a mathematics problem works, it was found that the majority of the pre-service teachers (93%) thought that if a person does not understand why an answer to a mathematics problem works; then he has not really solved the problem. Moreover, most of the pre-service teachers (90%) appreciated a demonstration of good reasoning rather than merely finding a correct answer, and believed that (85%) time used to investigate why a solution to a mathematics problem works is time well spent. When the pre-service teachers' beliefs were examined regarding problems that cannot be solved by following a predetermined sequence of steps, it was found that only half of the pre-service teachers (49%) reported their disagreement to the idea that mathematics problems are solved by following a step-by-step procedure (with the mean of 2.52). Even, a number of them (37%) thought that learning to do problems is mostly a matter of memorizing the right steps to follow, and that (50%) to solve most of the problems students should be taught the correct procedure.

When the pre-service teachers' beliefs were examined regarding time consuming mathematics problems, it was found that although the majority of the pre-service teachers (90%) supported the idea that hard mathematics problems can be solved if one just hangs in there, only half of the pre-service teachers (42%) were not bothered from time consuming problems, and did not believe that (55%) to be good in math, one must be able to solve problems quickly. When the pre-service teachers' beliefs were examined regarding problems that have more than one way of solution, it was found that the majority of the pre-service teachers (93%) did not support the idea that there is only one correct way to solve a mathematics problem. In addition, most of the pre-service teachers (93%) determined good mathematics teachers to be the one showing students lots of ways for solving the same question, and (93%) indicated that students can get the correct answer to a mathematics problem using methods other than the teacher or the textbook uses.

When the pre-service teachers' beliefs were examined regarding the kind of mathematics instruction emphasized in the new Turkish elementary curriculum, it was found that most of the pre-service teachers reflected positive beliefs about the importance of problem solving in mathematics classrooms. For example, the majority of the pre-service teachers (94%) indicated that students should share their problem solution approaches with other students, and (95%) that teachers should encourage students to write their own mathematical problems. However, only 67% of the pre-service teachers stated that problem solving is a process that should permeate the entire curriculum, and even, a majority of the pre-service teachers (80%) thought that problem solving is primarily the application of computational skills in mathematics education (with the mean of 2.11). Lastly, when the pre-service teachers' beliefs were examined regarding the usage of technologic equipments while solving mathematics problems, it was found that the majority of the pre-service teachers (83%) supported the appropriate usage of technologic equipments while solving mathematics problems, and (91%) supported the availability of such materials to all students at all times. In addition, nearly all of the pre-service teachers (93%) indicated that teachers can create new learning environments for their students with the usage of technology, and it can give students greater choice in their tasks.

Results Regarding the Mathematics Problems

The participant's evaluations about five mathematics problems and their written explanations for these evaluations were analyzed by giving a descriptive summary. Table 1 illustrates the frequencies and percentages associated with the pre-service teachers' problem evaluations, and Table 2 involves the mathematics problems that were evaluated.

Table 1. Pre-service teachers' evaluations of mathematics problems

	Poor		Average		Strong	
	f	%	f	%	f	%
Problem 1	21	8.6	118	48.4	105	43.0
Problem 2	76	31.1	53	21.7	115	47.1
Problem 3	38	15.6	86	35.2	120	49.2
Problem 4	43	17.6	91	37.3	110	45.1
Problem 5	108	44.3	93	38.1	43	17.6
Total	286	23.4	441	36.2	493	40.4

Table 2. Mathematics problems

Problem 1	Serkan was studying the Romans in history and came across an ancient document about a great army that advanced upon Alexandria. He was unable to read the size of the army as two digits were smudged, but he knew it was "45_ _ 8" and that the attacking army was divided into 9 equal battalions, to cover the 9 different entrances to Alexandria. What are the possible sizes for the attacking army?
Problem 2	How many rectangles are there on an 8 x 8 chess board?
Problem 3	A man wants to take her fox, chicken and a bag of corn across the river in a canoe. The canoe can hold only one thing in addition to the man. If left alone, the fox would eat the chicken, or the chicken would eat the corn. How can the man take everything across the river safely?
Problem 4	Five women participated in a 10 km walk, but started at different times. At a certain time in the walk the following descriptions were true. Melek was at the halfway point. Filiz was 2 km ahead of Canan. Nuray was 3 km ahead of Sibel. Melek was 1 km behind Canan. Sibel was 3.5 km behind Filiz. How far from the finish line was Nuray at that time?
Problem 5	In 2000, Ankara had a population of 4,007,860 and covers an area of 25,978 square kilometers. Yalova had a population of 168,593 with an area of 847 square kilometers. Which city was more densely populated?

As illustrated in Table 1, most of the pre-service teachers evaluated Problem 1 as average, whereas they evaluated Problem 2, Problem 3, and Problem 4 as strong, and Problem 5 as poor according to the problems' educational value and appropriateness to be used in elementary mathematics classrooms.

Almost half of the pre-service teachers (48%) evaluated the first problem as average, mostly because they believed that it has a moderate difficulty level, and does not require very high creativity and critical thinking (f=26). On the other hand, they appreciated this problem because they think it is interesting and different from ordinary mathematics questions (f=19), and covers a topic in elementary mathematics curriculum (f=7). Besides, almost half of the pre-service teachers (47%) evaluated the second problem as strong, generally because they believed that it is a challenging problem, and requires high level of mathematical thinking (f=30). Moreover, they proposed that it relates mathematics with different mathematical concepts (f=27), and direct students to think in multiple ways (f=23).

Similarly, almost half of the pre-service teachers (49%) evaluated the third problem as strong, mostly because they believed that it requires critical thinking, and develops students' long term skills such as creativity, intelligence, mathematical reasoning and problem solving (f=78). In addition, they suggested that it can help students to think in multiple ways (f=21). Likewise, almost half of the pre-service teachers (45%) evaluated the fourth problem as strong, generally because they believed that it is important for illustrating how to analyze the relationships between problem components (f=27). Besides, the pre-service teachers gave value to this problem because they believed that it is an enjoyable and thought-provoking problem (N=15), measuring both verbal and mathematical skills (f=7). On the other hand, almost half of the pre-service teachers (44%) evaluated the fifth problem as poor, mostly because they thought that it is an easy question, not leading students to make critical interpretations (f =46). Also, they believed that it is only about one subject area, and its solution depends only on operations (f =39). Even, a number of the pre-service teachers disapproved this problem because it contains very big numbers, and take a long time to reach a solution (f=6).

In summary, the pre-service teachers gave value to problems that are interesting in wording; offer a level of challenge; require mathematical thinking; and cover topics in mathematics curriculum as well as connecting mathematics with real life and with other subject matters. In a similar manner, the pre-service teachers did not appreciate the problems that have ordinary wording; do not fit in with elementary level curriculum; and not lead students to make interpretations. However, the results also revealed that the pre-service teachers did not prefer problems that do not cover any objective in mathematics curriculum; not involve numbers or operating with whole numbers; and take a long time to solve.

DISCUSSION

In general, the results of the questionnaire items revealed that pre-service teachers held positive beliefs about mathematical problem solving. That is, their beliefs were in line with the current reform movements in mathematics education. This finding might be an indicator of the significant improvements and innovations made in the new Turkish elementary curriculum. Most probably, the reform movements as well as the courses in teacher education programs may have positively influenced the pre-service teachers' views, assumptions, and values about mathematics teaching and learning.

Although the pre-service teachers usually indicated positive beliefs, actually they still hold several traditional beliefs about problem solving. Most of the pre-service teachers tended to view problem solving as a reason for practicing computation, and identified problem solving as being primarily the application of computational skills. Moreover, they seemed to support following predetermined sequence of steps while solving problems. One possible reason of these inconsistent views could be that although several reformist changes has been made on the Turkish curriculum, students in schools are still being assessed through traditional written exams and high stake tests are still of an important concern for students at all levels. Therefore, as the mastery of computational skills still poses great importance in students' lives, problem solving might have been considered as a reason for applying these computational skills. Moreover, a possible explanation of the pre-service teachers' belief in following predetermined sequence of steps might arise from a similar reason. In all high stake tests, students are expected to give the correct answer in an optimum time, in which case, knowing about methods of solutions that will help them to reach the correct answer in a short time with a less effort is highly valued by them. This rationale might have played a role in the beliefs of pre-service teachers.

Similar to the findings of the questionnaire items, the pre-service teachers' responses to the mathematics problems revealed that in general the pre-service teachers held positive beliefs about mathematics problems. In selecting problems for classroom use, it is important to consider that they are appropriate for students' level of skills and understandings (Henderson and Pingry, 1953), as well as appealing and meaningful from the students' point of view (Polya, 1966). In addition, problems should be relevant to students' daily lives and they should suitable for making connections among different mathematical concepts (Ministry of National Education, 2005). Therefore, regarding these points it is possible to conclude that in this study the pre-service teachers' preferences about mathematics problems were generally consistent with the theory and expectations cited in the literature, as well as in the new mathematics curriculum.

However, there were other findings indicating that the pre-service teachers held several traditional beliefs about mathematics problems. For example, a number of pre-service teachers did not appreciate problems that do not cover any objective in the mathematics curriculum. It might be mostly because of the fact that they view problem solving as an activity for practicing an introduced idea or algorithm in mathematics education, and find no use in asking such problems as they will not contribute to students' learning. However, it has been argued that problems should be given value "not only as a purpose for learning mathematics but also as a primary means of doing so" (Schroeder and Lester, 1989, p.33). Therefore, problems should be regarded more than "a vehicle to introduce and study the mathematical content" (Manuel, 1998, p.634).

The results also revealed that most of the pre-service teachers did not prefer problems that have big and complicated numbers, or the ones that do not involve any numbers. This might be mostly because of the fact that they highly value applying computational skills while solving mathematics problems. However, viewing problem solving as only dealing with numbers and looking for right answers is usually considered as a traditional view (Steele and Widman, 1997). Parallel with this idea, the new Turkish mathematics curriculum also values problems that do not involve numbers as long as they contribute to students' conceptual understanding (Ministry of National Education, 2005).

Lastly, this study also revealed that there were discrepancies between pre-service teachers' problem evaluations and their beliefs about problem solving. For instance, when the pre-service teachers' beliefs were examined from the questionnaire items, it was found that most of them believed hard mathematics problems can be done if one just 'hangs in there'. On the other hand, when their problem evaluations were examined, it was found that some of them evaluated hard problems as having low value in elementary mathematics education because they are time consuming. In a similar way, when the pre-service teachers' beliefs were examined from the questionnaire items, it was found that most of the pre-service teachers highly appreciated technology usage while solving mathematics problems, and believed that teachers can create new learning environments with the use of technology. However, when their problem evaluations were examined, it was found that none of them mention about any kind of technology usage that might contribute to the solution process. The discrepancies between these findings might be explained by the differences between the pre-service teachers' perceived beliefs and the actual beliefs.

CONCLUSION

In summary, the pre-service teachers in this study usually indicated positive beliefs about mathematical problem solving. For instance, they gave importance to understanding why a solution to a mathematics problem works, and appreciated developing different ways of solutions to the same problem. However, the results also revealed that the pre-service teachers held several moderate and negative beliefs. For example, they tended to believe that problem solving is primary the application of computational skills in mathematics education, and it is a matter of following predetermined sequence of steps.

In addition, although the pre-service teachers theoretically gave value to time consuming problems, their problem preferences revealed that actually they did not appreciate problems that take a long time to solve. Similarly, although they theoretically appreciated using technology in mathematics classrooms, they did not mention about any kind of technology usage while indicating their beliefs on the given mathematics problems. Even, their problem preferences showed that they did not appreciate problems that do not involve numbers, or require operating with whole numbers. Besides, when a problem does not cover any topic in mathematics curriculum, they evaluated it as poor according to its educational value to be used in mathematics classrooms.

Therefore, the results of this study indicated that the pre-service teachers gave importance to solving problems in mathematics education; however, they considered mathematics teaching and learning as focused on applying the knowledge gained during the lessons, as well as the mastery of computational skills through solving problems. Moreover, they gave value to problems that require mathematical thinking and reasoning; however, at the same time they prefer problems that are directly related with mathematics curriculum, and do not require spending too much time.

In order to gradually challenge pre-service teachers' negative beliefs about mathematical problem solving, adequate educational interventions should be planned and implemented in teacher education programs. For example, mathematics teacher educators need to examine their undergraduate courses both related to mathematics content and teaching, in order to offer courses more consistent with the underlying philosophy of the new mathematics curriculum. They can evaluate and modify their courses in terms of whether they pose non-ordinary mathematics problems that add a new insight and experience to students' mathematical thinking and understanding, as well as relating mathematics with other disciplines and real world situations. Also, they can engage pre-service teachers in activities where they gain both theoretical and practical understanding of the place and the use of technologies in mathematics education. A further research can be carried out as a case study to get more detailed picture of how pre-service teachers regard problem solving, for example during a methods course. A variety of data can be gathered from various sources such as observations, interviews, end-of-course questionnaires, and learner diaries.

REFERENCES

Altun, E. H. (1996). Information technology in developing nations: A study of lecturers' attitudes and expertise with reference to Turkish teacher education. *Journal of Information Technology for Teacher Education, 5(3)*, 185-205.

Altun, M. (2001*). Matematik Öğretimi* (2nd Ed.). İstanbul : Alfa Yayım Dağıtım.

Ball, D. (1998). Research on teacher learning: studying how teachers' knowledge changes. *Action in Teacher Education, 10(2)*, 7-24.

Brosnan, P., Edwards, T., and Erickson, D. (1996). An exploration of change in teachers' beliefs and practice during implementation of mathematics standards. *Focus on Learning Problems in Mathematics, 18*(4), 35-53.

Brown, N.M. (2003). A study of elementary teachers' abilities, attitudes, and beliefs about problem solving. *Dissertation Abstracts International, 64*(10), 3620. (UMI No. 3108818).

Emenaker, C. (1996). A problem solving based mathematics course and elementary teachers' beliefs. *School Science and Mathematics, 96*(2), 74-83.

Ford, M. I. (1994). Teachers' beliefs about mathematical problem solving in the elementary school. *School Science and Mathematics, 94*(6), 314-322.

Futch, L., Stephens, J., and James, C. (1997). The beliefs of Georgia teachers and principals regarding the NCTM standards: A representative view using the standards' belief instrument (SBI). *School Science and Mathematics, 97*(5), 112-121.

Gail, M. (1996). Problem solving about problem solving: framing a research agenda. *Proceedings of the Annual National Educational Computing Conference, Minnesota, 17*, 255-261. (ERIC Document Reproduction Service No. ED 398 890).

Grouws, D. A. (1996). *Critical Issues in Problem Solving Instruction in Mathematics.* In D. Zhang, T. Sawada, and J. P. Becker (Eds.), Proceedings of the China-Japan-U.S. seminar on mathematical education (pp. 70-93). Carbondale, IL: Board of Trustees of Southern Illinois University.

Handal, B. and Herrington, A. (2003). Mathematics teachers' beliefs and curriculum reform. *Mathematics Education Research Journal, 15*(1), 59-69.

Hart, L. C. (2002). Pre-service teachers' beliefs and practice after participating in an integrated content/methods course. *School Science and Mathematics, 102*(1), 4-15.

Henderson, K. B., and Pingry, R.E. (1953). Problem Solving in Mathematics. In H. F. Fehr (Ed.), *The Learning of Mathematics: Its theory and practice* (pp. 228-270). 21st yearbook of the NCTM. Reston, VA: NCTM.

Hollifield, M. (2000). The effect of NCTM standards based professional development in-service on elementary teachers' beliefs concerning the NCTM standards, mathematics anxiety, and classroom practice. *Dissertation Abstracts International, 61*(12), 4677. (UMI No. 9996478).

Karataş, İ., and Güven, B. (2004). 8. sınıf öğrencilerinin problem çözme becerilerinin belirlenmesi: bir özel durum çalışması. *Milli Eğititm Dergisi, 163,* 132-143.

Kloosterman, P., and Stage, F. K. (1992). Measuring beliefs about mathematical problem solving. *School Science and Mathematics, 92*(3), 109-115.

Korkmaz, E., Gür, H., and Ersoy, Y. (2006). Öğretmen adaylarının problem kurma becerilerinin belirlenmesi. *Balıkesir Üniversitesi Fen Bilimleri Enstitisü Dergisi, 8*(1), 64-75.

Lester, F. K. (1980). Problem solving: Is it a problem?. In M. M. Lindsquist (Ed.), *Selected Issues in Mathematics* (pp. 29-45). NCTM, Reston VA.

Lester, F. K. (1994). Musings about mathematical problem solving research: 1970-1994. *Journal for Research in Mathematics Education, 25*(6), 660-675.

Manuel, S. T. (1998). Instructional qualities of a successful mathematical problem solving class. *International Journal of Mathematics Education in Science and Technology, 29*(5), 631-645.

Martinez, M. E. (1998). What is problem solving?. *Phi Delta Kappan, 79* (8), 605-609.

Mathematical Sciences Education Board (MSEB). (1989). *Everybody counts: A report to the nation on the future of mathematics education*. Washington, DC: National Academy Press.

Ministry of National Education (2005). *İlköğretim matematik dersi 6-8. sınıflar öğretim programı. [Elementary Mathematics Curriculum for Grades 6-8]* M.E.B.: Ankara.

National Council of Teachers of Mathematics (1980). *An agenda for action: Recommendations for school mathematics of the 1980s*. Reston, VA: NCTM.

National Council of Teachers of Mathematics (2000). *Principles and standards for school mathematics*. Reston, VA: NCTM.

Polya, G. (1953). On teaching problem solving. In H. F. Fehr (Ed.), *The Learning of Mathematics: Its theory and practice* (pp. 228-270). 21st yearbook of the NCTM. Reston, VA: NCTM.

Polya, G. (1966). On teaching problem solving. In *The role of axioms and problem solving in mathematics* (pp. 123-129). Washington, DC: The Conference Board of the Mathematics Sciences.

Schoenfeld, A. H. (1989). Explorations of students' mathematical beliefs and behavior. *Journal for Research in Mathematics Education, 20*(4), 338-355.

Schoenfeld, A. H. (1992). Learning to think mathematically: Problem solving, metacognition, and sense making in mathematics. In D. A. Grouws (Ed.), Handbook of research on mathematics teaching and learning (pp. 334-370). New York: Macmillan Publishing Company.

Schroeder, T. and Lester, F. K. (1989). Developing understanding in mathematics via problem solving. In P. R. Trafton (Ed.), *New Directions for Elementary School Mathematics* (pp. 31- 56). Reston, VA: National Council of Teachers of Mathematics.

Soylu, Y. and Soylu, C. (2006). Matematik derslerinde başarıya giden yolda prolem çözmenin rolü. *Eğitim Fakültesi Dergisi, 7*(11), 97-111.

Sparks, D. (1999). Real life view: Here's what a rule learning community looks like. *Journal of Staff Development, 20*(4), 53-57.

Steele, D. F., and Widman, T. F. (1997). Practitioner's research: A study in changing preservice teachers' conceptions about mathematics. *School Science and Mathematics, 97*(4), 184-192.

Toluk, Z., and Olkun, S. (2002). Problem solving in Turkish mathematics education: Primary school mathematics textbooks. *Educational Sciences: Theory and Practice, 2*(2), 579-582.

Wilkins, J., and Brand, B. (2004). Change in pre-service teachers' beliefs: An evaluation of a mathematics methods course. *School Science and Mathematics, 104*(5), 226-232.

Zollman, A. and Mason, E. (1992). The standards' beliefs instrument (SBI): Teachers' beliefs about the NCTM standards. *School Science and Mathematics, 92*(7), 359-364.

In: Educational Theory
Editor: Jaleh Hassaskhah, pp. 109-120

ISBN 978-1-61324-580-4
© 2011 Nova Science Publishers, Inc.

Chapter 6

SYNTHESIS OF LEARNING IN THE PATCHWORK TEXT: PATCHWORK ASSESSMENT OR PATCHED WORK ASSESSMENT?

Kelvin Tan[1] and Chong Siew Fong[2]
[1]National Institute of Education, Singapore
[2]Ahmad Ibrahim Secondary School, Singapore

ABSTRACT

The Patchwork Text is a recent assessment innovation that seeks to enhance students' synthesis of learning over a period of time through engagement with progressive tasks culminating in a final synthesized assignment. However, this is not dissimilar to a form of plagiarism known as 'Patchwriting', wherein students unfamiliar with academic convention resort to paraphrasing pieces of published text and representing the consequent miscellany of text as their own. It is argued that students may likewise resort to Patchwriting in Patchwork Text assessment. In this article, the Structure of Observed Learning Outcomes ('SOLO') taxonomy is used to explain how certain forms of Patchwork text design may lead to Patchwriting, and suggests how Patchwork text assessment may be designed to minimize such risks. An example of minimizing Patchwriting is provided in the form of a Patchwork Text assessment for English Literature.

INTRODUCTION

The increasing modularization of courses and knowledge, fragments learning which risks losing sight of the bigger ideas in education and in life (Tan, 2008). Tests and examinations are typically conducted in controlled environments and this is useful and convenient from the view of managing students and handling marking loads. However, the cost of such administrative convenience is the tendency to isolate students through assessment practice and perpetuate the impression that knowledge can be reduced to periods of intense examination. Because tests and examinations need to reduce the assessment of learning to a fixed period of time, this in turn pressures the forms of learning to be demonstrated into isolated instances of different learning outcomes. Inevitably, a reductionist view of learning is constructed and communicated. Effective assessment on the other hand should persuade students to learn from each other, and insist that students connect and relate the different learning outcomes over a period of time.

Assessment should also be designed in ways that requires learners to make sense of different things in relation to each other for a "coherent learning experience that prepares learners to operate in intelligent and flexible ways." (Sadler, 2007, p. 389). Patchwork assessment is an example of an approach to assessment that emphasizes the synthesis and coherence of learning (Tan, 2007). The patchwork assessment method (originally known as the patchwork text) is claimed by Winter (2003) to "integrate the different assessment advantages of the essay and the portfolio" (p. 119). Darymple and Smith (2008) argue that the patchwork assessment method provides more opportunities for students to integrate theory and practice in light of teachers' feedback and significantly increases students' capacity for reflective practice.

The artificial segmentation of topics, ideas and knowledge into different assessment tasks is a common criticism of typical students' essays. The classical idea behind an essay is to prompt students to construct a series of coherent arguments to support a challenging contention. Winter (2003, p. 116) identifies the appeal of essays in its ability to test important intellectual skills such as "the selection of relevant facts, the evaluation of viewpoints, the structuring of arguments ..." Unfortunately, much of what students pass off (and pass up) as essays are clusters of text paraphrasing their textbooks or lecture notes without evidencing coherent thought.

An underlying premise of the essay, especially those performed in test controlled environments, is that learning, or the consolidation of intellectual activities required for essays, can take place within a short period of time. This may be true of low level cognitive tasks such as recalling facts and ideas and applying them in obvious contexts. It is argued that students can best achieve higher level cognitive tasks such as synthesizing and evaluating arguments over a period of time. Evidently, students will require more time to comprehend different ideas and arguments before attempting to synthesize and evaluate them.

Such a shortcoming of essays is traditionally addressed through the contrasting assessment method of student portfolios. Portfolios may be generally described as structured repositories of students' learning and achievements work over a period of time. Klenowski's (2002) description of portfolio assessment is in stark contrast with the "single episode" nature of essays:

> "A portfolio documents achievements over an extended period of time ... identifies work from an accumulated collection to illustrate achievement and to demonstrate learning for certification, summative assessment or formative assessment ... It is significantly more than a collection of assignments." (Klenowski, 2002, p. 26)

However, student portfolio assessment is not without its own limitations. Whilst it successfully extends the ambit of students' focus on assessment and learning beyond episodic instances, its scope and emphasis on extending learning over time risks protracting the learning and assessment process unduly. This may in turn lead to unfocused final outcomes which may not necessarily lead to students synthesizing all of their learning.

What would then be ideal is an assessment method that extends student learning beyond a single point in time, and yet structures student learning during the period of assessment to enhance the probability of achieving structured and relational learning outcomes? In short, an assessment method that combines the benefits of essays and portfolios whilst avoiding the shortcomings of both traditional methods.

The Patchwork Text Assessment Method

Such characteristic shortcomings with the traditional essay and portfolio assessment led some academics to design an assessment alternative – the patchwork text. The patchwork text is claimed by Winter (2003) to "integrate the different assessment advantages of the essay and the portfolio" (p. 119) whilst Tan (2007) argues that the patchwork text provides an assessment structure that places a premium on students constructing and synthesizing their knowledge. Ovens (2003) refers to the patchwork text as "a form of assessment where students write several short pieces, the 'patches', at intervals throughout the module and then at the end, the patches are 'stitched together' to make a patchwork text." (p. 546).

Typically, the patchwork text assessment method entails a series of tasks for students to complete over a period of time and culminates in a final task that requires them to synthesize what they had learned in the previous tasks. The example on the next page from Akister (2003) provides an example of what a patchwork text assessment looks like in the context of social work:

Patchwork Text Assignment Guidelines

Your assignment for the module will be assembled gradually in the semester through a series of written tasks, which you will share with your peers in small groups. There are several reasons for this:

- To avoid the last minute rush of having to write the whole assignment at the end of the semester
- To enable you to use a variety of different ways of writing
- To enable you to obtain feedback at an early stage

Your tasks are:

1. Discuss the advantages and disadvantages of all family members attending the first Family therapy interview and refer to at least one key text.
2. Write an appraisal of the life-cycle stage of the family you are assigned to.
3. With reference to one model of family therapy, what information would you need to gather to construct an assessment of a family's functioning?
4. Design a task which could be given to the family. How might this task impact on the family system?
5. Write a letter from one family member to an agony aunt.
6. Final synthesis – Using at least three of these pieces, write a retrospective summary of what you have learned about working systematically with families

Akister (2003)

Figure 1. Example of patchwork text assessment from Akister (2003).

Akister's (2003) reasons for introducing the patchwork text are clear and enlightening. Her objective was to try to "engage in a more formative, interactive assessment paradigm where learning could be shared and feedback received throughout the module delivery." (p. 202).

The final task requires students to synthesize what they have learned from the previous tasks. The preliminary tasks are designed to break the familiar linear patterns of thinking students frequently employ.

By prompting students to view the topic or subject from diverse perspectives, the preliminary tasks ensure that students can explore the various issues and nuances of different ideas in their own distinctive right. At the same time, the final synthesis task is critical for requiring students to construct a relational understanding of the patchwork text.

Is There Always Synthesis of Learning In Patchwork Assessment?

Is it possible that some students given patchwork text assignments would simply patch together different written outcomes in their prior tasks and submit a 'patched up' text as their final task outcome? Such a 'patched up' text is similar to the phenomenon of 'patchwriting' which Howard (1993) defines as "copying from a source text and then deleting some words, altering grammatical structures, or plugging in one-for-one synonym-substitutes" (p. 213).

As explained by Howard, students often turn to patchwriting when they are unsure of their understanding or lack confidence in the use of a particular language. It is submitted that students may likewise resort to patchwriting their final patchwork task by copying from their previous tasks because they may lack confidence in synthesizing their learning.

How can we tell the extent and quality of students' synthesis of their learning represented in preliminary patchwork tasks in their final synthesis task? The Structure of Observed Learning Outcomes (SOLO) provides an answer by describing a hierarchy of progressive levels of students' synthesis of learning. The SOLO taxonomy was developed by Biggs and Collis (1982) as a way of describing qualitatively different learning outcomes, and is useful for understanding what progressive levels of synthesis may mean in students' outcomes.

The key to greater understanding in the SOLO taxonomy focuses firmly on how knowledge is structured.

Hence, its shorthand labels for its different levels of learning outcomes articulates progressively more advanced understandings of structure – pre-structural (lack of structure), uni-structural (single dimension of structure), multi-structural (multiple structures), relational (complete synthesised learning) and extended abstract (understanding beyond complete integrated set of structures). The five progressive learning outcomes of the SOLO taxonomy can be briefly summarized as:

Pre-Structural

This concerns irrelevant or incorrect information. This may also be understood as pre-learning. The learner does not have sufficient understanding of any of the component pieces of knowledge to begin developing a structure of understanding.

Uni-Structural

This refers to relevant and correct information but in an isolated way. Learners understand a single concept in itself, but have no idea what that has to do with other related concepts.

Multi-Structural

Learners with a multi-structural level of learning understand relevant and correct information with basic connections with other relevant knowledge. However, they do not appreciate precise connections with other relevant concepts. For example, learners may know the basic similarities and differences but not the actual relationship between relevant concepts.

Relational

This holistic level of understanding represents an adequate integration of all relevant concepts in order to understand the larger complex idea. The learner is able to see how the different concepts are structured together to synthesise into a larger complex meaning.

Extended Abstract

As the most advanced level of the SOLO taxonomy, the extended abstract level depicts the understanding of a concept beyond the integrated concept itself. It refers to the understanding of a holistic concept (with all relevant relationships and structure) within a larger context. The larger context in turn provides the learner with a deeper understanding of the underlying influences of the relational complex idea. In the context of the SOLO taxonomy, the first five tasks in Akister's example prompt students towards uni-structural understandings of the various concepts which are eventually integrated by students into a relational level of learning in the final task. Hence, Akister's patchwork assessment design may be understood as requiring students to produce a series of unistructural outcomes which would then have to be synthesized into a relational outcome in the final task. It is possible that students may simply patch together (rather than synthesise) their previous outcomes in their final task, leaving the outcome in the final task something which would not approach synthesis as most of us would know it. In other words, the progression between several unistructural outcomes towards a single synthesized relational outcome may be a gap too far to bridge for some students. It is submitted that one way of assisting students to learn how to synthesise their learning would be to design a task with multi-structural outcomes that could then bridge the gap between uni-structural and relational outcomes. We will now go on to discuss how the use of patchwork text in English Literature may be designed in ways that specifically prompts students to synthesis their learning of preliminary assessment tasks into a final synthesis task.

Proposed Implementation of a Patchwork Text as Assessment for the Study of English Literature

The main aim of literature programs in schools is to get the students to enjoy Literature, to introduce them to the breadth and variety that is available, to expand their horizons and to capture their interest to start them on their life-long engagement with books. The following table sets out a proposed assessment design using a patchwork text in relation to the text of "To Kill A Mockingbird." It should be noted here that the following example seeks to explain the rationale of using SOLO Taxonomy in the teaching of Literature and how SOLO Taxonomy aligns with different theories of Literature. This example is meant to explain the planned curriculum; not the enacted one.

Patchwork Assignments for "To Kill A Mockingbird" by Harper Lee

For the next few weeks of Literature class, you will share with me what you have learned of the novel, "To Kill A Mockingbird."

There are two parts of what you need to do – *Part A and Part B. For Part A,* you will need to choose and do **3** out of 5 assignments *over 3 weeks*. As the breaking up of the tasks is meant for you to learn at your own pace with inputs from your friends and I, you should not be cramming all three assignments of Part A and doing all of them at the same time. You should spend on average one week for each assignment of Part A. Do make an appointment with me if you encounter any difficulty or would like to clarify any point as you are doing your assignments.

As for Part B, it is *compulsory* for you to do *question 6* as it will help you to put together what you have learned as a whole.

1. Create a montage based on your reading and understanding of the novel by cutting out pictures from magazines and newspapers that portray the events in the story. Find a partner and take turns to explain to each other your choice of the montage and how it relates to the story plot.
2. Imagine that you are a movie director and you are going to make "To Kill A Mockingbird" into a movie. Choose movie stars who are most suitable for the different roles. You will need to justify your choices and explain how you would dress the stars for their roles.
3. Rewrite the novel using a different setting (e.g. geographical, cultural, historical differences). Compare and contrast the new version and the original story and write an essay to explain the differences and their effects.
4. Look for 2 poems or novels that you have read on racial prejudice. Compare the viewpoints of these poems or novels with "To Kill A Mockingbird." Examine and evaluate which story or poem is most effective in expressing the writer's viewpoint in an oral presentation.
5. Imagine that you are a newspaper reporter. Write a newspaper account of what happened in the novel. How different do the news accounts differ from the original novel in style? Are there any differences in the effect or impact on the reader with the different styles?

Synthesis

6. Why do you think "To Kill A Mockingbird" is a popular, timeless classic? In an essay of 500 words, explain what makes this novel so powerful to the readers by discussing at least 3 aspects of the novel that you have learned from the assignments that you have done earlier.

Figure 2. Design of patchwork text for "To Kill A Mockingbird".

Literature Teaching and the SOLO Taxonomy

Besides crafting authentic tasks such as self and peer evaluation, another way to guide and assist students to synthesise their learning meaningfully is to build the assignments on the SOLO Taxonomy. In terms of the five progressive learning outcomes of the SOLO taxonomy – pre-structural (lack of structure), uni-structural (single dimension of structure), multi-structural (multiple structures), relational (complete synthesized learning) and extended abstract (understanding beyond complete integrated set of structures), the students should be at the pre-structural level for Assignment 1. Students at this level may not understand the novel every well. There may even be misreading for some weaker students. The task for Assignment 1 serves to surface the students' initial doubts of the novel besides honouring their initial responses to the novel. It should also be noted that this question requires the students to comment on the plot of the novel which is the most basic entry level in the reading and appreciation of any literary work. Asking the students to explain the plot to their partners also provides an opportunity for them to clarify their doubts and to learn from one another.

With Assignment 2, the students are at uni-structural level of SOLO taxonomy. While they understand the characters of the text, they are unable to see beyond the isolated concepts for a greater appreciation of the text. Similar to Assignment 2, Assignment 3 tests the students' level of learning at the uni-structural level of SOLO taxonomy. As the students rewrite a new setting and draw comparisons between what they have written and the original ending, they will understand and appreciate the text better. However, at this stage, they tend to see the concepts in isolation without meaningful connections with one another.

Assignment 4 requires the students to reach the multi-structural level of learning and be able to make basic connections across the concepts. In order to examine and evaluate two different genres on the same theme, students must achieve and internalise a higher level of understanding for both the main ideas and structure of the text. This is because the students will not be able to carry out a high order task such as evaluation if they do not see the connectedness of different concepts and ideas in the text.

In order to handle Assignment 5 well, students must reach a relational level of SOLO taxonomy. Students should demonstrate a good understanding of the text so that they can change it into another genre without losing the essence of the text. In this case, students must be able to appreciate the synthesis of the different concepts in order to fully explain the different impact on the reader with different styles.

With regard to the SOLO taxonomy, Assignment 6 forms the extended abstract which is the most advanced level of the SOLO taxonomy. In order to create a convincing and powerful argument of the novel as a "popular, timeless classic", students will need to tap on their deep understanding of the various concepts of the novel as required in the previous assignments and then build them up as a coherent whole. Besides the synthesis of all the relevant concepts, students must also show how this novel relates to the larger context or society. The two key words in this assignment "popular" and "timeless" serve as cues for the students to engage more deeply with the text and to apply their understanding of their texts together with their own opinions.

Unlike the typical summative assessment of writing an essay at one sitting for examination, students now have the benefit of understanding the various aspects of the novel before they synthesize the knowledge they have acquired. The SOLO taxonomy is especially useful for weaker students as they have the opportunity to reflect and improve on their work with the teachers' comments in mind. As for the teachers, they will have a more accurate assessment of their students' abilities as they have guided and mentored them in moving from one level of the SOLO taxonomy to another.

Literature Teaching, Literature Theories and the Patchwork Text

In addition, we would also argue that the proposed patchwork text assessment aligns well with fundamental principles of Literature teaching and Literature theories. Rosenblatt (1978) states that the real meaning of a literary text lies neither wholly in the text nor the reader, but in a "transaction" or "live circuit" set up between the reader and the text. A fundamental principle is for teachers to provide opportunities for students to fully immerse in the literary experience. One way of doing so is for teachers to allow room for, and to value and honor, the unique individual response of each learner as no two responses are exactly the same. The design of a patchwork text allows teachers to capture the individual responses of the learners. For example, assignment (1) of "To Kill A Mockingbird" which requires students to "create a montage based on (their) reading and understanding of the novel" aims to capture the individual responses of the students' understanding of the sequential development of events in the text; the significance and impact of individual scenes/events in a text on its overall plot and structure.

Another fundamental principle of Literature teaching that can be realized through the patchwork text is to provide opportunities for students to interact in pairs or groups so that they can discuss, give feedback to one another and recreate and share the reading experience. This is important as much of the value of the reading experience comes from thinking, talking and writing about the work. This is seen in the second part of assignment (1) whereby the students need to find a partner and take turns to explain to each other their choice of the montage and how it relates to the story plot.

Assignment 2 tests the learners' understanding of the characters in the text by asking the learner to recreate the characters as movie stars. Such a recreation exercise or the literature theory of "imaginative recreation" aims to extend the students' responses beyond their initial unsophisticated reactions without losing touch of their responses. According to this theory, students get inside the text and the characters, study them from different angles and extend their understanding with the recreation activity. Teachers can then assess the students' understanding of the text through the students' interpretation and re-enactment of the roles.

Assignments 3 and 4 explore the students' understanding of the setting and viewpoint of the text using the reader response theory. The reader response theory is concerned with the question of what readers do when they read books and the relationship between a literary work and its reader, both while and after the reading takes place. Therefore, by asking the students to change the setting and the genre, i.e. from novel to poems, teachers encourage the students to explore the influence and effect of the setting of a text; the significance of changes in setting and the writer's intention and point of view in the text.

Assignment 5 uses the stylistics theory whereby the students analyze how literary writing functions as a form of communication. By changing the text from a novel to that of a newspaper report which is a different genre, students will note the differences in style, register and the effects such poetic manipulations have on the readers.

Each assignment is designed to be self-contained and manageable by the students. In addition, the task requirements are varied and meaningful such that they can be pieced together at the end with the synthesis question 6. Some other possibilities of the synthesis question can be to invite the students to comment on the possible differences and effects on the readers with the removal of a crucial character in the novel such as Atticus or the removal of an important extract in the novel like the court scene. Such questions "force" the learners to re-examine all the key aspects of the text covered in the earlier assignments such as characters and setting and to make a critique of these aspects of the novel. In the process of doing so, the learners gain a deeper understanding of the text.

As for the time given to do the various tasks, it is intended that that the students will complete one assignment per week so that there is time for them to carry out self and peer evaluation whenever possible. In addition, students will receive feedback from their teacher to guide them in the learning process. The students are then given the opportunity to review and edit their tasks if necessary before the final submission. The final task (question 6) is a synthesis question which seeks to "stitch" the different patches of assignments that the students have done for Part A. Besides learning about the Literature text, the students will also benefit from indirect learning such as collaborative skills, presentation skills, and communication skills, critical and creative thinking skills.

Reader-Response Theory

Assignments 3 and 4 (refer to Appendix 1) explore the students' understanding of the setting and viewpoint using the Reader-Response Theory. The Reader-Response Theory is concerned with the "individual engagement" that is created between the text and the reader. Regarding the influence of literary texts on readers, Rosenblatt (1978) states that the reader's "primary concern is with what happens during the actual reading event…the reader's attention is (centred) directly on what he is living through during his relationship with that particular text." Probst (1994) adds that such a literary experience is "a respect for the uniqueness of the individual reader and the integrity of the individual reading" (p. 38) As such, teachers can honour the students' individual responses by inviting them to record their views in a Literature Journal. A Literature Journal is a record of the students' learning journey of Literature. If used properly, it should reflect a high degree of personal engagement and sophisticated understanding of the literary text. To guide students in their responses, the following questions which are adapted from Probst's article on "Reader-Response Theory and the English Curriculum" can be posed by the teacher:

1. Read "To Kill A Mockingbird" and record what you remember, feel and question in your Literature Journal.

With question 1, students are asked to observe themselves as they read and to examine the significance of their primary reactions.

2. What did you focus most intently as you read the novel? Is there a word, phrase, image or idea that captured your attention?

This question asks the students to concentrate on what is going on in the text. At this point, teachers recognise the unique responses of the students.

3. Write down your thoughts and feelings in your Literature Journal and share them with a partner. Did the novel call to mind different memories, thoughts and feelings?

By asking the students to share their thoughts, feelings and insights with a partner, the students will understand the importance of dialogue in the unique reading of each student.

4. Can you think of any other literary work that is similar to this novel? How are they related? Does it affect your reading?

This question highlights the fact that the construction of meaning of the text is a very complex one as external factors such as inter-textual understanding is needed to create meaning.

Besides facilitating and drawing out the individual responses from the students, teachers give the students the Reading Rubrics for Personal Response (Appendix 2). It is crucial for teachers to discuss the rubrics with the students and to clarify any doubts that they may have about the rubrics. This is because students need to understand the required standards and expectations for them to make a good evaluation of their performances.

After the students have recorded their responses in their Literature Journal using the questions as general prompts, they can then go on to do assignment 3 and 4 in the patchwork text. The possibility of plagiarism or patchwriting is kept to the minimum due to two reasons. Firstly, assignments 3 and 4 are creative products which discourage the students to "lift" or do a mere paraphrase of the novel. Secondly, having gone through the process of thinking and articulating their own responses in the Literature Journal, the students should have greater confidence to note their own authentic personal responses for the assignments.

Stylistics and Language Theory

Assignment 5 is based on the Stylistics Theory which emphasises on the analysis of language use in literary texts. One main aim of this theory is to employ the analysis of the forms of language in order to account for particular effects in a text. For assignment 5, in changing the genre of the text, students gain an insight into the unique quality of the literary text. Students should note that sometimes the changing of a single word changes the whole quality of the original. As such, this assignment makes the students examine and evaluate the effectiveness of stylistic devices present in the novel. This in turn enables them to develop an awareness of the variety of styles and sensitivity to literary expressions.

In order to facilitate the students' learning process, teachers can ask the students to carry out self and peer evaluation using the rubrics shown in Appendix 3. By evaluating their own work, students will take greater ownership of their work and be more aware of their abilities. McMillan (2007) highlights the differences between assessment of learning and assessment for learning. While assessment of learning is mainly concerned with summary judgments and the product, assessment for learning focuses on the process of learning and engages students in learning. Self and Peer Evaluation are types of assessment that belong to the latter. After their self evaluation, students can then carry out a conference with their teachers or peers. During these conferences, students account for or interpret the effects in changing the novel into a newspaper. Such dialogue platforms are crucial as feedback given to students provides direction for students' individual development and help them to further improve on their work.

By engaging in self and peer evaluation, the possibility of plagiarism is greatly reduced since students have the time to reflect and process their own thinking. In the case of the student-teacher conferences, teachers should be able to assess accurately how much learning has taken place due to their active participation in the learning process of their students.

CONCLUSION

The nature of a patchwork text which focuses on students constructing and synthesizing their knowledge over a period of time reduces the possibility of patchwriting or plagiarism. This is because unlike traditional assessment like essay writing, the patchwork assignments require students to build on their knowledge in a progressive manner over a period of time. In this article, we argue that for weaker students who need more guidance, teachers can further break down the patchwork assignments and provide scaffolds for their students in the form of Literature Journals and Self and Peer Evaluation. In addition, the teacher can design the tasks or assignments in such a way that the patchwork assessment progresses from a unistructural outcome to an extended abstract outcome in the final task. It should be noted that the Literature assignments mentioned earlier are not unique to the patchwork text. What is significant is that the patchwork text is a synthesis of various modes of assessments which provides various opportunities for students to showcase their talents and abilities. For instance, students who can learn better with music, sound and visuals can choose to do Assignment 2 which requires them to change the novel into a movie. As such, the patchwork text has the potential to better engage students as they become more aware of their own learning.

REFERENCES

Akister, Jane (2003) Designing and using a Patchwork Text to Assess Social Work Students Undertaking A Module in Family Therapy. *Innovations in Education and Teaching International*. 40, 2 202-207.

Biggs, J. B., and Collis, K. F. (1982). *Evaluating the quality of learning: the SOLO taxonomy.* New York: Academic Press.

Darymple, R., and Smith, P. (2008). The Patchwork Text: enabling discursive writing and reflective practice on a foundation module in work-based learning. *Innovations in Education and Training International, 45*(1), 47 - 54.

Howard, R.M. (1993) A plagiarism *pentimento. Journal of Teaching Writing*, 11(3), pp. 233-246.

Klenowski, V. (2002). *Developing portfolios for learning and assessment.* London: RoutledgeFalmer.

McMillan, J. H. (2007). *Classroom Assessment: Principles and Practice for effective standards-based instruction* (4th Ed.). Boston, MA: Allyn and Bacon.

Ovens, P. (2003). A patchwork text approach to assessment in teacher education. *Teaching in Higher Education, 8*(40), 545 - 562.

Probst, R. (1994). Reader-response theory and the English curriculum, *English Journal, 83*(3), 37 – 44.

Rosenbalt, Louise; *The Reader, The Text, The Poem*; Southern Illinois University Press, 1978

Sadler, D. R. (2007). Perils in the meticulous specification of goals and assessment criteria. *Assessment in Education, 14*(3), 387 - 392.

Tan, K. H. K. (2007). Patchwork Assessment. In K. H. K. Tan (Ed.), *Alternative Assessment in Schools: A Qualitative Approach*. Singapore: Pearson Education South Asia.

Tan, K. H. K. (2008). Assessment for Authentic Learning. In K. H. K. Tan and K. Koh (Eds.), *Authentic Assessment in Schools*. Singapore: Pearson Education South East Asia.

Winter, R. (2003) Contextualizing the Patchwork Text: Addressing Problems of Coursework Assessment in Higher Education. *Innovations in Education and Teaching International* 40 (2):112-122.

In: Educational Theory
Editor: Jaleh Hassaskhah, pp. 121-128

ISBN 978-1-61324-580-4
© 2011 Nova Science Publishers, Inc.

Chapter 7

E-MATHS

*Angel Garrido**
Departamento de Matemáticas Fundamentales
Facultad de Ciencias de la UNED, Madrid, Spain

ABSTRACT

Some reflections which proceeds from teaching and research on the areas of Mathematics and Computation, which have taken the author to conclude that both fields lose perspective and potential when they are kept disconnected, and only they have felt when they work coordinated, looking each of them for the natural support in other one.

Keywords: Mathematical Education; Computer Science; Game Theory; Fuzzy Logic; Artificial Intelligence.

1. INTRODUCTION

From the initial years of the introduction of the studies of Computation in Spain and many other countries one has come observing a difference every time major between the studies of Mathematics and those of Computer Science, being these increasingly foreign territories and unfortunately disjoints. So much it is so for example, the essential subjects that we were taking in our Department in the studies of this School have disappeared with the new Degree, absorbed by personnel of the same one, needed of hours. This is clearly harmful, so much to the mathematical studies as to them of those that are going to receive a devaluated formation.

This is clearly harmful, so much to the mathematical studies as to them of those that are going to receive a formation dubious by personnel not precisely expert in these matters, which can think that it is only an anecdote but it is many more. On one hand, it demonstrates of a loss of lamentable control -in our country, at least - of the mathematicians on an area that

---

* E-mail: agarrido@mat.uned.es

they have created and developed from his origins. On the other hand, they put as example on countries that the best mathematicians have produced, as Hungary, but supporting a tradition it combines of mathematics and computation, there being interrelated (Graph Theory, Complex Networks, and so on), that must use us as model.

All this rests on multitude of computational tools that serve to develop and to understand all these new problems, which or are approached mathematically, or they turn into mere pieces of manuals of recipes.

Therefore, which appears is the new one and more ambitious paradigm: of approaching the computation from a mathematical point of view and vice versa, which will make our science more attractive and rich, for the pupils and for the society [3].

It is not a question of adorning, so, the mathematical theory with IT tools, but one and another science never go jointly, and today they continue going, not only in the already mentioned Hungary, but in Japan, South Corea, China, India, etc., where there moves the gravity center of the science of the future.

2. MATHEMATICAL LEARNING

One of the fundamental problems which the teacher usually meets on Mathematical Education, apart from that of the discipline, and possibly sometimes connected him, is of offering a few attractive explanations for the pupil, with a modern and updated support. Also this is in the habit of happening to university level, which with successive decreases in the levels of effort and of exigency every time looks alike more at Secondary level.

This can that it happens, probably more that in no other matter, in the teaching of the Mathematics, though similar problems can appear in other disciplines, since it is the case of the relative ones to the Physics and to the Chemistry, but in these the grateful resource of support is had in the laboratory practices, which into certain way change at least the panorama (or the routine) of the class.

It is difficult to wake the interest up (and then, to support it in the time) of the pupils for these disciplines, which many people come like too abstract and untied from his daily life. Which is not true, but it looks alike to them, and it ultimately is what affects in his way of agreeing or rejecting that one that offers them.

The question would be to manage to change his vision of the same ones, and that were coming closer these matters for taste and not for obligation.

To obtain these aims, there is fundamental the attitude and the training of the educational futures of Mathematics in these levels. If they do not see this attraction, and they do not know the resources that help them to motivate the future pupils, evil they is going to go in his educational practice, and can be that they go inexorably towards the precipice. For it, we propose that the pupils who go for educational futures should be impregnated with this knowledge and simultaneously fundamentally with this enthusiasm that they have to transmit then. One does not forget that the teaching has great that to see with the scenic arts, and that the same role of the same theatrical work can be admirable or lamentable, according to the actor who interprets it.

3. NEW EDUCATIONAL PARADIGMS

The most effective tools can be those of the knowledge of the historical context where the problems appear and are solved, and all kinds of games and mathematical riddles, which stimulate and wake up the slept qualities that the pupils surely have in power [3]. But this must turn partly of the matter that explains, not in a more or less curious adornment. For it, we must try to blur the line of separation between these questions and the "classic ones" of the Mathematics, asking even it brings over of them at the moment of qualifying, which is very in the line of the "continuous assessment" that is claimed.

As for the games and mathematical riddles, there are many) and very good texts that contain them, apart from that we could know or happen to us on the march. We all have in mind some of the big ones [1, 6, 7, 8], as the works of Martin Gardner, Raymond Smullyan, Ian Stewart, George Pólya, Claudi Alsina, Miguel de Guzmán, etc. It brings over of if they have these tools, to be able to put them then into practice in the classroom, it must ask him the pupils, and encourage them for that they look always new someone. Since initially of his educational activity with every group it would be very suitable that they were giving a rapid and attractive vision of what it is the Mathematics, with the succinct panoramic historical one, which includes allusions to games, IT available tools, etc., the first activity that they can develop is to plan and to write the scheme at least of how they would focus the above mentioned motivating introduction.

Another very important aspect, which is in the habit of giving place to many disagreeable "surprises", resides in the skill to adapt the material to the hearing. This is an art, and is learned often by the time, apart from the more or less "innate" qualities in every person. But it is possible to promote and learn. What must not be done is to try that the pupils adapt to the same thing that they have given us in the Faculty, which is adapted neither for the level nor for often pernicious manners of giving it. Those who say that the pedagogy does not serve for anything, and that everything consists of giving up to the pupil a book and that it is learned, which it recognizes is that only they have memory.

The rejection and the difficulties that this incorrect route has caused to many teachers it tends to the infinite. That must bear in mind the hearing, which are his knowledge and his possibilities, instead of trying to organize an imitation of the old matter in the archaic group of his own University. For it, it would be a good exercise to take a topic written to a higher, or enclosed, more difficult level yet, to select an article of a scientific magazine and to try to turn it (that one that is digestible, obviously) in something that the pupils could understand, and even motivate them, predisposing them to favor, and not in against, of the Mathematics for the future. To propose this it can be a good training in this work of deciphered and fit to the level that we claim.

An example might be give them a general vision, and adapted to his age and his level, of the current topic of research of the Complex Networks, which is easily understandable for them and they are interested in it very much, for the increasing exponential development of the Social Networks, as Facebook, Twitter, etc., across that already one communicates almost the whole world. Also there exist the fascinating examples of the Web World Wide (WWW), of Internet, or of the expansion of the epidemics.

Another out-standing example would be that of the Fuzzy Sets. These, and the Fuzzy Logic, they have had a notable mathematical development in countries as Japan, giving place to great and admirable applications. To countries like ours it has been late and slowly, as the former trains, but lucky already it is coming. All this theory, apart from being a very useful generalization of the theory of Classic Sets of Cantor and Boole, is an essential tool in problems of contemporary mathematics, as that of the treatment of the uncertainty.

Another question that it is necessary to analyze is that of the Theory of the Complexity. In his computational version, it goes to one of the so called *Problems of the Millenium:* the famous *P versus NP,* still for resolving. It is possible to explain also without scarcely mathematical paraphernalia. Likewise, can be commented to them the problems that it approaches and sometimes it solves the Artificial Intelligence [4], or speak to them about the Theory of Automatons, about the Cryptography, about the Neuroscience, very mathematical and current all this.

But almost always on examples, or historical striking details, since they can be those of the secret work, in Blechtley Park, of Alan Turing and his team of mathematicians (the Codebreakers), Poles in the main, by means of that they managed to decipher the Code with that the messages were coded in the Enigma Machine, the movements of the submarine Nazi, advancing with it the end of the Second World war.

From Remote Times, the History of the Human Being Is Developed by a Successive Chain of Steps and Sometimes Jumps, Until the Relative Sophistication of the Modern Brain and Its Culture

The historical origin of the *Artificial Intelligence* is usually established at Darmouth Conference (1956). In this year, John McCarthy coined the term, and defines it as *"the science and engineering of making intelligent machines".*

But it is many more, multiply connected with many other fields, as Neuroscience or Philosophy. And we can find many more arcane origins, perhaps to Plato, Ramón Llull, Leibniz, Pascal, Babbage, Leonardo Torres Quevedo, …, with its attempts to create thinking machines. Also the construction of artifacts devoted to more quick, and based in logic computation.

So, A I will be interpreted as the area of Computer Science focusing on creating machines that can engage on behaviors that humans consider intelligent, with support in powerful tools, such as Fuzzy Logic.

Recall topics as Turing test, Strong vs Weak AI, Chinese Room argument, and so on. Until now, more than fifty years of modern AI. Researchers are attempting to create systems which mimic human thought, or understand speech, or beat the best human chess player. Understanding intelligence and creating intelligent artifacts are the twin goals of AI.

Also, we can consider, in more recent times, very great minds, as Janos von Neumann, Norbert Wiener, Claude Shannon, Alan Turing, Grigori Moisil, or Lofti Zadeh.

Frequently, AI requires Logic. But its Classical version shows too many insufficiencies. So, it was necessary to introduce new tools, as Fuzzy Logic, Modal Logic, Non-Monotonic Logic.

Recall that Mathematics should be a mere instance of First-Order Predicate Calculus, and therefore, belong to applied Monotonic Logic. So, we must show the limitations of classical logic reasoning, and the advantages of Fuzzy Logic.

4. MATHEMATICAL GAMES AND PUZZLES

Another interesting example, useful motivating the students, as connected with its diary life, can be the *Sudoku puzzle*. It has achieved worldwide popularity in recent times, and attracted great attention of the computational intelligence community. *Sudoku* is always considered as *Satisfiability Problem* or *Constraint Satisfaction Problem*.

It is possible to focus on the essential graph structure underlying the Sudoku puzzle. First, by the formalization of Sudoku game as a graph. Then, a solving algorithm based on heuristic reasoning on the graph may be proposed.

In order to evaluate the difficulty levels of puzzles, a quantitative measurement of the complexity level of Sudoku puzzles based on the graph structure and information theory may be proposed. Experimental results show that all the puzzles can be solved fast using heuristic reasoning, and that the proposed game complexity metrics can discriminate between difficulty levels of puzzles.

Origami is the art of paper folding. It also does have many educational benefits. Its connection with geometry is clear. But also the study of Origami and Mathematics may be considered into the field of Topology, although it may be more related with Combinatorics, or Graph Theory [2, 5, 10].

5. SOME RELATIONSHIPS WITH E-MATH

They are only a few ideas, which can develop, undoubtedly, but with this type of procedures we will avoid on the one hand to give a few too old Mathematics, though commodes for repeated, and for other one, we will manage to be introducing those who are already not the Mathematics of the future, but those who are done just now. Also we would stop somehow the bleeding that one comes producing in the last years of the pupils who traditionally were coming to Mathematics towards the studies of IT Engineering, which has occupied so to speak good part of our "ecological niche". One of the reasons is in having left them to occupy an area that naturally was ours to the new "invaders".

The mathematicians created and they have come developing in his most the rigorous and scientific bases of the Computation, and this way it should continue being in our domain. Because of it in the new universities, and in many of the "classic ones", of countries with great scientific and educational tradition, since it is the case of Romania, and typically of Hungary, or of the area of influence of his former regions (as Transylvania, for example), the faculties that are created are of Mathematics and Computer science, or of Mathematics and Computation.

But they have not to of it becoming before aimed from a teachers' mixing by the current ones of the schools of computer science. It should give a very mathematical profile, and give it those of us who are more qualified, together with that they are prepared. This way we will change the attitudes, slightly favorable in general, of the pupils towards these regions of the scientific knowledge. For these lines, now only outlined, I believe that we should continue advancing.

Everything before exposed has a strong support in tools and IT packages, between which we can emphasize as very illustrative those of Fuzzy Logic, or Fractals. So, we can mention the Fuzzy Logic Toolbox-MATLAB, with tools for designing systems based on Fuzzy Logic. Also with the support on fuzzy TECH, the world leading family of software development tools for Fuzzy Logic and neural-fuzzy solutions. Either, in the case of Fractals, we dispose of many possibilities as may be "Illuminations: Fractal Tool", or also on Java Applet, see for instance MathTools.

All this tools allow us a fruitful deployment of this wealth of mathematical ideas in the classroom, projected towards the future across the E- math.

6. ABOUT FUZZY LOGIC

Unfortunately, in the learning of Mathematics and Fuzzy Logic, they appear often as disconnected areas, when they are indeed two necessary and complementary branches of the same tree. Either of them alone produces only ethereal structures, or routines and ad-hoc programs. For this reason, it would be preferable to study, progressively, from the lower educational levels, both disciplines as naturally linked. So, it will be overrated the pure mechanistic of only give informatics to elementary level, as mere blind instructions, either too abstract pure mathematical constructs.

The Fuzzy Logic was introduced already many years ago. Because at least they can turn observations of her in the 1920s, when the logicians affirm that *"Everything is matter of degrees "*. But he was the great Polish logician Lukasiewicz who introduced, in the 1930s, the first three-valued logic, then generalized to many-valued logic. Also Max Black deserves to be mentioned, who was the first to such an about fuzzy sets membership functions. But the fundamental milestone was the article of Zadeh, *Fuzzy Sets,* in the 1960s. In the following decade also established the bases of the Fuzzy Control. Of this epoch they are already some of his more impressive applications. In both following decades there come the applications. In her of them 1990s, Fuzzy Systems was used to regulate many automatisms, appearing very prestigious publications. In the first decade of our century this theory started attracting the attention of the great public. The most advanced mathematicians and educators start being interested in these innovative concepts, with sight being applied specially in Mathematical Education. What we are going to study here is how the Fuzzy Logic, and the Fuzzy Set Theory, they are more fitted to the data processing that comes from the real world, as well as like functioning of the human thought and brain. Also we need to analyze the best way of these concepts being spread, with special attention to the educational area.

We say that a Language is Formal when their syntax is precisely given. Mathematical Logic is the study of the formal languages. Usually, it is called Classical Logic, being dychotomic, or bi-valuated, only either True or False. The Fuzzy Logic is a successful generalization of the Mathematical or Classical Logic. It deals with the problem of the ambiguity in Logic. Because Classical Logic shows many insufficiencies for the problems of AI.

A more flexible tool is needed, allowing for a gradation of certainty, indicating different degrees of membership to a set, or fulfillment of a property or relationship, and so on. The introduction of concepts and methods of Fuzzy Logic, where the idea of sets, relations and so on, must be modified in the sense of covering adequately the indetermination or imprecision of the real world. We define the "world" as a complete and coherent description of how things are or how they could have been. In the problems related with this "real world", which is only one of the "possible worlds", the Monotonic Logic seldom works. Such type of Logic is the classical in formal worlds, such as Mathematics. But it is necessary to provide our investigations with a mathematical construct that can express all the "grey tones", not the classical representation of real world as either black or white, either all or nothing, but as in the common and natural reasoning, through progressive gradation.

Fuzzy Rules are linguistic IF-THEN constructions that have the general form "IF A THEN B", where A, B are propositions containing linguistic variables. A is called the premise, or antecedent, and B is the consequent (or action) of the fuzzy rule. In effect, the use of linguistic variables and fuzzy IF-THEN rules exploits the tolerance for imprecision and uncertainty. In this respect, Fuzzy Logic imitates the ability of the human mind to summarize data and focus on decision-relevant information.

7. EDUCATION AND COMPUTING

By this new approach that we defend, Computer Science occupies, partially and in a natural way, the role Physics and its problems have played as support of mathematical reasoning, a fact in the past two centuries (although Physics do not disappear from the view, being a necessary aid). We propose showing such Methods through the parallel study of Mathematics and Computer Science foundation [9, 11, 12]. Other Computer Science subfields could be carriers of this method too, but perhaps AI is the current better choice, given its characteristics, which practically coincide with many mathematical techniques and objectives.

The creative learning permits to understand the development and practice of creativity. The possibility of founding new solutions is one specific characteristic of the creative process. It may consists in the art of formulate questions to obtain ideas, increasing capacities, defying the current conventionalism in the educative world. So, the benefits of such an innovative educative method must consist in a more progressive regard of Mathematical Education in modern times, with the final purpose of producing adaptive and creative minds, capable of solving new problems and challenges.

REFERENCES

[1] Courant, R. (1996), What Is Mathematics? *An Elementary Approach to Ideas and Methods.* Oxford UP.

[2] Chen, Z. (2009), *"Heuristic Reasoning on Graph and Game Complexity of Sudoku"*. The Smithsonian/NASA Astrophysics System.

[3] Garrido, A. (2010). "Mathematics and Artificial Intelligence, two branches of the same tree". *At the journal Procedia-Social and Behavioral Sciences*, pp. 233-240. Special Issue devoted to the WCES 2010 (World Congress on Educational Sciences), Bahcesehir University, Istanbul. Elsevier, Holland.

[4] McCorduck, P. (2004), *Machines Who Think* (2nd ed.), Natick, MA: A. K. Peters, Ltd.

[5] Mitchell, D. (2009): *Complete Origami. Firefly Books.*

[6]   Pólya, G. (2009): *How to Solve It: A New Aspect of Mathematical Method.* Ishi Press. First ed. 1945.

[7]   Pólya, G. (1990): Mathematics and Plausible Reasoning. Vol. I: *Induction and Analogy in Mathematics.* Vol. II: Patterns of Plausible Inference. Both in Princeton University Press.

[8]   Pólya, G. (1981): *Mathematical Discovery: On Understanding, Learning and Teaching Problem Solving.* Wiley and Sons.

[9]   Russell, S., and Norvig, P. (2003), *Artificial Intelligence: A Modern Approach* (2nd ed.), Prentice Hall.

[10] Samuel, A. L. (1959), "Some studies in machine learning using the game of checkers", *IBM Journal of Research and Development* 3 (3): 210–219

[11] Searle, J. (1980), "Minds, Brains, and Programs", *Behavioral and Brain Sciences* 3 (3): 417–457.

[12] Turing A. (1950), "Computing Machinery and Intelligence", *Mind,* LIX (236): 433–460.

In: Educational Theory
Editor: Jaleh Hassaskhah, pp. 129-141

ISBN 978-1-61324-580-4
© 2011 Nova Science Publishers, Inc.

Chapter 8

COGNITIVE DIVERSITY IN INTERDISCIPLINARY EDUCATIONAL THEORY DEVELOPMENT

Don Ambrose[*]
College of Liberal Arts, Education, and Sciences,
Rider University, Lawrenceville, NJ

ABSTRACT

Arguments over the nature and purpose of theory have abounded within and beyond educational fields. One counterproductive scenario is to leave education atheoretical and conceptually unguided. The opposite counterproductive scenario is to have education dominated by a grand hegemonic but inadequate, narrow theory. The phenomena of interest in education are highly varied and complex; consequently, educational fields require guidance from multiple theoretical perspectives, which can shed light on specific phenomena. Only an interdisciplinary search covering multiple levels of analysis can bring into play an adequate array of theories that can illuminate the intricate, complex, multiple dimensions of learners, educators, classrooms, school systems, and the sociopolitical, ideological, and economic contexts that influence them. Employing the concept of cognitive diversity, this chapter describes the conceptual territory from which useful theory can be drawn. This territory includes levels of disciplinary scope from macro-societal to immediate contextual, to the level of the individual, to the organic-biological, to the cellular biological, to the molecular-genetic, and possibly even to the subatomic. Examples of theoretical perspectives from these various levels are provided, along with some ways in which they can guide the work of educational researchers and practitioners.

---

[*] Editor, Roeper Review, Professor of Graduate Education, College of Liberal Arts, Education, and Sciences, Rider University, 2083 Lawrenceville Road, Lawrenceville, NJ, 08648-3099, phone: (609) 895-5647, email: ambrose@rider.edu

COGNITIVE DIVERSITY IN INTERDISCIPLINARY EDUCATIONAL THEORY DEVELOPMENT

Members of the general public and scholars in many academic disciplines mistakenly believe that education is a simple enterprise, which entails babysitting and mechanically shoveling content knowledge information bits into passive crania. This simplicity becomes evident in shortsighted, narrow-minded, superficial educational reform initiatives such as the No Child Left Behind legislation (see Apple, 2007; Meier & Wood, 2004; Ravitch, 2010). Such reforms are based on the assumption that learning occurs through transfer of precisely measurable content knowledge and skills into students' brains. Even if the intent of these reforms is good, which is questionable (see Berliner, in press), they leave students with an excessively mechanistic, shallow education that largely ignores the development of important knowledge, skills, and dispositions. Creative and critical thinking, the discovery of aspirations, and the development of talents tend to be suppressed in such environments.

Superficial, inadequate understanding of education can come from misguided adherence to grand, hegemonic theory or, conversely, from lack of sufficient theoretic guidance. Some scholars warn about the danger of grasping a single, dominant theory too tightly (e.g., Grant & Piechowski, 1999; Thomas, 1997). For example, when discussing root-metaphorical worldviews, which are macro theories shaping our philosophical assumptions about phenomena in the world, the eminent philosopher Stephen Pepper (1942) argued that no single world hypothesis (alternatively named worldview) could explain complex phenomena adequately:

> Post-rational eclecticism is simply the recognition of equal or nearly equal adequacy of a number of world theories and a recommendation to not fall into the dogmatism of neglecting any one of them. . . . Four good lights cast fewer shadows than one. (p. 342)

He went on to explain how those who can derive insights from more than one of the four worldviews (mechanism, ogranicism, contextualism, formism) can gain a better understanding than can someone trapped within only one of those worldviews. Following Pepper's advice, analysts have employed worldview analyses to encourage more eclectic, macro-theorizing in education (see Ambrose, 1996, 1998b, 2000, 2009b).

Others warn that research and practice in education can be too atheoretical. Coleman (2003) argued that the field of gifted education often falls prey to atheoretical initiatives, which can lead researchers and practitioners into barren conceptual territory. For example, educational professionals lacking theoretical awareness and guidance can end up simply replicating past practices based on implicit assumptions that commonly used psychometric measures can select the correct candidates for gifted programs. In actuality, such measures can ignore students who have impressive abilities that are not within the scope of the traditional instruments.

Einstein generated an insight that applies to either the case of grand, theoretic hegemony or atheoretical wandering in the wilderness. While lamenting the tendency of scholars to oversimplify and attend to the superficial he commented that "I have little patience with scientists who take a board of wood, look for its thinnest part, and drill a great number of holes where drilling is easy" (cited in Calaprice, 2010, p. 402). In the case of theoretic hegemony it is the overgeneralized theory that keeps scholars and practitioners from elevating their gaze to search for thicker, more knotty parts of the board in which complex, hidden, but important phenomena might be embedded. In the case of atheoretical disorientation, it is the lack of theoretical vision that keeps the professionals from moving beyond the thinnest part of the board.

WHY IS EDUCATION FAR MORE COMPLEX THAN COMMONLY BELIEVED?

There is a misconception in scholarly circles that seems to underlie the problem of oversimplification when it comes to education. Those who look beyond the borders of their own fields eventually come across the notion of the hierarchy of the sciences (see Ambrose, 1998a; Arecchi, 1996; Nicolescu, 2002; Schwartz, 1992; Simonton, 2004). Typical assumptions about this hierarchy are that the "hard," natural sciences (e.g., physics, chemistry) are at the top and the "soft," human sciences (e.g., the social sciences) are underneath. The hard sciences are assumed to be superior because they strive for and often achieve precision and clarity in their explorations of phenomena. In contrast, the soft sciences often become mired in the muck of imprecision and their methods of inquiry are assumed to be less impressive. Worse yet, education typically doesn't make it onto the hierarchy at all, and, if it is condescendingly considered, it is placed at the bottom of the soft sciences because of its lack of status in academia.

Although some argue in favor of the hierarchy of the sciences (e.g., Simonton, 2004), there are reasons to believe that the notion of a hierarchy is mistaken (see Ambrose, 2009; Schwartz, 1992). For example, Schwartz, a physicist, criticized the common tendency to assume that the natural sciences are superior to the human sciences, instead arguing that all disciplines have a place when it comes to contributing to knowledge. According to Gruber (1996), the eminent psychologist Jean Piaget also argued against the notion of a hierarchy claiming instead that the disciplines should be conceptually arrayed as the "circle of the sciences" so that all could contribute in a process of interdisciplinary borrowing. Piaget believed that the notion of the disciplinary hierarchy hindered interdisciplinary borrowing

From the viewpoint of the analysis in this chapter, there is another reason to lament the hierarchy of the sciences and the problem of education being mired at the bottom--if it makes the hierarchy at all. Assuming that education has a low-status position on the hierarchy implicitly reinforces the notion that it is a simple discipline, amenable to simple theoretical explanations. This reinforces the notion that superficial measures of educational progress, such as those employed through NCLB, are accurate and adequate. In actuality, education is immensely complex.

EDUCATION AS A HIGHLY COMPLEX, MULTIDISCIPLINARY PHENOMENON

In several detailed arguments (Ambrose, 1996, 1998a, 2003b, 2005, 2006, 2009a, 2009b, in press-a; Ambrose, VanTassel-Baska, Coleman, & Cross, 2010) I have made the case that educational research and theory should draw from multiple disciplines because important education-related discoveries can be made in those disciplines. Education is highly complex because it operates on multiple levels simultaneously. First, important phenomena relevant to education are embedded in disciplines throughout the questionable hierarchy of the sciences. These phenomena can be arrayed along a somewhat different hierarchy from micro to macro, which includes the following levels of analysis: broad contextual, immediate contextual, individual, organic systems, cellular, molecular-atomic, and possibly subatomic (Ambrose, 2005).

Starting in the middle of this alternative hierarchy we find the level of the individual where the psychological dynamics of students come into play. Here, theorists, researchers and practitioners are interested in cognitive, affective, motivational, and dispositional dynamics of the student that promote or suppress achievement. At the next level up, toward macro, is the immediate contextual level, which includes phenomena that emerge in local environments such as classrooms, schools, and families. At this level, educational professionals are interested in the nature of curriculum and instruction, the dynamics of interpersonal interactions, and organizational constraints on the thoughts and actions of learners and teachers. At both of these levels of analysis (individual and immediate contextual) theory and research tends to come from the fields of education and psychology.

At the broad contextual level of analysis, large-scale macro contexts come into play-- contexts such as national and international economic systems, political systems, and ideological, ethnic, and religious frameworks. Examples of important questions that arise at this level include:

- What dimensions of a child's intelligence are highlighted or obscured by the deprivation, segregation, and stigmatization he or she suffers in oppressive, dogmatic, sociopolitical and economic environments?
- How does the culture in a particular region shape or distort the aspirations of children?

Gaining more understanding of the phenomena that become visible at this broad contextual level requires theoretical insights from a number of disciplines including political science, sociology, economics, history, cultural anthropology, and ethical philosophy.

Moving back toward the micro levels of analysis, past the level of the individual where we started, we come to the level of organic systems where the structure and function of larger subsystems in the brain become visible. Here, theorists, researchers, and practitioners become interested in the influences of brain hemispheres, the prefrontal cortex, the limbic system and other brain components on student learning. Recent attention to "brain-based learning" is an example of navigation into this level of analysis. Insights here require direct borrowing from neuroscience and cognitive science.

The cellular level is the next stop on our trip toward the micro level of analysis. Here, we focus our attention on the structure and function of neurons and neural networks. For example, arguments between "connectionists" and symbolists" in cognitive science (see Baumgartner & Payr, 1995) could have some implications for education because connectionism seems to make more room for the unpredictable emergence of creativity while symbolism focuses more attention on rapid information processing. The relevant disciplines at this level are again neuroscience and cognitive science.

The next point in the hierarchy is the molecular-atomic level of analysis where genetic influences come into play. Educational professionals who gain a glimpse into this level might find some insights shedding light on the nature-nurture debate, which periodically emerges in the field of gifted education. They might discover some recent findings pertaining to the impact, or lack thereof, of genetics on the development and manifestation of various kinds of intelligences or other abilities. Insights at this level become most visible through the lens of molecular biology.

There is one more potential stop on the extreme micro end of this hierarchy of analytic levels. At the subatomic level, the strange paradoxes of quantum mechanics become visible. For example, in one of these paradoxes, the experimentally verified phenomenon of nonlocality shows that nonlocal influences can occur over large distances without relying on the physical forces or signals required for causality by the laws of Newtonian physics. Some scholars have theorized that nonlocality and other counterintuitive quantum phenomena could operate within the microstructures of the neuron thereby making room for expansion of our conceptions of human cognition. (e.g., Penrose, 1994, 1998). This theoretical connection runs counter to dominant, mechanistic theorizing in cognitive science and psychology, and it is speculative; consequently, it must be held lightly, with caution. Nevertheless, it should be kept in play because prematurely rejecting theory that has not been conclusively refuted is a scientific mistake (see Lakatos, 1978).

Overall, the levels of analysis discussed here reveal the immense complexity of the educational enterprise. In view of this complexity, we have two choices. One choice entails narrow-minded oversimplification of the educational enterprise and focusing only at the levels of the individual and the immediate contextual where educational and psychological theory prevail. This choice is not appealing for at least two reasons. First, it is based on dogmatic thinking, which prematurely narrows decision-making options (for recent, in-depth discussions of dogmatism see Ambrose & Sternberg, in press; Ambrose, Sternberg & Sriraman, in press).

The other choice entails an open-minded embrace of multiple, complex theoretical possibilities drawn from the multiple levels of analysis discussed earlier. This option is daunting because it requires high levels of tolerance of ambiguity. We can become lost in complexity when considering diverse theories from multiple disciplines. Nevertheless, this is the better option because it no longer confines us to the narrow, thin, excessively drilled and increasingly barren space on Einstein's board of wood.

The second option also makes sense if we think about educational inquiry as a process of creative problem solving. In essence, the creative problem solving (CPS) process (see Treffinger, Isaksen, & Dorval, 2000) can be thought of as funnel-like, beginning with broad, speculative exploration at the wide-open end of the funnel and moving toward highly refined, precise clarification at its narrow end. Work at the broad, speculative end of the funnel requires open-minded tolerance of ambiguity.

Applying the CPS model to our discussion of educational theory, navigating through multiple levels of analysis to extract theoretical insights from multiple academic disciplines for application to educational research and practice is analogous to working in the broad, speculative, "mess-finding" phase of creative problem-solving where ideas are held likely and probed for potential usefulness. Later, in the data finding, problem finding, idea finding, solution finding, and acceptance finding phases of the process we can attend more carefully to hypothesis-testing, empirical analyses that can support or refute theoretical insights. In order to make this process work, we must value broad, speculative, interdisciplinary theoretical exploration but keep it in its proper perspective so we don't become trapped within the parameters of new, untested theory. Analyses of the benefits that can be derived from cognitive diversity provide some reason for optimism about combining educational researchers' current penchant for drilling empirical holes in Einstein's board of wood with broader, interdisciplinary, speculative theorizing that can take us into the thicker, knottier sections of the board.

EMBRACING COGNITIVE DIVERSITY IN EDUCATIONAL THEORIZING

Page (2007) synthesized a great deal of research on the effectiveness of group problem-solving in a wide variety of settings, eventually coming to the conclusion that cognitive diversity is highly advantageous in this kind of work. A problem-solving group is cognitively diverse if it includes diverse perspectives or interpretations, diverse heuristics, and diverse predictive models. According to Page, cognitive diversity is at least as important as intelligence when it comes to the effectiveness of group problem solving.

Diverse perspectives or interpretations provide the group, collectively speaking, with diverse ways of viewing, representing, categorizing, or framing problems or issues. In the application of Page's findings to this analysis of educational theory, diverse perspectives or interpretations are analogous to diverse philosophies of education. For example, a cognitively diverse group of educational professionals would not be homogenous, including only constructivists or only essentialists. Diverse heuristics imply diverse methods of problem solving. For example, in our application of cognitive diversity to educational theory and research, a group of scholars would bring diverse heuristics to bear on educational phenomena if the members of that group included scholars with varying types of quantitative-empirical research expertise as well as various qualitative methodologies. Finally, a group of scholars would include diverse predictive models if the members of that group could bring into play a wide variety of theories that can apply to the various dimensions of education mentioned in the earlier discussion of levels of analysis.

A counterexample of cognitive diversity comes from the dominance of behaviorist psychological theory during the mid-20th century. While behaviorism provided some useful insights about teaching and learning it also was confining and became rather barren as the conceptual terrain it encompassed became excessively mined by empiricists.

SOME EXAMPLES OF INTERDISCIPLINARY BORROWING THAT CAN ENRICH EDUCATIONAL THEORY

As illustrated by the prior discussion of the multiple levels of analysis where insights can be drawn from multiple academic disciplines, exploration beyond current educational theory can be very broad indeed, encompassing a wide variety of new ideas. Again, this breadth is daunting and educational professionals could get lost in a broad, interdisciplinary search. Recall that this kind of interdisciplinary work should be considered exploratory and speculative, providing raw material for subsequent, more refined theoretic analyses and empirical inquiry. Given this caveat about daunting complexity, the following examples come from neoclassical economic theory, ethical philosophy, political philosophy, primatology, and cultural anthropology.

CRITIQUES OF NEOCLASSICAL ECONOMICS

For the past several decades, neoclassical economics has dominated the field of economics and has exerted powerful influences over the structure and dynamics of national, regional, and international economic systems (see Ambrose, in press-b; Chang, 2007; Freedman, 2008; Quiggin, 2010; Stiglitz, 2010). Neoclassical economists portray the human as a rational actor who makes rational decisions for selfish purposes based on complete information sets. These economists contend that a laissez-faire economic system unencumbered by significant government regulation should lead to the best economic outcomes. Supposedly, the decision-making of multiple rational actors in the marketplace becomes self-organizing through the manipulations of Adam Smith's metaphorical invisible hand. Ultimately, the unfettered free market should provide strong benefits for all.

Unfortunately, an excessively deregulated free-market system based on neoclassical economic theory isn't as perfect as its designers have contended. It leads to boom-and-bust cycles, promotes selfish, corrupt behavior, makes economic inequality intolerably severe, and has culminated in the recent global economic disaster, which was exceeded only by the Great Depression--itself an artifact of excessive free-market zeal (see Quiggin, 2010; Stiglitz, 2010).

Educational theorists can glean much from an excursion into neoclassical economic theory. First, they can come to understand with more clarity some of the daunting barriers facing deprived children in highly stratified nations. Children who face enormous socioeconomic barriers (e.g., deprivation, segregation, stigmatization) can find it very difficult or even impossible to discover productive, long-term aspirations that lead to discovery and development of talents. Neoclassical economic theory strongly highlights atomistic individualism making it easier for the haves in a stratified nation to claim that the have-nots are failing because of their own inadequacies on a level playing field. Critiques of neoclassical economic theory show instead that those who impose neoclassical economic systems on nations or regions actually are imposing barriers to the aspiration growth and talent development of large numbers of deprived children (see Ambrose, 2002, 2003a). Second, by gaining appreciation of the weaknesses embedded in neoclassical economic theory, educational scholars can see how a prominent, dominant theory in a neighboring discipline has created a sanitized, excessively mechanical model of the human as a very selfish but otherwise hyper-rational, Spock-like, atomistic individual. Of course, humans are far less rational and less selfishly atomistic than the neoclassical rational-actor model suggests. By using the weaknesses of this model as an example, educational theorists can look for similar weaknesses in their own conceptual models and theories, thereby critiquing them more effectively before following them down unproductive paths.

ETHICAL PHILOSOPHERS AND PRIMATOLOGISTS MAGNIFYING ALTRUISM

Altruism has little to no presence in the neoclassical economic theory discussed in the last subsection. It is, however, the subject of intense focus in the work of some ethical philosophers, political philosophers, and primatologists. For example, ethical philosopher Alan Gewirth (1998) distinguished between particularist and universalist morality. Individuals who are particularist in their ethical orientation may be kind and generous to others as long as those others are from their own identity group (e.g., ethnicity, nationality, religion). However, they can be dismissive of, or even cruel toward, outsiders who do not share their identity. Otherwise generous, kind individuals can be convinced somewhat easily in times of crisis to demonize "outsiders," thereby making it easier to exclude, punish, or even exterminate them (see Chirot & McCauley, 2006). In contrast, universalists may favor their own identity group somewhat but when things become serious (e.g., in times of resource shortages, crises, mass persecution) they do not distinguish between themselves and outsiders; instead they view everyone as members of the human race. Political philosopher Kristin Renwick Monroe (Martin & Monroe, 2009; Monroe, 2003, 2004) illustrated this phenomenon vividly by carrying out research on *rescuers*–those who risk their lives to rescue strangers. She found that those inclined to rescue strangers fit the universalist pattern.

We can even borrow from the field of primatology, which entails the study of our simian cousins. On the basis of several decades of research in this field, Frans de Waal (2009, 2006) has concluded that primates, supposedly lower on the evolutionary chain than we are, can and often do engage in altruistic actions. These findings seriously challenge the notion that nature is as red in tooth and claw as social Darwinists propose.

Educational theorists who borrow these theories and research findings about universalist morality and altruistic behavior can gain more clarity about educational philosophy and the ideology that influences it. For example, they may conclude that education should magnify generosity, cooperation, and altruism more than it currently does. They also could conclude that those who strongly promote competitive individualism as an educational goal might be missing an important part of the human experience. In addition, they could use this work from ethical philosophy, political philosophy, and primatology to build stronger cases when they argue against proposals that education should be driven more by hyper-individualistic competitive values.

CENTRIFUGAL ANTHROPOLOGY AND IMPRECISE DEFINITIONS

As in most fields, theorists and researchers in education continually seek for definitional precision in order to grasp more firmly the phenomena they are attempting to understand. This is particularly the case with scholars who have a mechanistic-positivistic bent because quantitative investigative methodologies typically rely on precise definitions or models. That is the reason for the sharply defined but rather sterile and misleading rational-actor model in neoclassical economic theory, for example.

Some excursions into interdisciplinary territory raise questions about even the possibility of precise definitions. It may be possible to define some phenomena precisely if they can be temporarily and efficiently severed from other phenomena and from contextual influences. But highly complex phenomena may resist definitional precision in the extreme. For example, the eminent cultural anthropologist Clifford Geertz (2000) discussed a definitional problem in his field, reporting that Harvard anthropologists once attempted to make sense of the various definitions of *culture,* which is the central concept of their field. They found 171 definitions that could be sorted into 13 categories.

Geertz eventually concluded that the field of cultural anthropology has a centrifugal impulse because investigators dig deeply into the particularities of specific cultures looking for unique variations instead of generalities that can be applied to humanity as a whole. Consequently, as findings emerge they spin the field outward centrifugally away from any possibility of a unified theory about culture.

Educational scholars tend to run into similar difficulty when they attempt to nail down precise meanings for complex concepts. For example, most of the scholars contributing to a volume on the topic of dogmatism in gifted education grappled with the difficulty professionals have experienced with the definition of "giftedness" since the inception of that field (see Ambrose, Sternberg & Sriraman, in press). Educational scholars tend to lament this lack of consensus and precision, and redouble efforts to achieve a "unified" definition. But in view of Geertz's insight about the centrifugal impulse of cultural anthropology it is possible that education also has some centrifugal forces and seeking definitional and theoretical unity could turn out to be a wild goose chase. At the very least, we should be open to the notion that agreement on definitions could be unattainable at our current level of understanding. We also should capitalize on the diverse understandings of particular findings in local settings that qualitative research studies can provide. After all, qualitative research in education was inspired largely by the inquiry methods of anthropologists such as Geertz.

CONCLUSION

Of course, the few examples of theoretical and research insights borrowed from foreign disciplines and imported into this chapter represent only a small sampling of what could be obtained by a long-term, broad-scope search for ideas that can inform theory development in education. For an introduction to many more examples, a recent book (Ambrose, 2009b) includes 79 theories and research findings borrowed from 29 different fields and academic disciplines. These ideas were forced together through a process of creative association to generate some ways in which awareness of a construct from one discipline can creatively impact a construct in another. Finally, the theories and research findings from outside disciplines were applied to theory and research in education to develop some speculative implications.

The limited scope of any single educational theory is helpful to an extent because it sheds light on particular phenomena and suggests ways to engage in productive investigations. Nevertheless, its limited scope also prevents vision beyond the current focus. When insights about teaching and learning can be had from multiple levels of analysis, from the micro levels of molecular biology to the macro levels of economic globalization, it seems shortsighted to hold firmly to a single educational theory.

REFERENCES

Ambrose, D. (1996). Unifying theories of creativity: Metaphorical thought and the unification process. *New Ideas in Psychology, 14*, 257-267.

Ambrose, D. (1998a). A model for clarification and expansion of conceptual foundations. *Gifted Child Quarterly, 42*, 77-86.

Ambrose, D. (1998b). Comprehensiveness of conceptual foundations for gifted education: A world-view analysis. *Journal for the Education of the Gifted, 21*, 452-470.

Ambrose, D. (2000). World-view entrapment: Moral-ethical implications for gifted education. *Journal for the Education of the Gifted, 23*, 159-186.

Ambrose, D. (2002). Socioeconomic stratification and its influences on talent development: Some interdisciplinary perspectives. *Gifted Child Quarterly, 46,* 170-180.

Ambrose, D. (2003a). Barriers to aspiration development and self-fulfillment: Interdisciplinary insights for talent discovery. *Gifted Child Quarterly, 47,* 282-294.

Ambrose, D. (2003b). Theoretic scope, dynamic tensions, and dialectical processes: A model for discovery of creative intelligence. In D. Ambrose, L. M. Cohen & A. J. Tannenbaum (Eds.), *Creative Intelligence: Toward Theoretic Integration,* (pp. 325-345). Cresskill, NJ: Hampton Press.

Ambrose, D. (2005). Interdisciplinary expansion of conceptual foundations: Insights from beyond our field. *Roeper Review, 27,* 137-143.

Ambrose, D. (2006). Large-scale contextual influences on creativity: Evolving academic disciplines and global value systems. *Creativity Research Journal, 18,* 75-85.

Ambrose, D. (2009a). Capitalizing on cognitive diversity in explorations of ethical high ability. In D. Ambrose & T. L. Cross (Eds.), *Morality, ethics, and gifted minds* (pp. 347-361). New York, NY: Springer Science.

Ambrose, D. (2009b). *Expanding visions of creative intelligence: An interdisciplinary exploration.* Cresskill, NJ: Hampton Press.

Ambrose, D. (in press-a). Finding dogmatic insularity in the territory of various academic disciplines In D. Ambrose & R. J. Sternberg (Eds.), *How dogmatic beliefs harm creativity and higher-level thinking.* New York, NY: Routledge.

Ambrose, D. (in press-b). The not-so-invisible hand of economics and its impact on conceptions and manifestations of high ability In D. Ambrose, R. J. Sternberg & B. Sriraman (Eds.), *Confronting dogmatism in gifted education.*

Ambrose, D., & Sternberg, R. J. (Eds.). (in press). *How dogmatic beliefs harm creativity and higher-level thinking.* New York, NY: Routledge.

Ambrose, D., Sternberg, R. J., & Sriraman, B. (Eds.). (in press). *Confronting dogmatism in gifted education.* New York, NY: Routledge.

Ambrose, D., VanTassel-Baska, J., Coleman, L. J., & Cross, T. L. (2010). Unified, insular, firmly policed or fractured, porous, contested, gifted education? *Journal for the Education of the Gifted, 33,* 453-478.

Apple, M. W. (2007). Ideological success, educational failure? On the politics of No Child Left Behind. *Journal of Teacher Education, 58,* 108-116.

Arecchi, F. T. (1996). Complexity in science: Models and metaphors. In B. Pullman (Ed.), *The emergence of complexity in mathematics, physics, chemistry, and biology* (pp. 129-160). Vatican City: Pontifical Academy of Sciences.

Baumgartner, P., & Payr, S. (Eds.). (1995). *Speaking minds: Interviews with twenty eminent cognitive scientists*. Princeton, NJ: Princeton University Press.

Berliner, D. C. (in press). Narrowing curriculum, assessments, and conceptions of what It means to be smart in the US schools: Creaticide by design In D. Ambrose & R. J. Sternberg (Eds.), *How dogmatic beliefs harm creativity and higher-level thinking*. New York, NY: Routledge.

Calaprice, A. (Ed.). (2010). *The ultimate quotable Einstein*. Princeton, NJ: Princeton University Press.

Chang, H. (2007). *Bad Samaritans: The myth of free trade and the secret history of capitalism* New York, NY: Random House.

Chirot, D., & McCauley, C. (2006). *Why not kill them all? The logic and prevention of mass political murder*. Princeton, NJ: Princeton University Press.

Coleman, L. J. (2003). An essay on rethinking theory as a tool for disciplined inquiry. In J. H. Borland (Ed.), *Rethinking gifted education* (pp. 61-71). New York, NY: Teachers College Press.

de Waal, F. (2009). *The age of empathy: Nature's lessons for a kinder society*. New York, NY: Random House.

de Waal, F. B. M. (2006). *Primates and philosophers: How morality evolved*. Princeton, NJ: Princeton University Press.

Freedman, C. F. (2008). *Chicago fundamentalism: Ideology and methodology in economics*. Singapore: World Scientific.

Geertz, C. (2000). *Available light: Anthropological reflections on philosophical topics*. Princeton, NJ: Princeton University Press.

Gewirth, A. (1998). *Self-fulfillment*. Princeton, NJ: Princeton University Press.

Grant, B. A., & Piechowski, M. M. (1999). Theories and the good: Toward child-centered gifted education. *Gifted Child Quarterly, 43*, 4-12.

Gruber, H. E. (1996). The life space of a scientist: The visionary function and other aspects of Jean Piaget's thinking. *Creativity Research Journal, 9*, 251-265.

Lakatos, I. (1978). History of science and its rational reconstructions. In J. Warrall & G. Currie (Eds.), *The methodology of scientific research programmes. Philosophical papers of Imre Lakatos* (Vol. 1, pp. 102-138). Cambridge, England: Cambridge University Press.

Martin, A., & Monroe, K. R. (2009). Identity, moral choice, and the moral imagination: Is there a neuroscientific foundation for altruism? In D. Ambrose & T. L. Cross (Eds.), *Morality, ethics, and gifted minds* (pp. 73-87). New York, NY: Springer Science.

Meier, D., & Wood, G. (Eds.). (2004). *Many children left behind: How the No Child Left Behind Act is damaging our children and our schools*. Boston, MA: Beacon Press.

Monroe, K. R. (2003). How identity and perspective constrain moral choice. *International Political Science Review, 24*, 405-425.

Monroe, K. R. (2004). *The hand of compassion: Portraits of moral choice during the Holocaust*. Princeton, NJ: Princeton University Press.

Nicolescu, B. (2002). *Manifesto of transdisciplinarity*. Albany, NY: SUNY Press.

Page, S. E. (2007). *The difference: How the power of diversity creates better groups, firms, schools, and societies*. Princeton, NJ: Princeton University Press.

Penrose, R. (1994). *Shadows of the mind: A search for the missing science of consciousness*. Oxford, England: Oxford University Press.

Penrose, R. (1998). Can a computer understand? In S. Rose (Ed.), *From brains to consciousness?* (pp. 154-179). Princeton, NJ: Princeton University Press.

Pepper, S. C. (1942). *World hypotheses.* Berkeley, CA: University of California Press.

Quiggin, J. (2010). *Zombie economics: How dead ideas still walk among us.* Princeton, NJ: Princeton University press.

Ravitch, D. (2010). *The death and life of the great American school system: How testing and choice are undermining education.* New York, NY: Basic Books.

Schwartz, J. (1992). *The creative moment: How science made itself alien to modern culture.* New York, NY: HarperCollins.

Simonton, D. K. (2004). Psychology's status as a scientific discipline: It's empirical placement within an implicit hierarchy of the sciences. *Review of General Psychology, 8,* 59-67.

Stiglitz, J. E. (2010). *Free fall: America, free markets, and the sinking of the world economy.* New York, NY: W W Norton.

Thomas, G. (1997). What's the use of theory? *Harvard Educational Review, 67,* 75-104.

Treffinger, D. J., Isaksen, S. G., & Dorval, K. B. (2000). *Creative problem solving: An introduction.* Waco, TX: Prufrock Press.

AUTHOR BIO

Don Ambrose is professor of graduate education at Rider University in Lawrenceville, NJ; editor of the *Roeper Review;* and past chair of the Conceptual Foundations Division of the National Association for Gifted Children. He serves on the editorial boards of most of the major journals in the field of gifted education. Most of his numerous publications are theoretical syntheses and philosophical analyses based on a wide-ranging, interdisciplinary search for theories, philosophical perspectives, and research findings that challenge, refine, and expand thinking about the development of creative intelligence. Among other outlets, his work has been discussed in *Wired Magazine* and *Scholastic.* His books include *How dogmatic beliefs harm creativity and higher-level thinking* (in press, Routledge, with Robert J. Sternberg); *Confronting dogmatism in gifted education* (in press, Routledge, with Robert J. Sternberg and Bharath Sriraman); *Expanding visions of creative intelligence: An interdisciplinary exploration* (Hampton Press); *Morality, ethics, and gifted minds* (Springer; with Tracy L. Cross); *Creative intelligence: Toward theoretic integration* (Hampton Press; with LeoNora M. Cohen and Abraham J. Tannenbaum); and *The Roeper School: A model for holistic development of high ability* (in press, Sense Publishing, with Bharath Sriraman and Tracy L. Cross).

INDEX

C

calculus, 48
candidates, 130
capitalism, 139
caricature, 54
case study, 81, 82, 106
cash, 90
causality, 133
Census, 1, 38
certification, 110
challenges, 48, 82, 86, 127
chaos, viii, 64, 72, 73, 74, 75, 79, 90
chaotic behavior, 72, 75
chemical, 40, 47, 61
chemicals, 84
Chicago, 33, 60, 139
chicken, 103
child development, 47
children, 3, 6, 8, 9, 12, 13, 17, 47, 61, 66, 69, 81, 92, 99, 132, 135, 139
China, 82, 107, 122
circulation, 85
cities, 54
City, 75, 76, 82, 138
clarity, 101, 131, 135, 136
classes, viii, ix, 63, 66, 69, 83, 84, 86, 87, 88, 89, 90, 91, 93, 94, 99
classical logic, 124
classification, 75, 90
classroom, vii, ix, 39, 40, 44, 54, 55, 56, 66, 69, 80, 83, 84, 86, 87, 88, 90, 93, 98, 101, 104, 107, 123, 126
classroom settings, 101
classroom teacher, vii, 39, 44, 55, 90
classroom teachers, vii, 39
cleaning, 85
climate, 84, 86, 90, 93, 94
clusters, 110
cochlea, 45
coding, 80
coffee, 54
cognition, 45, 46
cognitive data, 65
cognitive development, 46, 48, 49, 50, 55, 61
cognitive science, vii, 39, 60, 132, 133
cognitive skills, viii, 63, 64, 69
cognitive tasks, 110
coherence, 110
collaboration, 81
college students, 47
color, 76
commercial, 70

communication, 7, 65, 80, 94, 116, 117
communication skills, 117
communities, 5
community, 3, 46, 47, 49, 80, 85, 108, 125
compassion, 139
competition, 89, 91, 92
complexity, viii, 64, 73, 125, 133, 135, 138
compliance, ix, 83
complications, 49
composition, vii, 1, 2, 3, 4, 6, 7, 8, 13, 22, 23, 25, 26, 29, 30, 31, 32
comprehension, 71
computation, 104, 122, 124
computer, 72, 81, 125, 140
computing, 80
conception, 46, 59
conceptual model, 135
conference, 80, 119
confirmation bias, 48
conflict, 87, 92
confrontation, 87, 92
Confucius, 66
Congress, 79, 80, 127
consciousness, 45, 139, 140
consensus, 57, 87, 94, 95, 137
conservation, 85
consolidation, 110
construction, viii, 46, 48, 49, 53, 55, 63, 64, 69, 70, 72, 74, 101, 118, 124
constructivism, vii, viii, 39, 40, 56, 58, 60
content analysis, 69
contingency, 40
contradiction, 29
control group, 29
convention, ix, 109
convergence, 19, 21
conversations, 45, 89, 92
cooperation, 136
correlation, 4, 23
correlation coefficient, 4, 23
cost, 73, 109
course content, 65
covering, x, 126, 129
creative process, 127
creative thinking, 117
creativity, 56, 72, 73, 76, 103, 127, 132, 138, 139, 141
crises, 136
critical thinking, 72, 103, 130
criticism, 4, 110
cues, 47, 115
cultural heritage, 80

N

O

P